Failure's Opposite

Listening to A.M. Klein

Edited by

NORMAN RAVVIN AND SHERRY SIMON

McGill-Queen's University Press
Montreal & Kingston • London • Ithaca

© McGill-Queen's University Press 2011

ISBN 978-0-7735-3832-0 (cloth)
ISBN 978-0-7735-3862-7 (paper)

Legal deposit second quarter 2011
Bibliothèque nationale du Québec

Printed in Canada on acid-free paper that is 100% ancient forest
free (100% post-consumer recycled), processed chlorine free

This book has been published with the help of grants from the
Institute for Canadian Jewish Studies and the Aid to Research
Related Events (ARRE) program at Concordia University.

McGill-Queen's University Press acknowledges the support of the
Canada Council for the Arts for our publishing program. We also
acknowledge the financial support of the Government of Canada
through the Canada Book Fund for our publishing activities.

Library and Archives Canada Cataloguing in Publication

Failure's opposite: listening to A.M. Klein / edited by Norman
Ravvin and Sherry Simon.

Includes bibliographical references and index.
ISBN 978-0-7735-3832-0 (bound). – ISBN 978-0-7735-3862-7 (pbk.)

1. Klein, A. M. (Abraham Moses), 1909–1972 – Criticism and
interpretation. I. Ravvin, Norman, 1963– II. Simon, Sherry

PS8521.L45Z64 2011   C811'.52   C2010-907971-X

Typeset by Jay Tee Graphics Ltd. in 10.5/13.5 Sabon

FAILURE'S OPPOSITE

Contents

Acknowledgments

The editors would like to acknowledge the editorial work of Alicja Surzyn and Olivia Ward, which was crucial in completing this volume. Jonathan Crago's exacting work at McGill-Queen's University Press helped bring the book into being. The Klein family was sensitive and supportive throughout our work on their father. Loren Lerner aided in our finding a fine cover image, and archivists Shannon Hodge and Janice Rosen helped us gain access to illustrations. Funding was offered by Graham Carr at Concordia through his role at the Faculty of Arts and Science, through the Concordia Aid to Research Related Events, Exhibition, Publication and Dissemination Activities Program, and through the SSHRC workshop granting process.

In citations from A.M. Klein's *The Second Scroll*, contributors use the 2000 University of Toronto edition of the novel. An exception to this is Ian Rae, who also cites the 1994 McClelland and Stewart edition.

ARTS

A. J. MURRAY HONEYMAN

Born Dec. 13th, 1908, at Chelsea, Quebec. Attended the Hull Model School and Ottawa Collegiate. Came down to McGill in 1927. Honour course in Biology. Won Hiram Mills Scholarship for 1928. Hobbies: *Tennis and Badminton.*

GERALD FULTON HENDERSON HUNTER

"A kind and gentle heart he has To comfort friends and foes."

Forgotten by Joe Stork at Huntingdon, Que., July 20th, 1908. Educated at Huntingdon Academy. Entered McGill with scholarship, 1926. Activities: *McGill Daily* 1927-28-29; Class hockey 1927-28-29; Secretary English Literature Society, 1929-30; S.C.A. Board 1929-30; Class historian. Course: English Honours. Hobby: *Arguing fate.* Favourite expression: *"Yeah, I guess so."*

EDWARD H. JOHNSON

"His strength is as the strength of ten because his heart is pure."

Born Oct. 1st, 1909, in Westmount, where he received his early education. Graduated from Westmount High with scholarship. Entered McGill in 1926. Activities: Class Debating Executive '27-'28-'29; Arts representative on Students' Council 1929; Mission Study Group '28-'29, Chairman '29-'30; Winter sports team '27-'28-'29, '29, '29-'30, Captain '28-'29; Junior Rugby '26-'27 (championship); Intermediate Rugby '27-'28; Interfaculty Rugby '30; Gym Club '27-'28. Hobbies: *Vassar and canoeing.* Favourite expression: *"What the deuce."*

ABRAHAM M. KLEIN

And we will build Jerusalem again, In England's fair and pleasant land.

Born St. Valentine's Day 1909, in Montreal, Can. Educated at Mount Royal and Baron Byng High Schools. Came to McGill 1926. Activities: *McGill Daily* 1927-28; treasurer Maccabean Circle; secretary Debating Union. Hobbies: *Poetry, pig and whistle.* Favourite expression: *"It's the poor what gets the blyme."*

SIMON KLEIN

"And still they gazed and still their wonder grew That one small head could carry all he knew."

Born March 29th, 1908, at New York City. Educated at Bancroft Public School and Strathcona Academy. Came to McGill in 1926. Activities: Class hockey and Faculty baseball; McGill Senior Cricket Club 1927-27-28-29. Hobbies: *Bridge, reading and dancing.* Favourite expression: *"Let me explain..."*

BERNARD J. LANDE

"How long, Oh Lord, how long!"

Born May 16th, 1909, at Westmount, Quebec. Educated at Argyle School and Westmount High School. Entered McGill in 1925. Activities: Member of Political Economy; Players '26-'27 and Banjo-Mandolin Clubs, '26-'27. Hobbies: *Golf and bridge.* Favourite expression: *"Hello, girls."*

MONTY LEVENCROWN

"Ours not to reason why, Ours but to do and die."

Born March 29th, 1907, at Montreal, Quebec. Educated at Strathcona School and at Baron Byng High School. Came to McGill in 1926. Activities: Member of Boxing Club. Hobbies: *Track and basketball.* Favourite expression: *"All right, have it your way."*

THEODORE IRVING LEVINE

"One who never turned his back but marched breast forward. Never doubted clouds would break."

Born Dec. 21st, 1909, at Montreal, Que. Educated at Bancroft Public School and at Montreal High School. Entered McGill in 1926. Activities: *McGill Daily* '27-'28-'29. Junior football '28-'29. Class hockey and basketball. Arts '30 Debating Society. Hobbies: *Books and swimming.* Favourite expression: *"Let's talk it over."*

1930

Klein's McGill University yearbook with graduating comment. *Old McGill* 1930, McGill University Archives.

GOLDENBERG   COHEN   WASSERMAN   KLEIN

FRAID   SHLAKMAN   LANDE   LEWIS   GREEN

Klein with members of the Maccabean Circle, McGill University's Jewish students' organization. *Old McGill*, 1930, McGill University Archives.

Klein in the neighbourhood in which he lived, Montreal, early 1930s. Colman and Sandor Klein Collection.

To Head Zionist Youth Movement In Canada

Mr. Abraham M. Klein, B.A., LL.L., of Montreal, newly-elected president of the Federation of Young Judaea of Canada.

Mr. Abraham M. Klein, of Montreal, was elected president of Canadian Young Judaea at the Tenth National Convention of the Organization recently concluded in Saskatoon, Sask.

Mr. Klein has been an active leader for many years, and is well-known to the members of the movement throughout the country, having acted as Educational Director of the Organization for some years, and as Editor of the JUDAEAN magazine. He is an honour graduate of the University of McGill (B.A.) and of the University of Montreal (LL.L.) and is at present practicing law in Montreal. He has won wide recognition as a writer and lecturer.

Report on Klein's Zionist Activism, *The Canadian Zionist*, Montreal, October 1934. Canadian Jewish Congress Charities Committee National Archives.

Not only the C.C.F. but also LIBERALS ENDORSE A. M. KLEIN IN CARTIER!

HERE, IN BLUNT CLEAR-CUT TERMS A RENOWNED LIBERAL ORGAN PUTS INTO WORDS WHAT ALL CARTIER LIBERALS ARE THINKING !

FROM AN
Editorial in SATURDAY NIGHT,
Toronto, June 7, 1949

"News of the candidacy of A. M. Klein in the C.C.F. interest in the Cartier constituency of Montreal leaves us in a singularly divided frame of mind. We have no desire to see too large a C.C.F. delegation in the House of Commons, though we believe that by functioning as a third party it has had very useful effects upon the policies of both of the older parties and probably hastened the adaptation of our legislation to the rapidly changing character of the times. But if we had a vote in Cartier we should probably put Mr. Klein's name on the ballot.

"He is high up among our most original, sympathetic and deeply thoughtful poets . . . He is also a man who decidedly does his own thinking . . . He is a man who has shown a singular understanding of the French population of the province in which he lives. . . "

THIS IS THE EDITORIAL OPINION OF ONE OF THE MOST POPULAR PERIODICALS IN CANADA — A LIBERAL PUBLICATION. THIS IS WHAT PEOPLE ALL OVER THE COUNTRY THINK OF KLEIN. THE ELECTORS OF CARTIER SHARE THE SAME OPINION AND WILL VOTE FOR A. M. KLEIN ON JUNE 27!

Hear

A. M. KLEIN

Official CCF Candidate in Cartier

at a

MASS MEETING

Wednesday, June 15, 1949 at 8:30 P.M.

at the

WORKMEN'S CIRCLE CENTRE

4848 St. Lawrence Blvd.

OTHER SPEAKERS:

A. SHUREM • M. RUBINSTEIN

22

Campaign Headquarters: 5171 Park Ave., DO. 3413

Political poster for Klein's parliamentary run, 1949. Jewish Public Library Archives, Montreal.

Yiddish version, political poster, 1949. Jewish Public Library Archives, Montreal.

Klein at left; others present include, sitting, Maurice Hartt (member of Parliament), Sholem Asch, Melech Ravitch; standing, Yaacov Zipper, J.I. Segal. Jewish Public Library, Montreal, 1942. Jewish Public Library Archives, Montreal.

Klein with author Pierre Van Paassen at the Jewish Public Library, Montreal, 25 November 1945. Jewish Public Library Archives, Montreal.

FAILURE'S OPPOSITE

SHERRY SIMON AND NORMAN RAVVIN

Introduction

There can be no serious discussion of Canadian literary modernism, Jewish-Canadian writing, or the Montreal imagination that does not include mention of A.M. Klein. Since his death in 1972, he has remained an enduring presence in the Canadian literary consciousness – honoured by a steady stream of publications and gestures of recognition that have solidified and enhanced his reputation. That Leonard Cohen recently chose to record a lyric in honour of the man he called "his teacher," that Mordecai Richler made Klein a character in his novel *Solomon Gursky Was Here*, and that Klein is the only Canadian author to be highlighted in Ruth Wisse's *Modern Jewish Canon* – all of these are evidence of his continuing influence. In 1992, the Quebec Writers' Federation, the province's association of English-language writers, named its annual prize for poetry in honour of A.M Klein. In 1999, a volume of poems written for or about him by eminent Canadian poets, *A Rich Garland: Poems for A.M. Klein,* was published by Véhicule Press. Klein has been the subject of movies (most notably a 1980 film by David Kaufman) and of a play by Endre Farkas. The public figure and citizen of Montreal has also been remembered. In July 2007, Klein was named a Historic Figure by Parks Canada, through its Ethnocultural Communities History Initiative, and a plaque is to be installed in front of his former home on Hutchison Street. This designation is particularly precious because it will keep Klein's memory alive on the street in the neighbourhood that he loved, a lasting remembrance of his activities as an editorialist and public speaker but, especially, as the poet of the "jargoning streets" whose music he wove into his writing.

These signs of recognition confirm that A.M. Klein's engagement with language and history speaks powerfully to the issues of today's world. During his own lifetime, his influence as a writer and as a Jewish community leader through a tumultuous period of history was far-reaching. Readings of Klein since his death are marked by a series of important publications, the first of which appeared following the 1974 Klein symposium organized by Seymour Mayne at the University of Ottawa. This conference was especially important because it led to the formation of the Klein Research and Publication Committee, which, over the ensuing thirty years, published a series of invaluable scholarly editions: the *Complete Poems*; *Literary Essays and Reviews*; *Beyond Sambation: Selected Essays and Editorials*; *Short Stories*; the *Notebooks*; *The Second Scroll*; and, most recently, the *Letters*. Along with Usher Caplan's seminal biography *Like One That Dreamed* and Zailig Pollock's *A.M. Klein: The Story of the Poet*, these volumes, prepared by a group of distinguished and committed academics, form a rich and indispensable foundation for readings of Klein.

These publications (in addition to the 1984 issue of the *Journal of Canadian Studies* devoted to Klein) have broadened the landscape of Klein studies, providing both new primary materials (the extraordinary manuscripts of the *Notebooks*, for instance) and a wealth of secondary material (in the form of annotations and commentaries, adding to the already substantial number of studies on Klein's poetry and his novel *The Second Scroll*). The recent conclusion of this outstanding scholarly project provided the occasion for this volume. Now that the exegetical work has been done, and the connections have been made between Klein's writing and the heritage of Jewish learning from which it derives, what are the new issues that drive Klein scholarship? Why does Klein remain a compelling figure for critics and readers? And in a more speculative vein, one may also wonder why, despite the real attention Klein has received, the theme of failure continues to be associated with his career. What kinds of failure was Klein haunted by, and how are we to read his fears today?

The question of Klein's legacy to the brilliant group of Montreal Jewish writers who followed him remains fraught with ambiguity. What is Klein's role as the father of Canadian Jewish writing and what was the nature of his links with Leonard Cohen, Irving Layton, and Mordecai Richler? These questions remain a lively, though sometimes bitter, topic of debate. Each of these writers has reacted to Klein, but often by focusing on issues that are biographical rather than literary. In fact, the nature of Klein's influence on what has come to be known as the Montreal Jewish writing tradition remains very much open to question. Cohen, Layton, and Richler developed ambitions and aesthetics that were very different from Klein's. Klein was an experimental writer, a modernist, whose erudition and playful use of literary forms did not really find disciples. As Ian Rae suggests in the final chapter of this volume, it may be that Klein's influence skipped a generation and was most intensely felt by those known as postmodernists. And it may be that Klein's engagement with form was more relevant to readers who were not steeped in the discourses and materials of Jewish history.

Most vivid among the aspects of Klein's work that continue to resonate for new readers is no doubt his love for Montreal and the original ways in which he captured the atmosphere of his "jargoning city." This aspect of his appeal has taken a new turn with the "discovery" of Klein by francophone readers. Klein's work is now enjoying popularity with an entirely new readership and a new generation of literary critics, and Montreal has been the focus of much of this. It was, in fact, the explosion of interest in Montreal that was responsible for Klein's new prominence within the French-language world. Klein anticipated the questions that Montreal writers are even now asking themselves. How should the city and its increasing diversity be represented? What to make of its many competing tongues? Klein's life among languages found an apt setting in the neighbourhood of Mile End in Montreal, between the traditionally English-speaking West Side and the francophone East End. The linguistic and architectural hybridity of his immigrant neighbourhood confirmed his identity as a citizen of the Jewish Diaspora in North America. Drawing upon the strong traditions and languages that he knew – English, French, Yiddish, Hebrew – Klein was able to play "across" languages and to develop a poetic practice that was polyglot and innovative. The 350th anniversary of Montreal in 1992 became the occasion for a rediscovery of the city and the diversity of its populations. Quebec literature extended beyond the domain of a purely ethnic French-Canadian population to embrace the literature of a polyglot metropolis. The research program that became known as "Montréal imaginaire" at the Université de Montréal opened a new multicultural and multilingual field of study for francophone scholars, and one of the most "Montréalais" of authors was Klein.

Klein's commitment to and his grappling with the idea of the Diaspora also remain crucial to his legacy. The culture of Diaspora underlies much of Klein's writing, and it sustains his explorations of history and language. The meanings of the word have broadened considerably since Klein's time, but his investigations of both the emotional and historical dimensions of Diaspora remain richly suggestive for today's readers. In the following pages of this introduction, we enlarge on the issues raised by Klein's writing and the ways in which they are taken up by the contributors to this volume.

Polyphony

Zailig Pollock's contribution is invaluable in setting the scene for this moment of revaluation. As a participant in the 1974 symposium, and as one of the principal editors of the Klein publications and the author of a full-length study of Klein, Pollock is able to provide a broad and sensitive overview of Klein's critical reception. If many of the early commentators (including the important critic M.W. Steinberg) were concerned with defining Klein's relation to the Jewish tradition, explicating its references and deciphering difficult wordplay, later readers turned to the poetics of modernism. Many scholars have filled in important aspects of Klein's relationship to such precursors as Pound, Dante, and Joyce. Pollock leads us through successive periods of critical readership and concludes that today's readers have shifted away from Jewish history in favour of themes that transcend the Jewish experience, such as that of Diaspora.

That Zailig Pollock frames his argument with the idea of "reputation" points to an undeniable aspect of Klein's career. Klein was dissatisfied with his recognition as a poet during his lifetime. His own recognition of the difficulty of readership is put in heartbreakingly succinct terms in his major poem "Portrait of the Poet as Landscape." There, the poet is "cuckolded by the troubadour." "Is it the local tycoon," he wonders "who for a hobby / plays poet, he so epical in steel? / The orator, making a pause? Or is that man / he who blows his flash of brass in the jittering hall?" (*Rocking Chair* 54). Here, commerce and popular culture threaten the poet's audience, and the poem, often read as a broad prophecy of the decline of poetry, seems intimately connected with Klein's sense of his own cultural role. Famously concerned with his reception, Klein had two heavy strikes against him when it came to gaining a broader readership, but both of these fall under the rubric of difficulty, whether due to modernistic methods reminiscent of Pound or Eliot, or to rarified Jewish forms of reference and style.

Elizabeth Popham makes a strong case for the double portrait of Klein that emerges from his letters – the conflict between the demands of his life as a major spokesman for Canadian Jews and his vocation as a modernist with an obsessive engagement with history and ethnic identity. In this respect, says Popham, "he embodied the conflicting demands of artistry and identity, which are still at the core of Canadian multiculturalism." But because he was unable to bring his profession and avocation into alignment, because he experienced the continual frustration of this disjunction, the correspondence takes on unusual importance as an expression of his literary aspirations.

While Pollock and Popham both illustrate the complexity of Klein's voice, in particular the difficult passage between public and private expression, Robert Melançon celebrates the physical aspects of Klein's attention to voice in his writings – the colour and vitality of voices as they appear in his poetry and prose. Voice, in this reading, is primarily an expression of the diverse and the multiple, a way of showing that all expression emerges from a variety of sources. For Melançon, Klein's attention to the physical quality of voice, his understanding of the complex traditions that shape voice, and his experiments with poetic voice are all elements that speak directly to readers today.

Norman Ravvin explores a turning point in postwar literature by examining the formerly unpublished material of Kerouac and Klein and what it reflects about their attachments to literary and religious tradition. His chapter also considers the effect on a writer's legacy of publishing work shelved during the writer's lifetime as well as the role of failure in writerly lives. It includes a consideration of archival materials housed at the National Library of Canada as well as a consideration of the textual archival legacy left by Kerouac to his family trust.

Klein in French

One of the most singular and exciting chapters in Klein criticism has been the attention given to Klein by prominent francophone critics in Quebec since the 1990s. Klein's engagement with issues of language and translation have been of particular interest in this regard. Francophone critics have not only extended the reach of Klein readership – through essays on Klein and by translations of his work (*The Second Scroll* and *The Rocking Chair* have both appeared in French) – they have also opened Klein's writing to new interpretive perspectives. This is a development that would have delighted Klein, who, through his *Rocking Chair* poems, attempted to create links between the Jewish and francophone communities in Montreal. Robert Melançon, poet and professor of French studies at the Université de Montréal, was one of the first francophone critics to become acquainted with Klein. The circumstances were unusual: Melançon was a neighbour of Sandor Klein in Notre Dame de Grace and was drawn to investigate the work of this unfamiliar poet. With his wife, the translator and poet Charlotte Melançon, he translated *The Second Scroll. Le Second Rouleau,* a remarkable French version of a very difficult text, was awarded the Governor General's Prize for Translation. In his introduction to the volume, Melançon introduces the book to readers who would know little of the universe it evokes. He emphasizes the many levels at which the novel can be read, assuring the reader that no specialized knowledge is required in order to enjoy the book. Melançon places the novel in the most distinguished company – the great works of Kafka or Borges – because, like these, it "creates its own form." Marie Frankland's French-language translation of *The Rocking Chair* (*La chaise berçante*, Editions du Noroît, 2006) was originally undertaken as a master's thesis under the direction of Melançon.

Klein was acknowledged in French-language circles in Quebec during his lifetime. The spring 1946 issue of the journal *Gants du Ciel*, devoted to English-Canadian poetry, contained a substantial article on Klein by A.J.M Smith, which was translated into French. And "Huit Poemes Canadiens (en anglais)" had already been circulated by the Canadian Jewish Congress in 1948 with a preface by Jean-Marie Poirier. But the renewed interest in Klein that began in the late 1980s went far beyond this polite recognition of an eminent

Jewish-Canadian poet who was also "a friend of French Canada." Klein's recent reception in Quebec academic criticism signals a shift in perspective. Klein is no longer the outsider, the representative of a singular and alien sensibility. He is one of those who shaped the literary consciousness of Montreal and developed an especially effective language to express it.

Pierre Nepveu, the novelist, poet, and critic who has most assiduously brought Klein to the attention of the francophone world, has written of the "special genius" that allowed Klein to understand the nature of Montreal and to draw from this understanding "radical esthetic consequences": "the intellectual fireworks, the polyglot chaos are grounded in the pluralism of Montreal" (315). Philosopher and literary critic Anne Elaine Cliché has read Klein through psychoanalysis as an interpreter of the Jewish messianic tradition in her study *Poétiques du Messie, l'origine juive en souffrance* (2007), placing Klein among an unusual cast of subjects, from Don Quixote to the artisans of the Kabbalah, from Céline to Perec. Pierre Anctil has studied Klein's role as a political mediator. In a 1984 article, Anctil examines correspondence suggesting that Klein had written *The Rocking Chair* in order to take advantage of the postwar situation and to further rapprochement between Jews and French Canadians. In this volume, Anctil's own activities as a translator have led him to an in-depth analysis of Klein's methods as a translator from Yiddish.

Translation

Klein's writings show that he gave the broadest meanings to the task of the translator. This was not a simple task of mediation – of informing one linguistic group of the achievements of another – nor was it an attempt to translate North American Jewish experience *out of* or *away* from the past. His goal was to imbue the present with the forms and styles of the past, to express a culture traversed by many languages and histories. It was also, according to Ruth Wisse, to "render alien" what was to become the world's most powerful language. Wisse's praise for Klein in her book *The Modern Jewish Canon* focuses on his creation of "an alienating English to convey the Jewish experience" (265). Rather than "accommodating the Jewish subject to the requirements of English," he "exercises the right to appear alien to others rather than becoming alien to himself" (265–6). Klein's sensitivity to the power of language came from his situation as an English-language writer in Montreal, a situation similar to that of Kafka in Prague.

The chapters in *Failure's Opposite* that focus on translation open a new avenue of exploration in Klein studies, permitting fine analysis of his erudition and attention to language. Three chapters examine Klein's translation practices, giving texture and density to a career that could be characterized as *a targum leben*. *A targum leben* is the term used by Hirsch Wolofsky to underline the distance that the diasporic Jews of America experience in relation to their Jewish heritage. This is experienced, according to Wolofsky, as a translation whose original has been lost and that can only be regained through dedicated study of the biblical sources. The expression, which combines the Aramaic *targum* with the Yiddish *leben*, can also be understood in a more positive light as the possibility for creative interaction between the languages of the past and present. This is surely the meaning that Klein would have given the expression. And it is the basis for Ira Robinson's engagement with Klein's poetry and its *vorlage* – the pre-text or pre-language with which he plays. Using the term *vorlage* to refer to the underlying Yiddish or Hebrew text that Klein had in mind as he wrote in English, Robinson offers insight into the processes of translingual creation – the ways in which the cadence of verses from the Hebrew Bible, Talmudic phrases in Aramaic, and Yiddish conversational patterns constitute "crucial compositional factors" for him. Klein chose from the start, and never deviated from this choice, to write in English alone. He was among the first writers in Canada to express his Jewish identity in English. Yet, as Rebecca Margolis suggests, the shift from Yiddish to English did not come without ambivalence, and Klein not only maintained close ties with the Yiddish-speaking community but actively translated from Yiddish to English in an attempt to ensure the transmission of the Eastern European Jewish tradition.

Klein undertook many translations from Yiddish, including *Mayn lebens rayze* by Hirsch Wolofsky. As Pierre Anctil explains, Wolofsky was Klein's friend and employer, so this translation was surely undertaken as a personal favour. Anctil's close analysis of the translation (enriched by the fact that Anctil has himself translated the same text into French) reveals a great deal about Klein's relationship to Yiddish and his idea of what an effective translation should be. In fact, as Anctil shows, Klein "resisted" the original, elevating the diction and eliminating some crucial references to the Yiddish language itself.

Cities

The centrality of Montreal for Klein as a theme of his writing – as the milieu that shaped and sustained him – has been abundantly demonstrated. The Montreal milieu of the 1930s and 1940s has been less frequently studied as a network of reciprocal influences. Some of these are traced by Lianne Moyes in relation to the Yiddish poet J.I. Segal. Moyes reads Klein's Mountain poems – among the most anthologized and most beloved of his writings – in concert with similar poems and references by Yiddish-language poets, especially J.I. Segal. But what makes Klein's poems different, according to Moyes, is that they propose very personal narratives of the Mountain and therefore promote an idea of secular space. Her readings show how prominent the Mountain was for Montreal's Jewish poets, in both English and Yiddish.

The city is linked in Klein's thought to traditions of the Diaspora. Sherry Simon shows how the string of cities invoked in *The Second Scroll* are in fact moments of Jewish history, celebrated by Klein in counterpoint to the ideal messianic symbol of Jerusalem. Montreal, therefore, is "more" than Montreal: it is an instance among many of the polyphonic spaces that make up the continuing story of Jewish diasporic habitation.

Like Montreal, Winnipeg had a tight-knit and active Jewish intellectual community. It is not surprising, then, that there were strong links between the two communities and frequent moves from one to the other, as was the case for Miriam Waddington (who moved from Winnipeg, via Ottawa, to Montreal) and Klein (who travelled to Winnipeg on his frequent lecture tours). In his reading of the Winnipeg Jewish press during the 1930s and 1940s, Robert Schwartzwald discovers the relative prominence of Klein as a speaker and editorialist, and his solid reputation in western Canada. In investigating Klein's presence in the press, Schwartzwald discovers an unusual link between Klein and the Soviet Jewish enclave of Birobidjan. The rivalry between the English- and Yiddish-language presses in Winnipeg offers an interesting contrast with Montreal, specifically in light of Winnipeg's strong labour history and the spectacular 1919 General Strike.

Legacy: Klein as Jewish Writer

No aspect of Klein studies is as fraught with disagreement as is the question of his relationship to the writers that followed him, most notably Irving Layton, Mordecai Richler, and Leonard Cohen. This issue is given special momentum by Mordecai Richler's satirical attacks on Klein. Richler's caricatures of Klein were a backhanded reminder of Klein's prominence as a public figure, and they have stirred discussion about Richler's own understanding of his public role. The very richness of the relationship generated by this milieu, however, is confirmed by the vigour of these discussions as they are presented by Reinhold Kramer, David Leahy, Lawrence Kaplan, and Ian Rae.

But the notion of a local tradition and its meaningfulness for understanding Klein can be overblown. Certainly, Layton attended to Klein, positioned himself as an ephebe at his elbow, and was even tutored by him as a youth, yet Layton's own work, from the very earliest stages of his career through to its cantankerous end, differs from Klein's. Layton's relevance, his public persona, his relationship with aspects of a postmodern American poetic tradition can all be said to be enacted in resistance to Klein. And though Cohen did write a strange early elegy to Klein's late years, the same can be said of him: his poetic influences in Montreal, whether at McGill or through the jazz-inflected Bohemian nightclubs where he read his poems, American-style, to saxophone accompaniment, led him to become the kind of poet and young celebrity that Klein could not have dreamed of becoming. The late return, in Cohen's recordings, to Klein as mentor, is mysterious. One wonders what Klein would make of Cohen, who brought the Beat style – its rethinking of popular culture towards serious ends – to Canada.

How does Jewishness account for Klein's reception? One outcome is the tendency to dub Klein the "father of Canadian Jewish literature." Another is to describe his modernist methods – his self-interpretive and glossing strategies, for example, in *The Second Scroll*

– as "Talmudic" without an attentive or detailed effort to make this argument effective in reading Klein's work. Certainly Klein, like Richler, tells part of the story of the major decades of Jewish immigration to Montreal and the inception of an immigrant street – a *yiddishe gas* – that would set a model for waves of immigration to Montreal, Toronto, and Winnipeg. But it is Richler who tells this story with the greatest verve and provocation. Before him, we must look to Yiddish writers like Chava Rosenfarb or Yaacov Zipper for a sustained portrait of what it meant to arrive in Canada as a Yiddish-speaking Jew with one's life left behind in Eastern Europe. The early pages of *The Second Scroll* speak to these issues, though the novel veers off, once it has addressed the Holocaust, to suggest that new Jewish culture after the catastrophe will be taken from the Israeli model.

Recent developments, some of them reflected in this collection, suggest that it will be qualities other than Klein's relevance to Jewish North American writing that ensure his legacy. In the early years of his career, anthologies tended to highlight two aspects of Klein's poetry: the lyrical, multilingual portraits of Montreal life and Old World exotica – so the material must have seemed to readers in Canadian classrooms in the 1960s and 1970s – found in much-collected poems such as "Heirloom." T.S. Eliot and Ezra Pound, in their magpie methods and tendency to quote from abstruse source material, may be among the few moderns who were in greater need of footnoting than Klein. And though there were good critical studies of Klein's Jewish influences – most notably by M.W. Steinberg in the journal *Canadian Literature* – such specialized readings were a species of professional critical reception that had little impact or influence on a broader readership.

Klein is early, almost without peers, in his fictional reflections on Jewish life and history in light of what would come to be known as the Holocaust. He views the collapse of European civilization not only through the prism of his home – Montreal's Jewish immigrant streets – but also in relation to the rush of events that led to the declaration of the State of Israel in 1948. *The Second Scroll*, though highly stylized, attains a journalistic precision in its exploration of a Podolian massacre, the transport of European refugees to the Middle East, and the inception of a modern Israeli literature in Hebrew. These varied issues had yet to take their full role as pillars of postwar Jewish identity, yet Klein addresses them at a time when they are still remarkably painful and fresh.

For Klein, poetry was a public fact and an activity that he wanted his community to value. This is an important creative commitment, one that Mordecai Richler chose to satirize through his portrait of Klein in *Solomon Gursky Was Here*, and there is rich irony in the fact that Richler's backhanded characterization of Klein might have contributed to enhancing Klein's visibility today. It is true that the theme of failure haunts Klein's legacy, but it is also true to say that Klein led the way for an extraordinarily brilliant generation of Montreal English Jewish writers. Mordecai Richler's biographer, Reinhold Kramer, details the myriad ways in which the author positioned himself in relation to Klein, proving – as do several of the contributions here – that the trouble Richler took to satirize Klein was a mark of filial admiration. Indeed, if several of the same themes run through the contributions of Kramer, Lawrence Kaplan, and David Leahy, this is because the prominence of Richler and the nature of his parody forces critics to take sides. Lawrence Kaplan, however, reveals some startling crossovers when he shows in detail the resemblances in structure between *St. Urbain's Horseman* and *The Second Scroll*. David Leahy provides a rich and comprehensive reading of Richler's treatments of Klein. Together, these chapters ask questions about literary influence and, especially, about artistic independence. Richler's various uses of Klein – as a character, as a writer whose literary structures he mimicked – point to important questions about the ways in which writers interact with their communities. Both Klein and Richler were strongly attached to the world of Montreal Jewry. Both sought solutions to the dilemmas of artistic freedom. And Richler attained the kind of popularity and readership that Klein never did. On the other hand, Richler's journalism (especially *Oh Canada! Oh Quebec!*) alienated and angered his francophone readers in a way that Klein's writings never did.

In this volume's concluding chapter, Ian Rae introduces the theme of "failure" as the productive link between Klein and his postmodern followers. Though acknowledging the connections between Klein and younger Montreal writers such as Layton, Cohen, and Richler, Rae makes a strong argument for jumping straight to the aesthetics of another generation: "The genre of the novel has not defeated Klein; rather, he has reinvented it for subsequent poets, such as Cohen, Anne Michaels, Robert Kroetsch, Michael Ondaatje, Joy Kogawa and George Elliott Clarke, who also make use of the hybrid form to address the devastation and fragmentation of their respective cultures, as well as their reinvention in Canada." Klein's aesthetics and values are reflected in some of Canada's finest recent writing. And, indeed, the kinds of failure that are derived and mobilized from Klein's work begin to look like failure's opposite. In many ways, Klein's influence and relevance is being remade, refashioned, and reconstructed. As the first major consideration of Klein's oeuvre since 1974, *Failure's Opposite* reflects those processes of refashioning. The best outcomes of our efforts will arise from a true effort to listen to A.M. Klein.

PART ONE

Traces

ZAILIG POLLOCK

From Ghetto to Diaspora:
A.M. Klein in Our Time

In 2003, when Margaret Avison was presented with the prize for the year's best collection of Canadian poetry at the Griffin Awards Dinner, her comment to the audience was: "This is ridiculous." She then went on to explain that the experience of standing up in front of a rapturous crowd to receive a prize for her poetry was about as remote as she could imagine from her own sense of what poetry is. Anyone who knows Avison's poetry – deeply private, challenging, even esoteric in language and vision – will immediately understand what she meant. There is no poet for whom the kind of public recognition represented by the Griffin Prize is less relevant.

But what about A.M. Klein? What would he have said at future public events in his name? I suspect that, with typical Jewish irony, he might paraphrase "Portrait of the Poet as Landscape" and say "it is something" (*Complete Poems*, 2:639, line 158). For better or for worse, Klein, unlike Avison, cared deeply about public recognition. However, his ambitions, as he says in "Portrait," were never "mean" (line 158). He saw his function, and the function of all true poets, in grand, even grandiose, terms: to unroll "our culture from his scroll" (line 22). And from Klein's point of view one wonders if any tribute to a writer, conceivable in our contemporary world, would have entirely satisfied his ambitions. I think probably not. But I would like to argue that, although Klein's reputation and influence never attained the impossible heights he hoped for in his most ambitious moments, there is plenty of evidence that his work continues to engage and inspire readers, scholars, and writers – and that it will continue to do so in years to come.

There is something very human, but something disturbing as well, about Klein's lifelong concern – perhaps obsession is not too strong a word – with his reputation. This is especially striking in some of the previously unpublished writings included in the *Notebooks* volume of the *Collected Works*. It is also abundantly evident in his letters. To some extent this obsession may be explained as a response to what Klein saw, with some justification, as the lukewarm, even hostile, reception of his earlier works, *Hath Not a Jew ...*, *Poems*, and *The Hitleriad*. Be that as it may, Klein's obsession with public recognition continued throughout his career – even at the end, when, with *The Rocking Chair and Other Poems* and *The Second Scroll*, his reputation had reached new heights and was clearly on the rise.

A typical passage from the *Notebooks* expresses Klein's anger at what he saw as the public incomprehension of and indifference to his works; and it expresses, as well, his self-contempt for prostituting his talents as a speechwriter for the "maestro," that is, Samuel Bronfman:

> Rejoicing and drinks – the maestro's – at the planning of the final banquet of the annual philanthropic campaign. Everybody complimented by everybody, even me, who am only the author of its slogans – the proxy of the poor – the compiler of its sob-letters. Particular backslap for an anonymous poem about the grace of charity – Ah, the charm of gilded platitude – printed on the banquet souvenir-program. Poor me! poet parsleyate to a menu. Actually the sonnet was written only to avoid writing the sickening prose called for ... But that I should write it at all. ("From the 'Raw Material' File" 9–11)

In another passage, positively dripping with self-pity, the narrator imagines the rabbi's eulogy at this funeral:

> From behind my tears, I watch the entire ceremony, a stranger at my own funeral. Among the dead, I am beyond pain and pity, and am unmoved by the ululation which I have so unintentionally caused. But I feel a certain glow of mild satisfaction – Here, my whole biography has been recounted, but nobody mentioned the fact that I was a poet.

I have kept the secret well. Now, no one will ever know of
what I died. ("From the 'Raw Material' File" 26)

In reading passages like these – and there are many of them – we
may sometimes yearn for the austere indifference to public reputation of a Margaret Avison.

Klein himself was as fully aware as was Avison of the futility of
a serious artist's expecting immediate or widespread public recognition. Fame "has its attractions, but is not the thing," he says in
"Portrait of the Poet as Landscape" (line 126):

Fame, the adrenalin: to be talked about;
to be a verb; to be introduced as *The*;
to smile with endorsement from slick paper; make
caprices anecdotal; to nod to the world; to see
one's name like a song upon the marquees played;
to be forgotten with embarrassment
(lines 119–24)

However, as much as we, and Klein himself, may deplore his own
obsession with such trivia, there is a positive side to his concern with
his public role; and Klein's deepest ambitions and accomplishments
as an artist would be incomprehensible without it. For Klein – and
this is where he and Avison definitely part ways – the role of the poet
is *essentially* public; and public recognition, therefore, is essential
to the fulfilment of this role. Klein was raised in a Jewish milieu
that placed high value on community and on the duty of the educated members of the community to offer advice and guidance. Klein
saw himself as an heir not only of the great English poets such as
Chaucer, Shakespeare, and Milton but also of the great figures of the
rabbinical tradition such as ben-Zakkai, Hillel, Akiva, Rashi, and
Maimonides. It was precisely their influence on the ways of thinking and feeling of their community that constituted the greatness of
these figures. And it is a comparable influence that Klein desired for
his poetry. This view of the function of poetry recalls Shelley's claim
that poets are "the unacknowledged legislators of the world" – however, minus the "unacknowledged." When Klein speaks of the poet as
"bring[ing] / new forms to life, anonymously, new creeds" ("Portrait"

lines 155–6) he clearly sees the "anonymously" not as a permanent
feature of the poet's role but as one that he is forced to assume
"[m]eanwhile," (line 159) and that he must eventually transcend.

At the time of his retreat into silence in the early 1950s, while still
at the height of his poetic powers, Klein had come as close as he ever
would to the accomplishment of this role – and it is painful to think
of what he would have achieved, and of what his public reputation
would have been, if his career had continued to unfold over the next
twenty years or so. Klein's silence deprived us not only of a great
poetic voice but also of a great public voice, which would undoubtedly have enriched the debates on multiculturalism, on nationalism
– whether Canadian, Québécois, or Zionist – and on globalization
and social justice, which so concern us today. But to turn from these
perhaps idle speculations about what *we* have lost because of Klein's
untimely silence, there can be no doubt as to the loss this silence
entailed for Klein's reputation.

Klein's retreat into silence in the early 1950s meant that he was
effectively absent during the efflorescence of Canadian literature
that began some ten years later. His unwillingness or inability to participate in the rounds of readings, interviews, panels, prize commit-
tees, and debates that were so important to this efflorescence clearly
had a negative impact on his reputation.

Apart from this obvious biographical fact, there is a broader,
historical/sociological reason why Klein's reputation went into a
decline after the early 1950s. Through most of his career the primary audience for Klein's work, the public he most deliberately
and consciously addressed, was the Canadian Jewish community of
immigrants, or children of immigrants, from Eastern Europe, familiar with Ashkenazi traditions and customs and with the Yiddish language. This community had already begun the inevitable process of
assimilation, or Canadianization, by the end of Klein's career, threat-
ening to deprive him of his audience as initially conceived and of
his public role in relation to it. However, in *The Rocking Chair and
Other Poems* Klein had already shown his willingness and ability to
move beyond this audience, while remaining true to its core values.

But perhaps the most serious impediment to a full appreciation
of Klein's ambitions and achievement was a change in the zeitgeist
that was beginning to take shape by the end of his career. In retrospect, one can see in this change a foreshadowing of what has since

come to be known as postmodernism. A full articulation of the post-modernist aesthetic and epistemology by such thinkers as Jacques Derrida, Michel Foucault, Richard Rorty, and Jean-François Lyotard was, of course, still in the future when Klein fell silent. And Klein would, no doubt, have been deeply troubled by the implications for his exalted vision of the poet and his public role found in Lyotard's critique, offered in *The Postmodern Condition: A Report on Knowledge* (1979), of the metanarratives that had dominated Western thought, culminating in modernism and totalitarianism. However, here as elsewhere, the philosophers were responding to developments that the artists had already begun to sense. A classic example of a postmodernist *avant la lettre* is Jorge Luis Borges, whose major writings were all completed before the term "postmodernism" was invented, yet whose works are widely cited, by Foucault and others, as exemplars of the postmodernist vision. As I have pointed out in *A.M. Klein: The Story of the Poet* (233–4), Borges's story "The Approach to al-Mu'tasim" (1935) can be read as a detailed and insightful postmodernist commentary on *The Second Scroll*, even though the story preceded the novel by some fifteen years and Klein was entirely unaware of Borges's writings. It is in *The Second Scroll*, in fact, that Klein first begins to formulate a critique of the modernist assumptions that had underwritten his early works, though from a perspective that was to prove deeply unfashionable.

Throughout most of his career, Klein would have identified himself as a modernist, very much in the spirit of his hero James Joyce. Klein's relationship to modernism was a complex one, and certain aspects of modernism, not least the socially conservative and anti-Semitic leanings of many of its leading figures, had no appeal to him. But one aspect of modernism that clearly did appeal to Klein was its commitment to creating an art that, while rooted in the central traditions of European literature, was, at the same time, committed to renewing these traditions, to using a craft "archaic like the fletcher's" to "bring / new forms to life" ("Portrait" lines 153, 155–6). Klein believed, or struggled to believe, that modern poetry, even at its most challenging and experimental and adventurous, could maintain its roots in tradition and offer contemporary readers a much-needed vision of coherence and community. As he says of the poet in his late essay, "The Bible's Archetypical Poet": "Rooted in the common soil, he turns his eyes to new directions. He is, indeed, a fruitful bough; he springs from earth fed secretly by a well; but his branches run over the wall. Thus are the ideas of convention and revolt, of tradition and innovation, conjured up" (*Literary Essays and Reviews* 148).

However, by the end of his career (and even in the very essay from which I have just quoted), Klein had begun to lose faith in this vision. This loss of faith parallels widespread developments in literature, philosophy, and the arts in general in the latter half of the twentieth century. Already in *The Second Scroll*, Klein's most impressive exercise in modernism à la *Ulysses*, there are clear signs of dissatisfaction with this vision of tradition and innovation. And in later works, including "The Biblical Manuscripts," "In Praise of the Diaspora," "The Bells of Sobor Spasitula," and, perhaps most radically, his unfinished novel "The Golem," Klein's faith in the modernist vision seems shattered beyond repair. These works express Klein's sense of despair in the face of the chaotic fragmentation of the contemporary world, and they reject as a delusion the ambition to redeem the world through art. One is tempted to call these late works, in their critical self-reflexivity, postmodernist, even though Klein had never heard of the term. But if they are postmodernist, they are so in a tragic mode that is very different from the playful mode that characterizes postmodernism as it is generally understood today. Postmodernism, in this sense, is more likely than not to celebrate the irreducible multiplicity of the world. From this perspective the redemptive ambitions that dominated most of Klein's career seem alien, as does his tragic and despairing response to the apparent failure of these ambitions at the end of his career. Although Klein continues to have great appeal to students – when he is properly introduced – often their initial response to him, apart from bewilderment at his range of cultural references, is: "lighten up."

If my previous comments suggest a rather pessimistic picture of Klein's reputation, present and future, this picture is very incomplete. I am in fact optimistic that Klein, if he will never attain quite the central role in our culture that was his ambition (and what poet ever will?), nevertheless remains a powerful presence – a presence that I predict will continue to grow as the years go by.

Part of my reason for feeling this is based upon my experience teaching Klein. Klein's works, especially the works most steeped in Jewish customs and lore, do present difficulties to students whose knowledge of traditional culture in general, not to mention Jewish

culture, is limited. And Klein does not make it easy for his readers. For example, to fully appreciate "Gloss Gimel" in *The Second
Scroll* you should really be familiar, for starters, with: Michelangelo's paintings on the ceiling of the Sistine Chapel and the biblical and iconographic traditions upon which they draw; Charles de
Tolnay's commentary on these paintings; various kabbalistic doc-
trines, as formulated by Isaac Luria and expounded by Gershom
Scholem; and Joyce's *Ulysses* (and at least bits of *Finnegans Wake*). It
also helps to have more than a nodding acquaintance with Yiddish,
Hebrew, Aramaic, and Latin. "Gloss Gimel" is perhaps an extreme
case, but Klein *is* a challenging writer. However, it is my experience
as a teacher that once the initial barriers are breached, students are
fully capable of rising to the challenge that Klein sets them, and
they are deeply responsive to his vision, to the wit, passion, and
pathos of the language through which he expresses this vision. Our
best students are willing to work hard at mastering a text, be it
Klein, or Chaucer, or Milton, or Joyce, if they sense that there are
rewards for doing so. Interestingly, when I teach *The Second Scroll*
and *St. Urbain's Horseman* as a pair, dealing with Jewish responses
to historical and cultural crisis, it is *St. Urbain's Horseman* that my
students find the more remote of the two, with its dense web of references to historical events and cultural figures of the 1960s: "Who
is Sandy Koufax" they ask, "and why should we care?" And it is
quite a hard sell to convince them that they should take as much
interest in Jake Hersh's search for his cousin Joey as in the search
for Uncle Melech in *The Second Scroll*. For some reason, my twenty-
something students, most of them non-Jewish women, don't seem
to be all that fascinated by the mid-life crisis of a neurotic Jewish
man, especially when it is so much a reflection of a time and place
that seems as remote to most of them as does the War of the Roses.
I don't usually meet this kind of resistance to *The Second Scroll*
among my students. If they have any feel for language at all they
are drawn by the lyrical beauty, the wit, and the mastery of rhythm
and sound that mark *The Second Scroll*, and all of Klein's writing,
from the beginning of his career to its end. And the issues with which
Klein grapples in the novel – the nature of community and of the
struggle, both individual and communal, to make meaning out of
the apparently meaningless catastrophes of history – are big ones,
with an appeal that resonates beyond the increasingly distant Jewish

community of Klein's youth and maturity. These issues have engaged human beings throughout history – at least from the time of the *Iliad* – and I would guess that they will continue to do so for some time. As long as this is true, I suspect that Klein's eloquent and passionate explorations of these issues will continue to resonate among serious readers of any background.

Apart from my observations that, at least among my students, Klein's reputation is doing well, there is the evidence of continuing scholarly interest in Klein, drawing on a much broader range of contexts and perspectives than the scholarship in the years immediately following his death. More than that, there is evidence of a major shift in the focus of this scholarship, which suggests to me that Klein continues to speak to us but, because we are now listening for other things, in a different voice than in the past.

This shift is perhaps most strikingly evident if we compare the A.M. Klein Symposium held at the University of Ottawa in 1974 – the starting point in so many ways for the revival of interest in Klein's work – with the 2007 Concordia University conference, which marks a turning point in the development of that interest. The Ottawa Symposium was the first major reconsideration of Klein's achievement following Klein's death, and it set the groundwork for studies of Klein in the decades to come. During his lifetime, Klein's work had been widely discussed by most luminaries of Canadian criticism, including Northrop Frye, E.K. Brown, Roy Daniells, William Arthur Deacon, Leon Edel, Milton Wilson, Malcolm Ross, and Desmond Pacey, as well as by many of Klein's fellow writers – A.J.M. Smith, Irving Layton, Leon Kennedy, E.J. Pratt, Eli Mandel, Margaret Avison, Earle Birney, Robertson Davies, Miriam Waddington, Dorothy Livesay, and Louis Dudek. The most significant of the critical writings on Klein of this era were collected in 1970 by Tom Marshall in *A.M. Klein*, part of the *Critical Views on Canadian Writers* published by Ryerson Press. Although the essays in this collection were far from unanimous regarding the nature of Klein's achievement, the collection fairly represents what we might call the "Klein question" as it was seen at that time and the kinds of approaches typically taken to this question. Essentially, the question was: "What was Klein's relationship to Jewish tradition?" The answers were varied, but they all reflected a common conviction that Klein's relationship to Jewish tradition was of central concern to any discussion of his work. Moreover, there tended to be fairly wide-spread agreement that Klein was a spokesman for, or an embodiment of, Jewish tradition. This note had been sounded years earlier in Ludwig Lewisohn's comment in the *Jewish Standard* that Klein was "the first Jew to contribute authentic poetry to the literatures of English speech" (8). Klein included Lewisohn's comments as the foreword to his first book of poetry, *Hath Not a Jew ...*, and they were echoed repeatedly in criticism of this period and beyond.

Although Klein's Jewishness is obviously a central fact of his life and work, the nature of this "Jewishness" is perhaps not quite as unambiguous as his early commentators seemed to suggest. This is evident if we compare the first two critical monographs on Klein: Miriam Waddington's *A.M. Klein*, published in 1970, and Gretel Fischer's *In Search of Jerusalem: Religion and Ethics in the Writings of A.M. Klein*, published in 1975 but based on a dissertation completed in 1972. Both Waddington and Fischer attempt to place Klein in relation to Jewish tradition, but their views of what constitutes this tradition are very different. Waddington is heir to a tradition of *Yiddishkeit*, which, beginning in Eastern Europe in the nineteenth century, sought to define Jewishness in secular terms, with an emphasis on the central role of the Yiddish language, the common language of Ashkenazi Jews. From this perspective the culture of the Jewish people, although it is clearly rooted in the Hebrew Bible and in the religion of Judaism, no longer needed to express itself in primarily religious terms or, indeed, in religious terms at all. According to Waddington, "Klein's Jewishness resides not in his religion, but in his lifelong identification with ... a secular Yiddish, as well as a secular Hebrew culture" (*A.M. Klein*, 97–8).

In contrast to Waddington, Fischer sees Klein from the perspective of the religious tradition of rabbinnical Judaism. Fisher's Klein is essentially religious in his outlook and has an "ardent concern with ... divinity in the natural universe" (*In Search* 2). Although I personally tend more towards Waddington's view of Klein, I would argue that neither side of the debate is right. Or perhaps it would be more accurate to say that there is no real ground for debate since there are multiple traditions that can be identified as Jewish, and, throughout his life, Klein had shifting and contradictory relationships to many of them. The desire of earlier commentators to pin Klein down to a particular tradition or stance can, I think, be traced to at least a couple of sources. First, most of these earlier commentators were working within a dominant, though waning, critical tradition that emphasized universal transcendent aesthetic and ethical values, which they claimed to find in the canonical works of European literature. If Klein were to be taken seriously, he needed to be firmly identified with a great tradition that could be presented as addressing, in a worthy and recognizable way, such values – for example, Waddington's secular humanism or Fischer's Spinozistic pantheism. This view of the canon was already being challenged by the relatively new multicultural project in Canada as well as by the rise of postcolonial theory throughout the world, but neither of these, certainly not the latter, had much influence on the discussions swirling around Klein and his Jewishness at this time.

Something else that influenced the tenor of much of the discussions of Klein at this time was the fact that most of his published work, and all of his unpublished work, was inaccessible. *The Second Scroll* was available in the *New Canadian Library* reprint, but all the poetry was out of print, apart from a few widely anthologized pieces. Klein's numerous editorials (the bulk of his writing) had never been collected and neither had his fiction and critical essays. Perhaps most important, though, in this regard, is the fact that the large body of Klein's unpublished work, much of which is wholly different in character from anything Klein had published, was entirely unavailable at this time. Indeed, its existence was not even suspected.

All this began to change with the Ottawa Symposium. This symposium comprised a key moment in the history of Klein studies, partly because it provided the first account of the extent and nature of the Klein Papers (which had recently been deposited in Canada's national archives) and partly because it brought together Klein's contemporaries (A.J.M. Smith, Irving Layton, F.R. Scott, Leon Edel, Leo Kennedy, Dorothy Livesay, P.K. Page, Louis Dudek, David Lewis) and a new generation of scholars in a potent mix. Both the heated discussions that grew out of the symposium (which are barely reflected in the published proceedings) and the revelation that only a small fraction of Klein's work had previously been available for critical study made clear to the younger generation of scholars that the true nature of Klein's complex relationship to tradition variously conceived had scarcely been explored. One immediate result of the Ottawa Symposium was the establishment of the A.M. Klein

Research and Publication Committee, which has since overseen the publication of Klein's *Collected Works* – poems, essays, editorials, reviews, short stories, and previously unpublished notebooks and letters. These editions not only made Klein's writings available but, by establishing a chronology of the works, made it possible, for the first time, to grasp the shape of Klein's career. In the years following the symposium, the necessary tools for a proper assessment of Klein's achievement gradually appeared: Usher Caplan's biography, *Like One That Dreamed*; a bibliography, including annotated entries on the thousands of editorials that make up the bulk of Klein's writing; and my own *A.M. Klein: The Story of the Poet*, the first full-length study of Klein to be based on the complete body of his published and unpublished works. During this period, articles began to appear that evinced a new awareness of the previously hidden subcontinent of Klein's writings as well as the trajectory of his development. Some examples are the essays by Darlene Kelly on Klein and Ezra Pound (1998), by Lawrence Kaplan on Klein's translations of Hayyim Nahman Bialik (2005), and by D.M.R. Bentley on Klein's treatment of architecture in his unfinished novel "Stranger and Afraid" (2005).

Moreover, criticism in this period began to reflect a more nuanced understanding of Klein's relationship to the various Jewish traditions upon which he drew. Examples are the essays by John Kertzer on Klein's attempt to construct a poetic identity out of a variety of often contradictory Jewish traditions available to him (1984), by Linda Rozmovits on Klein's troubled relationship to Jewish modernism (1988), and *Third Solitudes: Tradition and Discontinuity in Jewish-Canadian Literature* by Michael Greenstein (1989), with its emphasis on subversion, resistance, and lack of closure.

However, the focus of these and many other Klein studies of this period is still primarily, almost exclusively, on Klein's relationship, however troubled, to Jewish traditions, however defined. What is perhaps most significant about recent Klein studies is that they reflect an important shift in critical perspective, in this case from a "Jewboy['s...] ghetto streets" ("Autobiographical," *Complete Poems*, 2:564) to "other kids of other slums and races" ("Lookout: Mount Royal," *Complete Poems*, 2:687).

One way of describing this change is to say that recent studies of Klein are, to borrow the title of one of Klein's most powerful essays, "In Praise of the Diaspora" (*Beyond Sambation* 463–77). But the

Diaspora being praised is no longer just the Jewish Diaspora but the
much broader Diaspora of peoples of various origins throughout
the world that has come to be seen as one of the defining aspects of
our postcolonial, increasingly globalized, world. Perhaps the most
important influence on the view of Klein as an exemplary figure of
the Diaspora in this sense, is the work of Pierre Anctil, who began
with a social-anthropological study of Jack Kerouac and the French-
Canadian Diaspora and has since gone on to become the leading
authority on the relationship between the Yiddish-speaking and
writing community of Klein's youth and the francophone culture of
Quebec. Anctil's work provides a model for thinking about the relationships between different ethnic and linguistic communities in the
contemporary world, of which the complex interaction between Yiddish-speaking and francophone Montreal exemplified and explored
by Klein is just one example. Sherry Simon's *Translating Montreal*,
with its account of Klein as a translational figure, is an example of
this new critical approach, which does not attempt to root Klein in
a particular tradition but, rather, sees him as creating "new mixtures out of diverse traditions. These are loose blends, suspensions,
whose originating elements do not dissolve" (89). This postcolonial
celebration of Klein's hybridity foreshadows the approach taken by
a number of young critics, who suggest that, as the ghetto streets
that Klein celebrated and critiqued fade from view, his relevance to
the other worlds that have taken their place is clear and strong.

However, there is one other kind of engagement with Klein's
achievement, which, in the end, I think is even more significant than
that of scholars, or even of serious readers in general, and that is the
engagement of his peers – of his fellow practitioners in the fields of
poetry and fiction. Perhaps more than any other Canadian writer,
Klein's life and works have evoked powerful responses – and not
always positive ones – from his fellow writers, who seem to have felt
the need to define Klein's achievement as a way of placing their own.
Obvious examples are P.K. Page's Klein as a Sufi sage and Miriam
Waddington's Klein as a radical socialist from the North End of
Winnipeg, in spirit at least. These and other "almost meetings" with
Klein are a significant indicator that Klein is a force to be reckoned
with. Evidence that this engagement with Klein continues is pro-
vided by *A Rich Garland: Poems for A.M. Klein*, edited by Seymour
Mayne and B. Glen Rotchin, a volume of poetic responses to Klein

by poets of his day and ours. With the exception of Leonard Cohen, who himself has written one of the most moving tributes to Klein, "To a Teacher," it would be difficult to put together such a volume for any other Canadian poet.

Arguably, the two Canadian writers whose engagement with Klein is most intense – and most negative – are Irving Layton and Mordecai Richler. I will not say anything about Layton, apart from pointing out that his achievement would have been impossible without Klein's example; and that his attacks on Klein's supposed naivety and lack of a sense of evil are rooted partly in Layton's sheer competitiveness and partly in his own very different relationship to the Montreal Jewish community. Richler's case is more striking, and it is no surprise that Klein scholars focus upon it. It is a well recognized fact, though not one explored in any detail until recently, that Richler's two most ambitious novels – *St. Urbain's Horseman* and *Solomon Gursky Was Here* – provide strong evidence of his continued engagement with Klein. The search for Joey in *St. Urbain's Horseman* clearly echoes the narrator's search for Uncle Melech in *The Second Scroll*. And in *Solomon Gursky Was Here*, Richler's engagement with Klein is even more obvious since the novel includes a cruelly satirical account of Klein in the figure of the poet L.B. Berger, a pathetic and mediocre sellout. Richler's attitude to Klein and to the community Klein represents for him calls to mind V.S. Naipaul,[1] the colonial who, like Richler, couldn't wait to shake the dust of home from his feet as a young man and make for the big city at the heart of Empire. From this perspective, Richler's attack on Klein is reminiscent of Naipaul's dismissal of Derek Walcott as a limited provincial because, like Klein, Walcott chose to celebrate and mythologize his hybrid roots: there certainly is no term of greater contempt in Richler's lexicon than "provincial." But there is an intensity, a nastiness, to the attack on Klein (Richler doesn't even bother to change the name of Klein's wife Bessie) that demands our attention. Where does this passionate intensity come from? Without getting too Freudian, it seems to me that the Oedipal is unavoidable. Like Jake Hersh, Joshua Shapiro, and Barney Panofsky, heroes of the bulky apologias that Richler produced every decade or so in the latter years of his career, Moses Berger is one of Richler's Self-Portraits of the Artist as a Flawed but Loveable Human Being. And, of course, Moses Berger is the son of the despised L.B. Berger. What this means is that Richler intended to define himself and his own deeply ambivalent relationship to his community by attacking Klein, the father figure, whom he saw, as rebellious sons tend to do, as his exact opposite (ironically, Klein's relationship to his community, as revealed in the *Notebooks*, was at least as ambivalent as Richler's).

Like all lovers and admirers of Klein, I was annoyed at what I saw as Richler's cheap shots when I first read *Solomon Gursky*; however, I am forced to admit that, in the end, Richler's novel is, in fact, one of the most significant testimonies to the continuing centrality of Klein's achievement in our literature.

In support of this perhaps paradoxical and controversial claim I would cite "What Is a Classic?" by J.M. Coetzee, one of the greatest of our contemporary writers, and one who, like Klein, is deeply concerned with the public role of the artist. The essay, which is too rich in its movement and thought to summarize here, ends with a meditation on the status of Johann Sebastian Bach as a classic and on the fact that, for many years, Bach's music fell out of public view. Coetzee argues that the traditional account of the decline and ultimate revival of Bach's reputation is misleading because, even when Bach was little known to the general public, his peers, such as Mozart and Beethoven, continued to study his music and to respond to it in their own works, whether or not the general public was aware of this. Coetzee goes on to say that "the interrogation of the classic, no matter how hostile, is part of the history of the classic, inevitable and even to be welcomed. For as long as the classic needs to be protected from attack, it can never prove itself classic." Criticism, Coetzee concludes, "is duty-bound to interrogate the classic ... criticism, and indeed criticism of the most skeptical kind, may be what the classic uses to define itself and ensure its survival. Criticism may in that sense be one of the instruments of the cunning of history" (16). From this perspective, Richler's attack on Klein – as much as any celebration of him that we scholars can offer – is an instrument of the cunning of history. This will ensure the survival of Klein's reputation as a classic.

NORMAN RAVVIN

On Being Published in Heaven: The Case of Klein and Kerouac

It is the literary scholar, the biographer, and the archivist who have interested themselves in the unfinished and unpublished works left behind after an author's death. Whether these are youthful efforts that proved embarrassing, fragments that did not receive full attention, or simple failures, the role such artefacts should play in our understanding of a writer's work and life is ambiguous and difficult to define. Certain writing lives are consumed with unpublished and unfinished works. A cursory reading of Franz Kafka's biography marks him as, in ways both sad and darkly funny, the prime model for this – with major works incomplete at his death alongside the famous letter to his friend Max Brod that "enjoined him, as his last request, to burn all his writings without reading them – diaries, manuscripts, letters ... as well as sketches" (Begley 2). Almost five decades after his death, the status of Ernest Hemingway's posthumously published *A Moveable Feast* is still shifting, as repeated generations of editors and family members reorder its manuscript and argue for a text that the author would have acknowledged as his. Some writers prepare for the day their papers will enter an archive with a bookkeeper's anxiety, filing copies of letters and consecutive drafts as carefully as a banker might shelve his bullion. This was the case with Jack Kerouac, a famously itinerant and, in later life, dissipated character, who was visited in 1966 by his biographer Ann Charters as she worked on a bibliography of his writings. At Hyannis, where Kerouac lived with his mother, he told Charters, "I've kept the neatest records you ever saw." And there, in his study, Charters found "a meticulously preserved literary archive, as carefully organized as the archives [she] used a few years later while researching his biography" (Charters, *Jack Kerouac*, vii). There was a time, too, when much of Kerouac's major prose work was unpublished, including the many versions he would write of the novel that appeared in 1957 as *On the Road*. In 1955 he prepared for his literary agent a "List of Manuscripts," which carefully accounted for each title, relevant page number lengths, number of copies extant, and associated "Data" related to each: "Rejected by ..."; "Whereabouts unknown"; "'Unpublishable'" (Charters, *Jack Kerouac*, 467–8). Kerouac conceived of the list in order to ask to have everything on it back. This was two years before the breakthrough brought about by *On the Road*, a time when Kerouac was consumed by a sense of his own irrelevance, if not failure. "Clearly," he wrote to his agent Sterling Lord,

> publishing is now in a flux of commercialism that began during World War II; for instance I wonder if Thomas Wolfe's wild huge books would be published today if he was just coming up, like me ... Besides, publishing to me (the big kind like *Town & City*) is like a threat over my head, I know I'll write better when that whole arbitrary mess is lifted out of my thoughts and it's like early morning again, Saturday, no school, overalls and nothing to do but let the imagination play. (Charters, *Jack Kerouac*, 466)

Here, alongside the list-making of a creative artist clearly aware of his work as an oeuvre, a weighty output, is the tantalizing notion of writing purely for writing's sake – an audienceless, individual, almost mythical childhood game of making things up.

Just as Kerouac's formative years can be bracketed by the war years and the beginning of the new, prosperous but culturally ambiguous era of the mid-1950s, so Montreal poet and prose writer A.M. Klein undertook his major projects during these years. Although one can point to successes – in particular the 1948 publication of *The Rocking Chair and Other Poems*, which won the Governor General's Award, and Knopf's release in 1951 of Klein's lone novel, *The Second Scroll* – the decade of Klein's finest accomplishments was underwritten by failure, which was self-perceived and ultimately self-imposed through his total withdrawal from literary and public life in the mid-1950s. Klein left many unfinished works at the time of his death in 1972, most of them untouched and unremarked upon for as many as twenty-five years. Klein's personal archive, upon his death, was not, like Kerouac's, a model of completeness and neatness, nor was it a straightforward treasure trove for biographers and bibliographers. Usher Caplan, who would become Klein's biographer, received the task of organizing and cataloguing Klein's papers when the author's family donated them to Canada's national archives in 1973. Reporting on his labours for a conference on Klein staged in 1974, Caplan noted that the papers were remarkable for what they excluded as much as for what they included. What was there, Caplan tells us, was "*mostly ... the working papers* of a writer at a particular moment in his career – the mid-fifties. Hence there are a large number of both unfinished and unpublished manuscripts from the late forties and early fifties" ("A.M. Klein Papers," 31, emphasis in original). Caplan adds two revealing remarks to this otherwise prosaic list of documents. Klein, he says, seemed "to have looked down upon" the prospect of his work arriving in an archive "as a kind of literary graveyard." And more provocatively, he acknowledges that "there *may* be many items in the files which Klein indeed *would have* destroyed, had he known that they would end up where they did" (31, emphasis in original). The place where Klein's papers ended up was the relatively sequestered Library and Archives Canada – might we think of it as the Fort Knox of national culture? – where the papers were curated and protected from deterioration. The most dedicated Klein reader, and certainly the average citizen, is as unlikely to visit this vault as she is to go to the Royal Canadian Mint, a short distance away on Ottawa's scenic riverside, to view the way the country shelved its gold. Yet, following the A.M. Klein Symposium, the establishment of the A.M. Klein Research and Publication Committee ensured the willingness on the part of editors, in tandem with the University of Toronto Press, to bring much of this material out in annotated scholarly editions. The volumes that have appeared in this series are fine examples of editorial management, and even filial care, whose argument for their raison d'être is not only that they shed light on Klein's published work but also that they bring to light valuable work that readers had yet to see.

It is worthwhile and even a bit sad to consider the state of these materials upon Klein's death. Caplan provides us with an image of them, pre-archive, worthy of a scenarist:

> Most of the collection comes from a four-drawer cabinet that
> used to be in Klein's study. The cabinet contained all of Klein's
> personal and professional papers, excluding those having to do
> with his law practice. By personal papers, I mean literary manu-
> scripts, literary notes, speech and lecture notes, letters, clippings,
> and various personal documents. ("A.M. Klein Papers" 31)

It would not be too romantic a claim, I think, to say that, in this
description, we recognize a truer archive or, at least, something
intimately reflective of a writer's working life, its graveyard quality, where the unfinished and abandoned efforts of real literary
struggle are mixed with more basic and everyday clippings, notes,
and "personal documents," a kind of unintended bricolage. Might
we not imagine, even yearn for, a bare white room overlooking the
Ottawa River, whose only object might be the "four-drawer cabinet"
(what colour was it? were its fittings impressive or cheap, its work-
ings smooth or rough?) to which the interested visitor could apply
to open and gaze inside if not actually remove anything from its
drawers? No publications, scholarly work, or critical bibliographies
would arise from such an archive: only descriptions of visits to the
room itself and musings about the edges of files, note paper, scattered handwriting. And if Caplan is correct in his surmise, things
Klein never intended to publish would remain hidden, tantalizingly
so, from the public eye.

When Caplan approached the collection upon its arrival at the
national archives, he found it in a "disordered state." Manuscripts
were "broken up and scattered through any number of file fold-
ers .... In the end, some of the jumbled files were intentionally left
intact, while others were completely taken apart and reordered."
Caplan made inventories of the collection's "original ordering," and
it occurred to him that "perhaps some hidden order was being tam-
pered with" ("A.M. Klein Papers" 32). If not a hidden order – and
most likely this was the case – at least the real texture of failure,
of things finished with because they were unfinishable. Such things
reflect the dark side of a writing life that is entirely connected with
inwardness, with private struggles and even with heartbreak. All
this is lost, impossible to recover, though Caplan, in his early dealings with Klein's archive, is able to offer us a few pointers on the
orthography of failure. Poems that were "never typed up," he tells

us, reflect "Klein's own dissatisfaction with them" (33). The first chapter of an unfinished novel built upon autobiographical details from Klein's youth consisted of "fourteen numbered sheets ... in the same ink throughout. There are numerous revisions in that ink, as well as a few in a second ink and in pencil" (Klein, *Notebooks*, 203). Further work on this manuscript includes several "sheets of preparatory material ... a plot summary ... and notes and drafts of various episodes" (204). This is all redolent of the peculiar habits of the writing life, but it is that first chapter, with its revisions in two colours of ink as well as in pencil, that best evokes the lost time of discarded drafts. These different working-throughs result in a personal trail, like the impressions of an animal as it passes again and again along a familiar pathway, leaving tracks that are inevitably covered by wind and the changing seasons.

From the foregoing remarks we begin to recognize some of the particular experience of failure and misdirection that lurked in Klein's career and that led Kerouac to claim that he was "coming up" at the wrong time for his work to gain broad acceptance. Kerouac's first novel, *The Town and the City*, appeared in 1950 from Harcourt Brace in New York, a maker of the kind of books that Kerouac dubs "the big kind." It received largely positive reviews but was no breakaway success. It was followed by an outpouring of creative work that made up the list of unpublished manuscripts Kerouac sent to Sterling Lord in early 1955: "Doctor Sax," "Mary Cassidy," "The Subterraneans," "Visions of Neal," and "On the Road." The latter went through numerous major redraftings and rejections. Describing it on his "List of Manuscripts," Kerouac notes that the book, as it stood in 1955, had been "[r]ejected by Harcourt Brace, Farrar Straus & Viking" (Charters, *Jack Kerouac*, 467). The appearance in 2007 of a publication entitled *On the Road: The Original Scroll* allows non-archivists and those without the resources to send a stand-in to Sotheby's to bid on the artefacts of literary celebrity, to read and understand the meaning of failure, of faltering, of rejection, review, and rewriting, with relation to Kerouac's finished 1957 novel *On the Road*. Kerouac's book is, ironically, one of the twentieth-century texts whose reputation promotes the myth of creative momentum at the expense of writerly reworking and editorial influence based on conventional market expectations. It is commonly said – at times by Kerouac's compatriots – that he wrote *On the Road* in a non-stop three-week burst of work in April 1951 (Cunnell 23). In his introductory essay to *The Original Scroll* Howard Cunnell accounts for the mythic status of Kerouac's "clattering typewriter" alongside "Jackson Pollock's furious brushstrokes and Charlie Parker's escalating and spiraling alto saxophone choruses in a trinity representing the breakthrough of a new postwar counterculture seemingly built on sweat, immediacy, and instinct, rather than apprenticeship, craft, and daring practice" (2). Kerouac promoted the myth himself: "'I wrote that book on COFFEE," he told his friend and muse Neal Cassady, guessing that he'd averaged six thousand words a day (Cunnell 24).

Both Kerouac's friends and enemies grasped hold of this myth of creative outpouring. "First thought, best thought" became Allen Ginsberg's guiding poetic mantra, while Truman Capote dismissed *On the Road* as typing, not writing. But Cunnell is quick to discount the possibility that *On the Road* appeared, magically, "out of clear blue air" (3). He tells us that Kerouac worked on early versions of the novel – one would not yet call them drafts – in 1948. In his notebooks in 1949, Kerouac writes: "I'm stuck with On the Road .... I DON'T KNOW WHAT TO DO" (14). In early 1950, he completed a ten-page hand-written manuscript in French, which he then translated, under the tentative title "On the Road ECRIT EN FRANCAIS" (15). At this point he considered a French-Canadian narrator and envisioned the book as being in pursuit of his own francophone roots. Among the outcomes of these various efforts was a range of decisions regarding the nature of his autobiographical fiction. In the 1951 draft that we now have under the title *The Original Scroll*, details like Kerouac's father's death, his own lifelong attachment to his mother, and the real names of his compatriots and friends are all unchanged. This may have been one aspect of the scroll version that assured its rejection, which was forthcoming from editor Robert Giroux at Harcourt, Brace in 1951 (Cunnell 32–3). The manuscript would go through at least two more major re-drafts before the substantial editorial going-over it received from Malcolm Cowley and others at Viking. Cunnell suggests that the scroll version of *On the Road* is a "markedly darker, edgier, and uninhibited text than the published book. The original version of *On the Road* is also ... a younger man's book. Kerouac was still only twenty-nine in the spring of 1951. By the time the novel was published he was thirty-five" (31). And one shouldn't expect that the spectre of rejection was waved away with the novel's completion. While *On the Road* was in press Viking rejected a newer work entitled "Desolation Angels."

The long period of writerly challenge – from the 1950 appearance of *The Town and the City* until the 1957 publication of *On the Road* – is a part of Kerouac's life that fits only loosely with the myth of the young, ever-wandering literary adventurer. Allen Ginsberg turned those years of rejection into something inspirational in the lengthy dedication he added to the 1956 publication of his poem "Howl." Though Kerouac's period of rejection was soon to end (in part with Ginsberg's help) Ginsberg dedicates his own breakthrough text to

> Jack Kerouac, new Buddha of American prose, who spit forth intelligence into eleven books written in half the number of years (1951-1956) – *On the Road, Visions of Neal, Dr. Sax, Springtime Mary, The Subterraneans, San Francisco Blues, Some of the Dharma, Book of Dreams, Wake Up, Mexico City Blues*, and *Visions of Gerard....*
>
> All these books are published in Heaven. (*Howl* frontispiece)

Here we find a response to failure with some similarities to Kerouac's own notion of great writing, which needed no audience, no conventional reception. Yet Ginsberg goes further, beatifying Kerouac's kind of writerly labours. The phrase "published in Heaven" has slipped out into the culture, and there are many (possibly too many) would-be authors making themselves known via blogs and websites who celebrate their own or their best friend's unpublished masterpiece using Ginsberg's phrase, unattributed.

Failure in Klein is a more tangled theme. For Klein there was no Allen Ginsberg, friend and guardian agent, to send out the good word regarding unpublished work. And Klein was far more concerned, even obsessed, with the idea of his own failure and the lack of an audience than was Kerouac. His fears regarding failure expressed themselves in prose works that were themselves failures – most of them unfinished, unread by anyone other than Klein himself. We know of these following the 1994 publication of *Notebooks: Selection from the A.M. Klein Papers* by editors Zailig Pollock and Usher Caplan. The *Notebooks* include a set of incomplete drafts begun in the early 1940s. Among the earliest of these, the editors tell us, is a

portrait of a profoundly frustrated poet, named Kay, whose
poetry is of no interest to his community, which values only his
hack work as a speech-writer and lecturer. Klein's anger at his
community for failing to appreciate the true value of his work
is expressed in a number of sardonic portraits of his family, his
associates, and the Montreal Jewish community as a whole,
revealing a side of him which one would hardly suspect from his
published writings (Klein, *Notebooks*, xi).

In 1945, Klein approached this material anew and attempted a prison
novel he entitled "Stranger and Afraid." Towards the end of the
decade Klein is at work on another draft – this time an untitled novel
– which shares thematic similarities with the earlier projects. Its date
of composition places it in proximity to the development of material
for *The Second Scroll*, and it addresses the Holocaust and the importance of religious ritual life and the calendar of Jewish holidays to an
emotional understanding of contemporary Jewish Montreal.

Unlike Kerouac's scroll, the drafts in Klein's papers were never
considered, much less rejected, by an editor. In his *A.M. Klein: The
Story of the Poet*, Zailig Pollock points to how these reveal a tendency towards a more autobiographical kind of fiction than that
undertaken in *The Second Scroll*. In one case, the names of the writer's parents appear as part of a sketch of the narrator's home (Klein,
Notebooks, 130), and the Chevra Thillim Synagogue, which recurs
in the drafts, was the name of the synagogue at which Klein's father
was a founding member (Klein, *Notebooks*, 221).

In his writerly progress towards *The Second Scroll*, Klein's
reworkings of previous material included a substantial downplaying of the autobiographical character of his fiction. In Kerouac's
case, publishability included Viking's demands that real names be
changed to avoid libel accusations. The lost father is no longer the
narrator's, but his friend's; and the beloved mother of early drafts is
transformed into a far less affecting aunt in the final version of *On
the Road*.

The unfinished fictional drafts found in Klein's papers are, like the
original version of Kerouac's novel, darker and more cryptic than the
book they may have helped him write. In this, I would not think of
them as works "culminating in *The Second Scroll*" (Pollock, *Story*,
140). In certain ways they represent what had to be cast out so that

a novel like *The Second Scroll* could take shape. Kerouac's "original scroll" had a similar character, as writing that set itself outside mainstream publishability. When looked at by his friend and writer John Clellon Holmes, the draft drove Holmes to: "walk by the East River, cursing Kerouac in my head for writing so well in a book which, I was firmly convinced, would never be published.... I recall that I cursed *him*, rather than the publishers, or the critics, or the culture itself that was excluding him" (Cunnell 36). Whether one agrees that Kerouac and Klein write well in their unpublished drafts, one can certainly appreciate Holmes' recognition of writing that is too strange, too out of step with contemporary styles, to be published. This was, arguably, the key writerly experience shared by Kerouac and Klein. Their fiction took shape at odd angles to the mainstream. Each followed recognizable models: in the case of Klein the structure of *The Second Scroll* is Hebraic, its diction Miltonic; while in Kerouac's work, one senses the streetwise documentary impulse of John Dos Passos and the incantatory long line of Walt Whitman. In both cases, these influences were of little use in popular terms since such literary models were either largely irrelevant or, worse, noxious to the contemporary reader. Neither Klein nor Kerouac were representative men of their times; rather, they distilled aspects of tradition into something unique and strange, what Harold Bloom calls the uncanny, the thing so original it seems to have no true antecedents.

Bloom's notion of the uncanny in literature is evocative in this context for a number of reasons. It accounts for how a creative work can be strange and great at the same time; in the case of a literary voice it implies uniqueness and the accomplishment of overgoing one's predecessors, to use Bloom's terminology — an obliteration of them through an original use of those predecessors' greatest creative triumphs. In Bloom's work on biblical literature the notion of the uncanny evokes an otherness, especially in the Hebrew Bible, of characters like Yahweh, and certain scenarios, like Moses' appearance before the burning bush. An uncanny creative force, according to Bloom, is greatness bound to strangeness, a singularity that somehow overcomes its own idiosyncrasies and breaks free of tradition, making tradition over in its own image. These are tantalizing terms in which to view both Klein and Kerouac. But in order to better understand each writer's role and relevance it is worthwhile to consider in what way they each found themselves strange, at odd angles to the cultural mainstream, in some way ahead of their time. Klein addressed these issues in a poem, first published under the title "Portrait of the Poet as a Nobody," which found its way in revised form into his 1948 collection *The Rocking Chair and Other Poems* as "Portrait of the Poet as Landscape." The context of the lesser-known early version of the poem is revealing, if a little ironic. "Portrait of the Poet as a Nobody" took up six pages in the June/July 1945 volume of *First Statement*, the literary magazine edited by the young Irving Layton. In 1952 Layton, with his influential co-editor Louis Dudek, brought out an anthology entitled *Canadian Poems, 1850–1952*, which aimed to present an appreciation of the country's literature "both critical and new in spirit" (Dudek and Layton 13). The anthology's introduction, co-signed by "THE EDITORS" but full of a characteristic Laytonesque rhetoric and wit, is cutting with regard to some of the poetry included in the pages that follow. The first decades of the Canadian twentieth century are said to have been spent "waiting in snowed-in silence" (14); the influential E.J. Pratt, a major mid-twentieth-century Canadian poet, is given qualified support though his work is marred by the fact that he is "a lusty narrative poet of the old school" (14); and Earle Birney, whose poem "David" was becoming a popular standard, shows "little verbal sparkle and excitement" (15). The "most arresting figure" the editors can proffer is A.M. Klein:

> A fecund writer, Mr. Klein has produced five books, each of them as idiosyncratic as his own signature. In the tragic history and martyrdom of his people he has found a powerful subject to hand – and the gifts of wit and imagination, it should be added, to make use of it. It is to the frail, the insecure, the disappearing, to the what-was-and-will-no-longer-be, that Mr. Klein habitually addresses himself and from which his poems derive their infectious charm. They have the charm, the slippered urbanity, of reminiscence, of pathos, of the happy stories one tells oneself when one is alone and sad. For Mr. Klein has consistently written about hard-pressed minorities romantically fighting for survival – Jews, French Canadians, Indians, poets – in that order of fractional distillation – in a prosaic and heedless world. His best poems are full-bodied and civilized and have the arresting excellences of verve, originality, and compassion. His recently

published *The Second Scroll* and *The Rocking Chair* (second edition) are landmarks in the development of Canadian letters. (15)

So the editors feel, seven years after Klein confirmed his own feelings about the poetic pursuit as the purview of Nobodydom:

Not an editorial-writer, bereaved with bartlett,
mourns him, the shelved Lycidas.
No actress squeezes a glycerine tear for him.
The radio broadcast lets his passing pass.
And with the police, no record. Nobody, it appears,
either under his real name or his alias,
missed him enough to report.

It is possible that he is dead and not discovered.
It is possible that he can be found some place
in a narrow closet, like the corpse in a detective story,
standing, his eyes staring, and ready to fall on his face.
It is also possible that he is alive
and amnesiac, or mad, or in retired disgrace,
or beyond recognition lost in love.

We are sure only that from our real society
he had disappeared; he simply does not count....
("Portrait of the Poet as Nobody" 3)

The ironies here are multiple: in a wonderful poem, straightforward in its diction, at the same time dark and brightly evocative, which would go on to become a classic of our literature, much anthologized and discussed, Klein confirms creative collapse. His tendency, worked out in greater detail later in the poem, is to compare poetic accomplishment to "the fletcher's" craft, to things hopelessly outmoded (8); or to the breakthrough undertakings of postwar prosperity – the "local tycoon ... epical in steel" or the jazzman "who blows his flash of brass in the jittering hall" (6). He links his literary ideals to the past, to "his great-grandfather's ghost," rendering himself a "throwback, relict, freak" (4). Lurking behind all this is Klein's notion of literary work as something that could be rightly called uncanny, beyond the everyday:

Therefore he seeds illusions. Look, he is
the nth Adam taking a green inventory
in world but scarcely uttered, naming, praising,
the flowering fiats in the meadow, the
syllabled fur, stars aspirate, the pollen
whose sweet collision sounds eternally.
For to praise

the world – he, solitary man – is breath
to him. Until it has been praised, that part
has not been lived. O item by exciting item –
air to his lungs, and pressured blood to his heart. –
they are pulsated and breathed, until they map,
not the world's, but his own body's chart! (7)

Conveyed in the above stanzas – entangled with the more troubling issues of personal defeat – is an appreciation, whether accurate or not, of a change in culture. Klein's poem points to a pattern that one should be able to trace, as well, in contemporary social history: the writer finds his role and influence suddenly transformed in the wake of a perceived shift in ideals, in economic system or social context. Such a transformation is given dramatic and particular shape in Abram Reitblat's provocatively titled essay "The 'Novel of Literary Failure.'" Reitblat's historical tableau is specific: Russian literary life between the 1860s and 1890s, when social and economic revolution transformed key elements of national literary life. Reitblat tells us, relying in part on the literary history conducted by N.V. Shelgunov, that, in the first years of this period, the role of writers in "social reforms and vigorous social movements" placed them in a "'position of honor'" as "'society's teacher, educator, and prophet'" (Shelgunov qtd. in Reitblat 19). In a new way,

the classless ... intelligentsia, minor and middle-ranking officials,
and the gentry began to view literary work as both honorable
and prestigious. We note that in the 1860s many provincial
teachers abandoned their fairly well-paid positions, moved to
St. Petersburg, and became writers (Aleksei Suvorin, Aleksandr
Kruglov, Aleksandr Shkliarovskii, Oktavii Mil'chevskii, and
others). In the late 1850s fee scales began a rapid ascent, and by
the early 1870s they had risen by approximately 150 percent.

Soon several hundreds of people were making a living from literature. Our estimates indicate that in 1855, 8.9 percent of authors supported themselves with their writing, while by 1880 that number had risen to 32.9 percent.

In the 1880s and the 1890s, as the number of newspapers and illustrated weeklies grew, the basic call for writers came from these publications. But the substantial number of writers who had internalized the notion of the writer as prophet and teacher, as public bellwether, and as servant of the highest ideals were having difficulty shifting to the role of purveyor of entertaining and sensational texts, cherishing no particular ambition and aiming only to satisfy the desiderata of a different culture. (19–20)

Following these developments, through the 1880s and 1890s, when reforms were quashed after the assassination of Czar Alexander II, Reitblat points to the appearance of a tradition of novel writing based directly upon these changes. The "Novel of Literary Failure" not only reflected reality but also created a shift in literary focus. In a reading of a number of these novels from the 1880s and 1890s, Reitblat points to their presentation of how the

"committed" writer gradually becomes convinced that, since it is impossible to write how and what he wishes and still make a living from literary honoraria, he must either "sell" himself by taking a job at a newspaper or illustrated magazine and producing pieces that will make it (or even by accepting specific writing commissions), or he must quit literature entirely (that is, stop writing, die, etc.).

.... But the writer has a family, is accustomed to a certain lifestyle, and often would like to be well received by the readership. As a result, he frequently elects to work for a newspaper or illustrated magazine, caving in to circumstances while recognizing as he does so that this represents a moral failure on his part. (12–13)

This description is uncanny in its applicability to Klein's inner life and sense of his writing life, especially as it relates to the predicament in which he saw himself during the final decade of his active literary life. Can we then, as concisely as Reitblat has done, convey a context and the specifics of Klein's own movement away from idealism into a perception of defeat so complete that he ceased to write altogether? Reitblat's argument is well supported by the degree of social and historical detail he brings to it: it is, arguably, the story of a time and place, inhabited by a generation of writers who, at least unconsciously, understood themselves and their work in similar ways. Klein's position is in many ways singular and solitary; his views can be seen to be narrowly focused on himself and not reflective of a generation of literary workers with whom he shared similar challenges. But certain key social and historical determinants are worth raising. One can assume that Klein's inherent idealism regarding literary life arose from a number of his formative experiences. The Montreal of his youth was an important centre of Yiddish literary life, and Klein's Old World upbringing, his leftist inclinations, and his facility with Yiddish allowed him a view of the rich cultural creativity of his surroundings. In the unfinished prose work "Stranger and Afraid" the narrator's childhood neighbourhood is viewed through "the windows of the big cafeteria" where "philosophers sat stirring the livelong tea" (Klein, *Notebooks*, 81). Literacy and the life of the mind were promoted, too, by his childhood religious home life, where a learned father's library became the subject of "Heirloom," one of his best known poems:

> My father bequeathed me no wide estates;
> No keys and ledgers were my heritage;
> Only some holy books with *yahrzeit* dates
> Writ mournfully upon a blank front page –

Klein attended McGill University from 1926 until 1930, where he studied classics, political science, and economics; played an active role in the Debating Society; and founded the *McGilliad* literary magazine. These formative years placed him at the centre of a rising tide of literary modernism – a kind of renewal of Canadian national literary life – that confirmed Montreal's role as the centre of Canada's creative avant-garde. It is not difficult to devise from these details some sources of Klein's literary idealism, but it is less easy to recognize, as Reitblat does for his Russian writers, the social shifts that might quash such idealism. Canada before the Second World War was no more inclined towards its writers than it was after 1945, and postwar prosperity brought about an increase in publishing, editing, and journalistic work, whether through such institutions as the CBC or via the kind of independent literary careers that a growing national literature could support by the onset of the 1950s. Klein's accomplishments, as celebrated in Dudek and Layton's anthology, reflect these possibilities. It is tempting to understand Klein's dividedness over his reception as the outcome of his varied allegiances, his willingness to do community work, his commitment over many years to the journalistic and editorial work he did for the *Canadian Jewish Chronicle*, his decision to maintain a day job as a lawyer and to avoid the sort of academic career many of his contemporaries chose. These commitments proved divergent rather than complementary. To this predicament Zailig Pollock adds an element of Klein's personality that he calls a "lifelong disturbing obsession with his reputation" (Arnold n.p.). Lurking behind all of these considerations are the unknowns related to Klein's emotional life, whose effects began to show themselves most severely in the early 1950s. These issues – entirely private so unresolvable – prove a distraction. They are crucial yet they play no part in the structure of Canadian literary society following the Second World War. Like the four-drawer cabinet, which Caplan surmises Klein may have wished had remained closed, these concerns are among the author's true secrets.

Though Jack Kerouac viewed his literary apprenticeship as reflective of his outsider status, developments in New York City literary culture after the Second World War placed him at the centre of what would become a major movement in postwar American fiction. True, his compatriots in the late 1940s were beat in the old-fashioned sense of the word. Times Square, where Kerouac first heard Herbert Huncke refer to himself as "beat," inspired the sense of rejection, diffidence, and marginality felt by many of his compatriots. But as early as 1948, commentators in such mainstream venues as the *New York Times* were recognizing a new literary and cultural development – the first postwar youth movement — which was confirmed in Kerouac's *On the Road*: "They were like the man with the dungeon stone and the gloom, rising from the underground, the sordid hipsters of America, a new beat generation that I was slowly joining" (54). Kerouac's transformation through his fiction of failure, of outsiderness and idiosyncrasy, into the figurehead of a mainstream movement is a pattern different from that described by Reitblat. According to Kerouac, the hipsters of the late 1940s were "serious, curious, bumming and hitchhiking everywhere, ragged, beatific, beautiful in an ugly graceful new way" (Kerouac, "About," 559). But by the final third of the 1950s, following the success of Kerouac's novel, a new version of these characters had taken shape, both in the media and in the culture more broadly. "In 1958," one critic among many tells us of *On the Road*, "as a paperback, it was the hip-pocket bible of the *beat generation*, the bridge between the hipsters and the hippies" (Tamony 274).

With the success that arrived with *On the Road* came the seeds of Kerouac's personal failure. The unpublished work that he had demanded back from Sterling Lord found its way into print, but fame hit hard. He persisted as an itinerant, moving, often with his mother in tow, as if he could not abandon his years as a "bum, a brakeman, a seaman, a panhandler, a pseudo-Indian in Mexico" (Kerouac, "Beatific," 570). As he achieved ever greater centrality and influence, Kerouac descended further into alcoholism and self-destructiveness, which contributed to his death at forty-seven in 1969. Success included the "horror" he "felt in 1957 and later 1958 naturally to see 'Beat' being taken up by everybody, press and TV and Hollywood borscht circuit" (571). These latter media protagonists, viewed as exploiters by Kerouac, are the antagonists in Klein's "Portrait" poem. Like Kerouac, Klein felt these antagonists robbed him of his relevance.

Failure bookends Kerouac's career, in the decade of rejection before the breakthrough of *On the Road* and in his period of drunken decline in the 1960s, when he dedicated himself to his mother and shut out the compatriots who had aided him in his work and daily life in the immediate postwar period. Like Klein, he chose (or was chosen by) silence, irrelevance, darkness.

There is one final context against which we can measure the balance of literary idealism and the sense of failure in the work and lives of Klein and Kerouac. It is their relationship to the broader literary tradition and its sources in religious life. Here there is a shared motif – the scroll – which is emblematic of both authors' oeuvres. In Klein's case the scroll plays a central role in his effort to model the narrative structure of *The Second Scroll* after the Hebrew Bible. With its messianic story-line divided into five books, each bearing a name of one of the five books of the Bible, *The Second Scroll* is a major and singular postwar effort to link the Holocaust and previous Jewish catastrophes to the canon of Jewish religious literature. Both the first American edition of the novel, released in 1951, and a Canadian paperback imprint, which first appeared in 1961, made much of the Torah scroll on its cover art and typography. This intrigue and investment in the idea of the scroll finds its way into Klein's lesser works, too. An early short story, which appeared in 1933 in the Toronto-based *Jewish Standard* provides a portrait of the life of a scribe and his dedication to creating what will be his "seventh scroll," in honour of the saintly wife he has lost. A more complete, even exhausting, exploration of such themes appears in the long essay Klein published in parts over a period of a month in the *Canadian Jewish Chronicle*. Entitled "The Bible Manuscripts," it offers a somewhat idiosyncratic investigation of the possibility of tracing back from the Torah as it is known today to its ostensible source at the hands of Moses. In a tone of both high-flown rhetoric and irony, Klein inquires of "the two tablets of stone, which Moses [received] ... at Horeb":

> *These* tables, are they extant?
> No.
> What! Lost? Misplaced? ....
> Who did hew them? How is that known? Failing exhibit of the stone tables, how is it known that they ever were?
> From Scripture.
> But the scripture in our hands, which attests to the existence and the disappearance of its own original, is but a transcript.... Have we the name of the copyist? .... was he – world-destroying thought! – of that tribe of copyists who would themselves be authors, who add to their texts what in their arrogance they deem to have been overlooked ... and subtract therefrom what in their obtuseness they deem to be superfluous? (Klein, *Literary Essays*, 135)

Klein follows these questions with a consideration of the customary response to scribal mistakes in the process of making a Torah scroll as well as a loving rendering of the way the scroll, when in use in a synagogue, is dressed: "Its two rollers – trees of life! – project ivory, and on them, royal, the Crown of the Law, silver, behung with hushed bells, like flowercups. Upon the mantle itself – thoracic the Breastplate" (*Literary Essays*, "The Bible," 138). Klein ultimately overcomes the problem of the lost original by a wholehearted embrace of the notion of continuity in tradition: "from the Table of Moses to the Stone of Joshua to the Scroll in the Ark to the writings of Aristeas to the calligraphy of the youngest scribe – the image is repeated and the latest is facsimile of the first. The tradition, then, is an unbroken tradition" (138–9).

These ideas gain remarkable clarity and importance when the time of their publication – late 1951 – is recognized to be contemporary with the appearance of Klein's own *Second Scroll*. In it he supplies a host of images and narrative motifs that can be seen as "the latest ... facsimile of the first" (Klein, *Literary Essays*, 139). His long piece on biblical manuscripts can be seen as a kind of nest into which he would have readers place his novel, which should be read as part of a tradition imbued with continuity, regularity, and reliability.

The scroll plays a less central role in Kerouac's work than it does in Klein's, yet it remains a concrete part of the mythology and legacy associated with the composition of the final version of *On the Road*. Kerouac was a maker of scrolls; in particular, for completing *On the Road*, he worked with "thin, long sheets of drawing paper" taped together so that he was able to turn the work of typing handwritten notes and revising drafts into a kind of endurance sport as the unending ribbon of white wound through his Underwood (Cunnell 24). Kerouac built *On the Road* from a myriad of sources, which included notebook entries, letters he sent and received from friends, and then an ongoing redrafting process, which culminated in the now legendary three weeks in April 1951, when he worked at a typewriter in what his compatriot Clellon Holmes called a "large, pleasant room in Chelsea" (qtd. in Cunnell 24). Howard Cunnell's introduction to *The Original Scroll* points us in interesting directions with regard to the meaning of the scroll as writing work. He likens the "long roll of paper" to the "remembered road," evoking Kerouac's own urge to abandon the "big kind" of publishing in favour of writing that would be "free of all worldly & literary motives" (Cunnell 24; Charters, *Jack Kerouac*, 466). The clattering, sweating, coffee-driven work that Holmes recalls being undertaken in the pleasant room in Chelsea shares certain characteristics with conventional writing work, but it recalls, too, the kind of itinerant labour that Kerouac undertook in the fallow years of the 1950s, when he rode trains as a brakeman. The scroll, like the rails or the American highway Kerouac plied with his friends, is an avenue for breaking through to the new – a new style and voice unburdened by the literary tradition he felt had formed his first novel. Cunnell characterizes the scroll as "something consciously *made* by Kerouac" (24), a personal artefact fashioned for a particular use, which he links to the "intimate, discursive, wild" sentences of *On the Road*. With "improvised notations – dots and dashes – to break sentences," they "pile upon themselves like waves" (25). Kerouac's scroll lacks the tradition-bound qualities of Klein's. It pushes outward, forward, into the vague future, while Klein's is ever conscious of, and bonded to, the past. Their two great mid-century books – *The Second Scroll* and *On the Road* – point in opposite directions.

ELIZABETH POPHAM

"Myself in Time ... and Space": The Letters of A.M. Klein

In *The Silent Woman: Sylvia Plath and Ted Hughes*, Janet Malcolm conveys the vitality of letters as a biographical resource:

> Letters are the great fixative of experience. Time erodes feeling. Time creates indifference. Letters prove to us that we once cared. They are the fossils of feeling. This is why biographers prize them so: they are biography's only conduit to unmediated experience. Everything else the biographer touches is stale, hashed over, told and retold, dubious, unauthentic, suspect. Only when he reads a subject's letters does the biographer feel he has come fully into his presence, and only when he quotes from the letters does he share with his readers his sense of life retrieved.
> (Malcolm, *Silent Woman*, 110)

The lure of authenticity is particularly strong in the case of prominent people, whether poets or politicians. We are intrigued by the possibility that in their letters we can hear the personal intonation often masked in the public voice, that we can piece together the "narrative" of their lives from the evidence of preserved moments in time. And, as Malcolm goes on to speculate, part of the attraction is "the feeling of transgression that comes from reading letters not meant for one's eyes" – in spite of the inseparable "discomfort and unease" (110). This is certainly my experience as a reader of the letters of A.M. Klein.

Today many readers will first become aware of Klein through his literary avatar L.B. Berger, speech-writer to Bernard Gursky, the fictional stand-in for Samuel Bronfman in Mordecai Richler's *Solomon*

Gursky Was Here. The poet L.B. is self-important, parochial, and artistically compromised by his association with the Gursky family. Richler's narrator and alter-ego, Moses Berger, is L.B.'s son, a character whose whole adult life is shaped by his disappointment in his father. While Richler's anger is an extreme manifestation, Irving Layton, Leonard Cohen, and many other Jewish-Canadian writers exhibit Oedipal relationships with A.M. Klein. By allowing us unmediated access to Klein's own voice in the moment, his letters provide a useful corrective. In the narrative that emerges from these fragments of a life, we are reminded that, between 1938 and the early 1950s, A.M. Klein was, albeit somewhat indirectly, a major spokesman for Canadian Jews. He was also perhaps the best poetic technician of his generation – a modernist with an obsessive engagement with history and ethnic identity who was fully aware, as his friend Leo Kennedy repeatedly warned him, that this could potentially ghettoize his work.[1] In this respect, he embodied the conflicting demands of artistry and identity, which are still at the core of Canadian multiculturalism. He was a Zionist who was firmly rooted in Diaspora and a secular Jew who explored the case for faith in the language of Torah and Talmud. In his masterwork, the poetic novel-cum-travelogue *The Second Scroll*, he established a powerful dialectic between autobiography and fiction, documentary and theodicy, outrage at the Holocaust and qualified hope that the messianic potential of the new State of Israel might yet be realized. And he was a public relations consultant for Seagram's and once composed an acrostic for Mr Sam's birthday.[2] He was, in short, a complex and puzzling figure.

For that reason, he was fortunate in his biographer, Usher Caplan, whose documentary approach in *Like One That Dreamed: A Portrait of A.M. Klein* (1982) allowed Klein to speak for himself in excerpts from his published and unpublished writings, speeches, and letters.[3] The A.M. Klein Research and Publication Committee, established shortly after Klein's death in 1972, has worked very much in this spirit: the first three volumes of Klein's collected works – *Beyond Sambation* (1982), *Short Stories* (1983), and *Literary Essays and Reviews* (1987) – made his literary and political journalism and short fiction accessible, while a genetic editorial strategy focused on the evolution of the text has characterized the volumes published since Zailig Pollock assumed the position of general editor – *Complete*

Poems (1990), the collection of unpublished work in *Notebooks* (1994), and *The Second Scroll* (2000). The final volume in the series will be a comprehensive selection of Klein's letters, drawn from the Abraham Moses Klein Fonds in Library and Archives Canada, additional material gathered by Usher Caplan as he prepared to write his biography, and correspondence unearthed from other sources. These letters have been used to establish the genesis of Klein's poetry, fiction, and critical writing; and, in turn, the published volumes have proved useful in the work of annotating the letters.

Profession and Avocation

Klein was fond of making the distinction between his profession – the law – and his avocation as a poet and scholar. With very few exceptions, his letters are the product of this avocation, evidence of his ongoing attempts to balance the necessary business of making a living with service to his community and with his love of language and literature. They are, in one of his favourite expressions, a sort of *apologia pro vita sua* – in legal terms, a defence of his life. Frustrated by the demands of editors and anthologists that he define the source of his poetic inspiration, Klein bristled and balked. However, as Harold Heft observes in his examination of the "lost" Guggenheim application of 1943, the prospect of funding loosened his tongue:

> My ultimate purpose as a writer?
> To express myself; and thus, being in all essential things, save in expression, like my fellows, to express mankin[d]; myself in Time, as centre-point between ancestry and posterity; and in Space, myself in relation to my environment, animate and inanimate, seen and Unseen. ("Lost" 81)[4]

Ironically, while always conscious of his position "as centre-point between ancestry and posterity," Klein was not convinced that posterity would be interested in his papers, and the Klein collection in Library and Archives Canada is characterized as much by what is missing as by what is preserved. He destroyed all the drafts of his early poems, and likely would have done the same with drafts of later ones had he not suffered his breakdown in the mid-1950s. There are no drafts of his masterwork, *The Second Scroll*, although it went through a major structural revision between its initial submission and Knopf's acceptance of the second draft for publication; and there is no manuscript of the line-by-line exegesis of James Joyce's *Ulysses*, which Klein describes to Joyce scholar Ellsworth Mason on 8 June 1948 as "three quarters finished" (Mason Fonds, LAC).[5] On the other hand, as a lawyer, Klein ensured that his letters to editors and publishers were treated in a business-like manner. More often than not, these were written (or dictated) in the law office and typed on letterhead by the firm's secretaries, with carbon copies filed to enable tracking of submissions.[6] As a result, an unusually detailed history exists of Klein's negotiations with editors and publishers about which poems will be published and in which version.

The correspondence associated with his law practice – confidential, and of little literary or personal interest[7] – is largely absent from the Klein collection. The exceptions are Klein's terse letters on 6 March 1956 to his partners, Samuel Chait and Harry Aronovitch, and to the bar associations of Montreal and Quebec, resigning from the firm he had joined sixteen years earlier and signalling his intention to cease practising law (Klein Fonds, LAC, MS 852–57). These letters are the most telling documentary evidence of Klein's tragic withdrawal from the world until his death in 1972. Also missing from the collection are family letters that have been sealed until 2022. Access to family material in the Klein Fonds of Library and Archives Canada is restricted.

Except for a brief stint in Rouyn between 1937 and 1940, Klein spent his entire life in Montreal. As a result, the few personal letters in the collection are to close friends from high school or university whose careers had taken them away from that centre. In these letters, there are a few profoundly personal moments: jubilant congratulations on David Lewis's marriage and elation as Klein announced the birth of his first son (telegrams dated 24 November 1934 and 5 July 1937, respectively; David Lewis Fonds, LAC). However, almost all of his letters move quickly to some aspect of shared business: his candidacy for the Co-operative Commonwealth Federation (CCF) in the case of Lewis; the activities of the Canadian Jewish Congress and, later, the internal politics of *Contemporary Jewish Record* in the case of Samuel Abramson; his "avocation" as a poet in the cases of Leo Kennedy and A.J.M. Smith, fellow poets supporting themselves in copy-writing and academia, respectively; and his dream of making a major contribution to Joyce scholarship in the case of Leon Edel, who had published on Joyce and, although working as a journalist, had by 1939 begun to establish himself as a major commentator on Henry James. Yet these letters are deeply felt and passionately expressed. It soon becomes evident that the "personal life" of A.M. Klein, the lawyer, is supported by the life of words and ideas – of poetry – and driven by the politics of making his voice heard.

Occupying a middle ground between the practice of law and his literary enthusiasms was Klein's ongoing work on behalf of the Jewish community and, as an offshoot, his public relations work for Samuel Bronfman and Joseph E. Seagram and Sons. By the early 1930s, Klein was an experienced organizer for Canadian Young Judaea and was editor of the *Judaean*; by 1937, he was director of "Publicity and Propaganda" for the Zionist Organization of Canada, editing the monthly *Canadian Zionist*; by 1938, he had graduated to the position of editor of the *Canadian Jewish Chronicle*, a position that, until 1955, provided him with both a weekly forum to address Canadian Jews in a crucial period in Jewish history and a venue to publish his own poems and stories. As assistant and speech-writer for Samuel Bronfman, then president of the Canadian Jewish Congress, Klein exercised his rhetorical muscle and soon made the transition to freelance work for Seagram's. In each case, the work was occasionally literary, and often political, as well as administrative.

The inherent complexity of his work for the Congress is perhaps best illustrated by a series of letters in the summer of 1939, when Canadian Jews were reeling from Britain's adoption of the MacDonald White Paper with its restrictions on Jewish emigration and ownership of land in Palestine. Klein's editorial on the subject, "The White Paper," appeared in the *Canadian Jewish Chronicle* on 26 May 1939. In it, Klein voices the outrage of Jews at the British government's *volte-face* – "[a] ghetto is planned where a homeland was contemplated" (*Beyond Sambation* 51) – but he calls for restrained political action to oppose and alter the policy:

> For sensation-seeking journalists, therefore, to speak of boycott
> and war against Britain is dangerous, irresponsible, prima-facie
> demagoguery. The battle against the White Paper is to be fought,
> not with boycott and Anglophobia, but with all those instru-
> ments and modalities which the Government opposition, for

example, employs against unjust legislation of Governments in power. (52)

The next few months show the strategy in action. On 24 August, Klein wrote Oscar Cohen of the Central Division of the Canadian Jewish Congress to inquire whether the Ontario press had covered Samuel Bronfman's recent address to the Western Conference in Calgary (Canadian Jewish Congress Papers). This inquiry takes on a certain irony when we recognize that Klein had no doubt written Bronfman's speech. The irony intensifies when, on 11 August, as a member of the Jewish press, Klein argues strenuously in an editorial for the *Canadian Jewish Chronicle* that the speech was a crucial communication by Canadian Jews to their countrymen that, despite "disappointment ... in the foreign policy of England, as it is applied to Palestine," "we" are a "loyal opposition":

> It is well, too, that at a time when so many malicious tongues seek to describe us with venom rather than with veracity, that our positions should be made clear, and made clear by one who is authorized to speak in the name of Canadian Jewry. That our fellow-Canadians were waiting for some such expression of our national stand, moreover, is evidenced by the echo of approval which the Congress President's remarks received in the Canadian press. Such public relations work, indeed, does more than tomes of apologetics and crates of pamphlets; it speaks that language of the day, and touches the things that count. ("Words in Their Season" 3)

Then, fast on the heels of this editorial, Klein composed and distributed Bronfman's New Year's message to the Jewish community.

As evidenced by this carefully managed sequence of public statements, the "public relations work" for which Klein praises Bronfman was Klein's own. While Bronfman, in his role as president of the Canadian Jewish Congress, was establishing himself as the official spokesman for Canadian Jewry, Klein was working in parallel as their speech-writer and press agent – their coordinator of public relations. Given his commitment to negotiation, it should be no surprise that, in the poetry of this period, Klein experiments with ways to reconcile images of Jewish identity under siege with key figures of the English poetic tradition – Shakespeare, Marlowe, Byron, and Fitzgerald. Echoing Edmund Spenser's praise of Chaucer as that "wel of English undefiled," as Klein explains in his application to the Guggenheim Foundation in October 1943, he "sought to bring to the well of English that mineral content – the wrath of righteousness – which is my heritage from my biblical forefathers" (*The Faerie Queene*, 4.2.32).

Klein's work for Seagram's began in 1939, about the same time that he was attempting to manage the debate over the White Paper. Under Bronfman, the company expanded its in-house publishing to include not only internal newsletters and materials on distillation designed for wider distribution but also – during and after the Second World War – high-profile projects designed to enhance its reputation as a responsible corporate citizen and to further the political ambitions of its president. The most prominent of these was Stephen Leacock's *Canada: The Foundations of Its Future*, which was commissioned and, despite wartime rationing of paper, sumptuously produced with full colour plates by prominent Canadian artists.[8] In 1941, Klein had reviewed the manuscript on Bronfman's behalf to ensure that it would have the desired public relations effect, and he helped to negotiate revisions with the author. In 1944, the Seagram's correspondence shows him reviewing the French translation for potential problems. Once again, these letters evince Klein's anxious attention to appearances – in this case, concern over how to contain potential damage to the reputation of the firm and Sam Bronfman, which might result from Leacock's sometimes racist, if humorously expressed, opinions, which ran entirely counter to the intention that the translation build bridges with French-speaking Quebec. Diplomatically, Klein writes of "passages which permitted of two versions," saying that "in all instances, I preferred and recommended a rendering which would eliminate any possible controversy and offence, or ambiguity – and yet not be false to the original ... there still remain, however, certain sections of the translated version which do trouble me, having regard to the unpredictable nature of national sensitivities" (letter to Bronfman, 20 January 1944, Klein Fonds, LAC, MS 251).[9] While he had written Bronfman's preface to the English edition, he declines to write the French preface but makes detailed and specific recommendations on its contents.

Bronfman acknowledges this service in his dedication of Klein's copy of Leacock's history, which, as Usher Caplan points out, was drafted by Klein himself:

> To my dear friend Abe Klein,
>   In whose soul there is Poetry -
> in whose mind there is truth -
> in whose heart there is loyalty.
>   Who helped me so much with
> my thoughts and immortalized
> them with his golden pen.
>   Sam Bronfman
> Dec 7/42[10]

It is impossible not to hear autobiographical resonance of this work in Klein's depiction of the devalued role of the poet in "Portrait of the Poet as Landscape." Klein may often have felt "menial, a shadow's shadow," the dummy "upon the knees of ventriloquists, ... own[ing], / of [his] dandled brightness, only the paint and board" (*Complete Poems*, 2:636, lines 65, 81–2). The metaphor of ventriloquism is central to Richler's infamous lampooning of Klein in *Solomon Gursky Was Here* as well as to his angry articles on "Mr. Sam" in *Saturday Night*.[11] However, as Colman Klein has maintained, "if there was a sell-out, it was ... for influence .... A hack speech-writer is penning the thoughts of someone else ... this is not what my father was doing."[12] As demonstrated in the small sampling of letters from 1939, Klein may well have felt – especially early in their professional relationship – that he was the ventriloquist, putting policy as well as words in Bronfman's mouth. He certainly can be seen manipulating the intersection of Bronfman's role as spokesman and his own as an editor and journalist to forward a mutual agenda. Indeed, Klein could take heart that many prominent members of the community did recognize and appreciate his voice. For example, when Rabbi Stephen S. Wise, the editor of *Opinion*, wrote on 9 October 1942 to ask him to contribute a monthly column (Klein Fonds, LAC, MS 193), his appeal for "something special, with a little of the Bronfman spirits in it!" tacitly acknowledges not only Klein's association with Bronfman's company but also that Klein was the source of Bronfman's stirring rhetoric for Jewish concerns and causes.

As the correspondence makes clear, Klein's work for Samuel Bronfman and Seagram's was also an increasingly important source of financial support. As Klein explained to his friend Joseph Dainow on 27 August 1943, "I labour at my daily tasks, and unlike a poet support my wife and children" (Lavy Becker Fonds, LAC). Two years earlier, on 24 March 1941, shortly after the birth of his first child, Klein wrote a witty thanks to Bronfman for an unexpected cheque, laughingly indicating that his impulse to an "arrogant gesture of refusal" had been tempered by imagining his wife's reaction (Klein Fonds, LAC, MS140). Klein dreamed of becoming sufficiently established as a writer to leave the practice of law or, failing that, as he joked to Leon Edel, finding a "patron" (15 February 1949, Edel Papers, McClennan Library). When financial success as a writer did not materialize, he accepted the limited patronage of an academic position at McGill, arranged by Bronfman, and found university life an unsatisfactory alternative. In the mid-1950s, once Klein had resigned from his law practice, his work for Seagram's was necessary to sustain the family. Ironically, as he lapsed into silence, it also provided him with at least some engagement with words. While the letters of 1956–58 make a sad contrast with his vibrant interactions with poets, scholars, editors, and publishers in the late 1940s and early 1950s, they show Klein still active, if indirectly, in the world of words and ideas as a consultant on such corporate publication projects as a history of distillation and volumes commemorating Seagram's hundredth anniversary. During this period he worked from home, with his wife Bessie serving as his secretary.

In a letter to Sam Bronfman dated 6 January 1958 (Klein Fonds, LAC, MS 1042–7), Klein recalls his careful scrutiny of Leacock's history. The pamphlet under review was one of the series of publications celebrating the centenary of the House of Seagram, which included a scientific symposium sponsored by the company. "The Next Hundred Years" featured Nobel laureates and ideas that, in 1956, would have seemed like science fiction. If Klein's reactions to the prospect of genetic manipulation, in-vitro fertilization, cloning, and population control to divert environmental disaster seem timid, one should recall – as he advises Bronfman to do – that many readers would recall all too vividly that similar arguments had recently been used to justify genocide.

Apologia pro vita sua

If we are to understand the current fascination with the relation-ship of Klein and Richler's L.B. Berger, we must attend to the let-ters that reveal Klein's work for the Canadian Jewish Congress and Seagram's. However, such considerations serve as a preamble to a discussion of the core of the collection, the "literary" correspon-dence in which we truly reap the benefits of Klein's separation of his profession from his avocation. Here we have reports on works in progress, submissions of manuscripts, negotiations of texts to be published, meditations on poetics and politics that evolve into manifestos, an informal record of Klein's Joyce scholarship, and evi-dence of a growing demand for readings and speeches. Affirmation of his poetic vocation came early: Klein was only nineteen when his "Sequence of Songs" was accepted for publication in *Poetry: A Magazine of Verse*, the leading modernist journal in North America. Yet early success and mainstream acceptance of his distinctly Jew-ish "mineral content" was followed by years of frustration with the difficulties of finding time to write and a receptive audience for his work. He was caught between two stools. His poetry was perceived as too "Jewish" for modernist journals, too modern for the Jewish Publication Society, and occasionally too erudite for either.

For contemporaries like E.J. Pratt, who spent his professional life in a department of English literature, discussion of literature was often work-a-day. However, Klein's letters to other poets, scholars, and publishers are passionate (sometimes overly so) and detailed. Until he actually experienced it during his three-year term as "Visit-ing Professor of Poetry" at McGill University (1945–48), he ideal-ized the academic life. However, on 22 January 1948, he wrote to decline an invitation to deliver a lecture in the United States, while indicating that he might be able to commit to a later date:

> I do not intend to renew my association with McGill – although I was offered a promotion – because all of the excitement and novelty of the thing has gone out. This year I am teaching the same thing I taught three years ago – such a psittaceous existence is not for me. I could, of course, give new courses every year – but who wants to work like a horse even if the horse is Pegasus?

So I am returning to the practice of law where the duties are less
onerous and the rewards – when they come – more generous.[13]

Having experienced academia, he found it to be as humdrum as his
detested law practice. His ideal gravitated towards true freedom,
and he wrote to Henry Allen Moe of the Guggenheim Foundation
on 7 July 1948 to ask his advice about possible sources of funding
for his research on Joyce (Klein Fonds, LAC, MS 391–5). By December, in a letter to Joyce scholar Ellsworth Mason, his frustration is
evident:

> My manuscript is growing apace, and Joyce's wonders do not
> cease. Hardly a week passes by without its revelation. The man
> is inexhaustible, has the true gift of tongues. But when I shall
> finish the work I do not know; again and again I am interrupted
> by having to make a living, not only for myself, but my wife,
> my three children, and my dog. O that my father had left me an
> estate! (Mason Fonds, LAC)

In a letter to Leon Edel dated 15 February 1949, he indulged in a
playful fantasy that he might find "a patron! Somebody who can, for
a dedication, a tribute, or for its own sake finance the completion of
my annotation" (Edel Papers, McClennan Library).

Because he was unable to bring his profession and avocation into
alignment, Klein came closest to living his ideal life as a poet and
scholar – if only indirectly – in his correspondence. Old friends,
A.J.M. Smith and Leon Edel, had established themselves as literary critics; Joyce scholars Mason and John J. Slocum acknowledged
him as an authority on *Ulysses*, providing him with resources to
pursue his goal of producing the ultimate commentary on that notoriously difficult text; James Laughlin, who, as the founder of New
Directions Press, was one of the most important patrons of American modernism, was his publisher and mentor. His ego was fed by
their respect, and he blossomed in dialogue with them. But these
letters also provide evidence of a volatile mixture of delusions of
grandeur and extreme insecurity. There is a bit of L.B. Berger in
these moments. Klein is, by turns, outraged, defensive, and raging
against critics, personal "squibs," betrayals of all sorts. However,
there are also moments when Klein's delivery of his *apologia pro*

vita sua – his explanation or "defence" of his life – gives the reader a true sense of what Malcolm calls "presence," of "a life retrieved" (*Silent Woman* 110).

There is, for example, the analysis of *The Second Scroll* that he – not without self-interest – directs to A.J.M. Smith and Leon Edel, close friends from their days at McGill and a fellow poet and scholar, respectively, but also influential critics who made certain that the novel would be reviewed in the non-Jewish literary press. There is an extraordinary letter (surviving only as a draft) to American poet Karl Shapiro, whom Klein had previously described in articles in the *Canadian Jewish Chronicle* as a "lost Jew,"[14] exhorting him of his responsibility to write as a Jew in the historical moment (Klein Fonds, LAC, MS 227–33):

> Now the continuation of our own culture stands before the Jewish writer as *the* challenge. The hiatus of the Diaspora has been closed – closed even for those who still remain therein. We do not write any longer *in vacuo*; we write in the aftermath of a great death, European Jewry's, and in the presence of a great resurrection. Our miracle, moreover, owns to a miracle's greatest virtue – contemporaneity. (27 December 1948)

Klein's own response to the call is *The Second Scroll*, and the letter shows Klein working through one of the central images and concerns of his novel – the "miracle" of the establishment of the new state of Israel and the paradoxical threat it poses to the culture of the Diaspora. There are also some insights into Klein's modernist poetics in his detailed response to A.J.M. Smith's ground-breaking *Book of Canadian Poetry* (1943) (Klein Fonds, LAC, MS 227–33). He begins with a compliment to the maker of the new canon of English-Canadian poetry:

> I think you have done for Canadian poetry what Palgrave did for English – you have prepared the classic anthology. Not that I compare your standards of criticism with those of Palgrave; he was no slouch, it is true, but he could not escape the Victorianism of his time. By dint of ancestral restraint, you, of a later age, have the advantage over him. The parallel is, however, true insofar as the classical nature of both volumes is concerned.

After your anthology, all other Canadian "flower-collections," hitherto intrinsically suspect, now become comparatively value-less. What I was particularly pleased about is that your approach to your subject, as so admirably illustrated in your well-thought-out and fundamentally sound preface, was eclectic. You did not come to your work with the fixed ideas of a single school, even of a school of seven. You did not, merely because you stole into this century, damn with one devastating gesture, all the fathers that begat us. In every period, you found something worth while remembering; in some, you even resurrected the dead, as you did for me in the case of Heavysege. This is a tribute to your good taste; the peasant can stomach only one diet; the epicure enjoys all delicacies. (5 November 1943)

Noting that "a number of thoughts struck me on first looking into Smith's Homeriana," Klein proceeds to provide a comment on virtually every poet – and the relative wisdom of Smith's selection – in the anthology. There is, however, one major exception: "I skip the new nationalism and the whole period of the pundits, the foster-fathers of Confederation. I cannot read them as carefully as the other poets in the anthology. They have upon me a narcotic effect. They produce in me not only that suspension of disbelief of which Coleridge spoke, but what is worse, a total suspension of all my reacting faculties." And for those who assume that Klein's persistent focus on Jewish culture precludes modernity, his commodious definition of the term is suggested by his activities in the summer and fall of that same year. His 30 November letter to Smith (Smith Papers, FRBL) about the uncertain critical reception of the more "modern" verse in the *Book of Canadian Poetry* – including his own – appears amid a series of letters in which he negotiates revisions to *Poems* (1944) as it is prepared for publication by the Jewish Publication Society;[15] submits *The Hitleriad* to the definitively modernist New Directions Press, which had just accepted nine poems for its Annual;[16] and applies to the Guggenheim Foundation for a grant that would allow him to write "A long poem of homage to James Joyce, rhymed, and employing the linguistic technique of *Finnegans Wake*," in which he would "pour his unconventional language into conventional forms" (October 1943, Guggenheim Foundation Archives).

As this eclectic combination illustrates, while Klein might voice to Smith his wish that influential modernist critic E.K. Brown and anthologist W.E. Collin would stop "flaunting my circumcision" (letter of 30 November 1943, Smith Papers, FRBL), he was deeply committed to maintaining the Jewish focus of his writing. His plans to write a poem in honour of Joyce and a six-hundred-line satiric "Essay on Law" appear first and second on the list in his 1943 Guggenheim grant description of "themes which have been clamouring within me for utterance." They are followed by "an updating of the fourth act of *The Merchant of Venice*, a one-act play set in Prague at the time of the Nazi invasion, and an 'Askenazate Anthology.'" Two years earlier, this commitment to Jewish subjects meant that Klein found himself obliged to defend his decision to write in English rather than in Yiddish. On 21 January 1941 (YIVO), he responded to a critique by eminent Yiddish writer Shmuel Niger (Samuel Charney) that the "difficulty" of the poems included in *Hath Not a Jew* ... "lies in wanting to untie the *culture* of one people, with the *language* of another people" (Klein Fonds, LAC, MS 130–3):[17]

You are right when you say that my book pre-supposes on the part of the reader a knowledge of the Hebrew tradition. Apart from being written because I wished to write it, the book is addressed precisely to those who have that knowledge or those who may acquire it. In English literature reference to a so-called alien culture is not a novelty. Milton's *Paradise Lost* pre-supposes great Biblical knowledge. A better example, – large tracts of English poetry assume on the part of the reader an intimate knowledge of Greek mythology and the close relationship between the various Gods and Goddesses of Greek lore. To amalgamate factors, therefore, of two cultures does not to me appear to be an impossibility – it becomes a certain failure however only when the attempt is stretched to ridiculous extremes, as for example, James Joyce's attempt – in his *Finnegans Wake* – to write in a language which although essentially English is a composite of all the tongues and dialects of Europe. Per contra, Joyce's *Ulysses*, where every chapter has its counterpart in a similar chapter of Homer's *Odyssey* is to my mind a completely successful literary merger of the values of two cultures.

As Klein goes on to explain, the combination of cultures is entirely natural to him as a North American Jew:

> Certainly in a world where one culture impinges upon another, and where time and space have been considerably constricted, it is not surprising that the synthesis should be attempted.
>
> Of course, I make all these remarks as a contribution to a theoretical discussion of the subject and not in relation to my work. Upon its success or failure I will have to let others judge. Suffice it to say that I did not set out of purpose to accomplish a *tour de force*; to show that Hebrew values could be translated into English terms. The above remarks too are not to be considered as an attempt by myself to draw parallels between Milton and Shakespeare and Klein.

However, perhaps the most extravagant commentary Klein offers on his struggle to become a successful Jewish poet is his detailed strategizing with James Laughlin of New Directions Books about how to get *The Hitleriad* into broader circulation. His letter dated 18 October 1944 is a full-blown rant on the anti-Semitic politics of the commercial book trade in the mid-twentieth century. When sending copies of the book to Churchill and Roosevelt failed to elicit an endorsement, and the Book-of-the-Month Club turned them down, the two speculated freely and a bit nuttily on the anti-Semitism of the largely Jewish elite controlling the American market:

> You are right, right, full-face, dead-centre, bullseye right! Myself I never would have volunteered that analysis of the Fadiman, Untermyer, Cerf, Keimberg attitude[18] – you may think of this junta as the composite of their initials – myself, I had deluded myself into believing that this phenomenon was a social, a family secret – but if you, a non-Jew have observed it, have noted it, have written about it, – well, then the shame is out! Let it be discussed. (18 October 1944, James Laughlin Papers)[19]

This is part of an exchange that both participants are clearly enjoying – a joint exercise in the satiric method.[20] As the letter continues, Klein's rhetoric intensifies into a parody of his more philosophical declarations of cultural identity, culminating in his insistence that, while he does not "showcase" his Jewishness, he refuses to hide it "under the counter, like contraceptives." Then the tone becomes more serious:

Let me make myself clear. I am myself not one of those I-am-proud-to-be-a-Jew Jews. A Jew I am; the whole world knows it, and I accept that fact like the fact that I have two arms. I don't go about envying and simulating octopi. I am the possessor, because of the education which my bearded father gave me, of a rich legacy. The burden of Jewry, for me, is not all sorrow; I own – and I am not being arrogant or literary – vast stores of cultural wealth. My grandfather may have been a peddler; but my great-great grandfather was a prophet. As for myself, I believe I still have a contribution to make as a Jew, a contribution to the culture of the group – the whole group – in which I dwell. To my country Canada I am bound by a thousand bonds, infancy, habit, nostalgia, association, *paysage* – all the little things that constitute true patriotism. Other cultures, therefore, I meet as an equal, not as an interloper. I travel on my own passport.

The rhetoric is appropriate to *The Hitleriad* – extreme and outrageous, simultaneously self-mocking and in deadly earnest. It provides evidence of a concerted attempt on Klein's part to make space for both his ethnic and national identities. However, in the context of a personal letter, it suggests a precarious balance between arrogance and a dreadful anxiety that his work will not be accepted.

"Myself in Time ... and Space"

In retrospect, Klein's achievements are extraordinary. Along with other members of the "Montreal Group," he was in the vanguard of Canadian modernism: his poems anchored the modernist anthology *New Provinces* and were staples in the anthologies of the 1940s, which were remaking the canon of Canadian literature. James Laughlin anthologized his verse and issued *The Hitleriad* as a separate volume in the New Directions "Poets of the Year" series, which, in 1943, also included volumes by Dylan Thomas, Yvor Winters, Bertolt Brecht, and George Barker. Laughlin also expressed interest in publishing his commentary on *Ulysses*. *The Rocking Chair* (1948) had been published by Ryerson Press, bringing Klein long-awaited public acceptance in Canada, including the Governor General's Award in 1948 and the Lorne Pierce Medal for contributions to Canadian literature from the Royal Society of Canada in 1956. *The Second Scroll* (1951) was published by Alfred A. Knopf, who had an option on a second novel. And, for a time in the late 1940s and early 1950s, Klein was one of a select group of scholars to whom John J. Slocum was providing photostats of Joyce's letters and manuscripts; he had published three installments of his commentary on *Ulysses* and had given an invited address to the James Joyce Society at the Gotham Book Mart in New York. He was in demand on the lecture circuit, both as a speaker on Jewish politics and culture and as a poet and novelist. But, as the "unmediated experience" of the letters illustrates, success came in fits and starts and required a tremendous expenditure of energy (Malcolm, *Silent Woman*, 110).

The cumulative effect of reading Klein's letters is a palpable sense of his exhaustion due to many years of over-commitment. The extremely positive reception of *The Rocking Chair* and the composition and publication of *The Second Scroll* in 1951 coincided with Herculean efforts to raise funds for Israel and refugee relief. On 2 October 1952, letters to Leon Edel and Ellsworth Mason show him desperately attempting to reassert his own priorities – his research on Joyce. But on 15 October, one day after cancelling nine lectures because of a "slipped disc," he writes to Edel of "putting my Joyce work aside." He begins to withdraw from the many responsibilities he had juggled so effectively over the years. In the fall of 1954, he again sets up a series of speaking engagements, which he then reschedules to accommodate a trip – never taken – to Europe and Israel to research a novel on the legend of the golem. Letters increasingly focus on editing projects for Seagram's rather than on his own writing, and, in January 1956, he writes that he may be unable to accept an invitation to speak because, rather than being "a practising lawyer and able to dispose of my time as I [wish]," he is now "a salaried employee of an industrial concern, where my duties are such that I must be available for its purposes at all times."[21] The few final letters after this point are disappointing for those seeking answers. They are dispirited, without Klein's distinctive wit and energy, his passion, even his outrage. To use his own metaphor, he seems to have lost his "centre," his defining sense of himself "in Time" and "in Space."

ROBERT MELANÇON

A Writer for our Age: Notes on Voice in A.M. Klein's Poetry and Prose

In A.M. Klein's oeuvre, in his poetry, his prose, and even in his journalism and occasional writings, constant attention is given to voice
– that is, to language as a physical phenomenon, to language as it
is performed by one person as it passes through the mouth, thus
acquiring a colour, a rhythm, a resonance unmistakable with any
other, and is transformed in the process into a powerful mark of
individuality. Voiceprint is not less defined than fingerprints. For
Klein, language is not merely a code as a means of communication;
rather, it is the individual speech of a singular person in particular
circumstances, for which none other could be substituted. Reading
any page he wrote, one always *hears* his voice, with its musical qualities of phrasing and its characteristic rhythm. Klein liked sonorous
and complex sentences, developing their subordinate clauses in a
well balanced syntax, symmetrical and numbered:

> Who knows it only by the famous cross which bleeds
> into the fifty miles of night its light
> knows a night-scene;
> and who upon a postcard knows its shape –
> the buffalo straggled of the laurentian herd, –
> holds in his hand a postcard.[1]

There is more than a touch of rhetoric in this opening stanza of "The
Mountain" in *The Rocking Chair*, with its somewhat convoluted
sentence, symmetrically built and twice echoing itself, but there is
much more in it than mere rhetoric. The syntactical symmetries conceal metaphors that are unexpected and unsymmetrical: the cross on

the top of Mount Royal "bleeds" its light into the night, re-enacting the Passion of Jesus, and the mountain itself is a "buffalo" impersonating the North American wilderness in the middle of the city.

Consider the particularities of Klein's voice, in prose, from an article published on 14 May 1948, entitled "The New Jewish State":

> Conceived two thousand years ago on that same day the long agony of exile and dispersion began, – throughout the centuries nurtured in the very body and beneath the heart of the people, – borne, through suffering, with patience, – in its own blood sustained, – the Jewish State is at long last about to enter into life.[2]

Here Klein did not want merely to say something, to convey meaning; he wanted language to embody its meaning, to play it like an actor upon the stage. Hence, in this second example, the postponement at the end of the sentence, after some anticipation has been created, of its principal clause. The reader has to wait before discovering the passage's topic.

Klein likes to play with words, blending their sounds and their meanings in virtuoso performances. There is almost always an unpredictable turn, and the reader can never fully expect what is to come, as in the opening line of "Annual Banquet: Chambre de Commerce": "And as the orators, rewarded roars, scored, soared, bored – ."[3] The semantic progression, sustained by rhymes that are almost too conspicuous, breaks itself on the last unexpected word, when it is on the verge of becoming pompous. Klein often picks a word that is rare, precious, even obsolete if it fits his sentence, but he does so in such a way that the meaning is never obscure for the reader, as in "Soirée of Velvel Kleinburger": "My brother Velvel vigils in the night."[4] Language is not simply a means of communication, but it does convey meaning. For Klein, writing is not what later critics will call mere deconstructionist play; rather, language conveys meanings, in the plural, layer upon layer. In "Portrait of the Poet as Landscape," the editorial-writer is "bereaved with bartlett."[5] One understands at once that the writer cannot look into *Familiar Quotations* for some commonplace to dispatch his eulogy, but why? Because the poet who just passed away was not famous enough – indeed, he disappeared into the landscape – to have his lines inserted in Bartlett's famous compendium. So, as Klein notes dryly, though with deft wordplay, the radio broadcast lets his "passing pass."[6]

Klein was an inspired poet and a technically competent writer who played with all the possibilities of language and, by doing so, put on it the stamp of his personality. At the beginning of "Notebook of a Journey," the diary of his travel to Israel, he produces ten narrations of his departure ("Reportorial, Rhetorical, Sentimental, Ironic, Satiric, Poetic, Biblic, Mishnaic, Talmudic, Cabbalistic") before stating "the plain unvarnished fact. I'm going to Israel!!!"[7] These variations offer an astonishing display of virtuosity, but they are by no means unwarranted: Klein does not only say that he is going to Israel, he lets loose upon the page the tempest of feelings that this event arouses in him ("Reportorial, Rhetorical, Sentimental, Ironic, Satiric, Poetic ..."), and, at the same time, he suggests the impossibility of coming to terms with the varied meanings that can be drawn from the mere fact that the State of Israel now exists, is a place where one can travel or settle, and is no longer an impossible dream. Far from being a purple patch or a bag of sonorous and empty words, such a page compresses meaning as much as possible: try to say and suggest as much in fewer words if you can. And, it should be added, Klein's apparently showy rhetoric is a display of modesty. Where a less subtle writer might be solemn and ponderous, Klein sings a Mozartian aria in prose and ends it with light irony directed at himself: three exclamation marks express his glee upon stating "the plain unvarnished fact."

Quite often, he plays with contrasts, mixing tones and levels of style with a ferocious irony, as in "Annual Banquet: Chambre de Commerce":

And as the orators, rewarded roars, scored, soared, bored –
The man of capital:
You certainly have a wonderful country. Why don't you
Exploit it?[8]

In these four lines, the reader is brought from grandiose rhetoric – slightly too grandiose to be taken at face value – to the most prosaic utterance. The rest of the poem will deflate further any pretension to heightened language and sentiments, culminating in the dryly ironic rewriting of the sublime last line of Dante's *Divine Comedy*, "O Love which moves the stars and factories."[9]

Voice is a mark of individuality and Klein uses it deftly to define a character with vivid immediacy, as in this Chaplinesque portrait of "M. Bertrand" in *The Rocking Chair*:

> Oh, but in France they arrange these things much better!
> M. Bertrand who always, before kissing the female wrist
> rolls the *r* in *charmante*
> admits he owes everything to those golden Sorbonne years.[10]

Each voice is as unique as a face. When describing a character, Klein makes sure he conveys his voiceprint. One has only to think of the mellifluous Monsignor Piersanti encountered in Rome by the narrator of *The Second Scroll* as he pursues his elusive uncle Melech,[11] or of the poultry seller doing his best to lure customers in "A Market Song," a poem in which Jewish life in Montreal in the early 1920s is vividly captured.[12]

Klein often mixes many voices, placing them side by side so they are heard together in euphoric cacophony. The gathering of many languages at once always inserts a burst of happiness into Klein's text: the sentences become musical, light, fast. For instance, in the third chapter of *The Second Scroll*, "Leviticus," the narrator, who is in Rome looking for his uncle Melech, goes to the American Joint Distribution Committee where survivors of the Holocaust from all over Europe are looking for help:

> For here, waiting on the various landings and in the ante-
> chambers of this building, which housed also consulates and
> international societies, were numerous groups of jargoning Jews
> engaged in conversations loud, gesticulative, or whispered. The
> groups overflowed also into the street, and there, in front of the
> little restaurants displaying in their windows straw-girt wine
> bottles and basketed bread, broke up into dialogues, triumvir-
> ates, family scenes. As I made my way up the stairs – the elevator
> was out of order – snatches of their talk reached me to make in
> my mind a polyglot echoing of the more palpable anxieties of the
> exodus.

"Der yid beim tzvaten tisch iz zeir a simpatisher ... Treren...."
"Mais oui, on parle français à Québec."
"In Detroit ich habe eine uncle gefunden."
"Derveil macht er a leben mit di Amerikanski dollaren ... Flei-shige un milchige."
"Az Amerikai di vat magazin nagya jo izlesu."
"Basta!"
"Un restaurant mic, si se poate un bar de coctail."
"Yehudai hagalut, dorshai hagalut ... zocharnu et habtzolim v'et hashomim."[13]

More than any other characteristic, human speech embodies human difference, desire, and dreams. One can almost say that humankind is defined by language or, rather, languages.

In "Montreal", Klein presents himself as the "auditor of [the] music" of the city:

Grand port of navigations, multiple
The lexicons uncargo'd at your quays,
Sonnant though strange to me; but chiefest, I,
Auditor of your music, cherish the
Joined double-melodied vocabulaire
Where English vocable and roll Ecossic,
Mollified by the parle of French
Bilinguefact your air![14]

One must note that Klein "cherishes" most "the joined double-melodied vocabulaire" in which English and French mix, enriched by the "multiple ... lexicons uncargo'd" at the port. Thus, Montreal, "the jargoning city,"[15] where so many languages and communities meet, becomes a summary of the world, a compendium of human diversity. This is the "suaver voice"[16] of his city, a voice made of many voices.

A city is a collective being, yet an individual is no less the result of many encounters and the product of his or her history. This is magnificently conveyed in "A Psalm Touching Genealogy":

Not sole was I born, but entire genesis:
For to the fathers that begat me, this

Body is residence. Corpuscular,
They dwell in my veins, they eavesdrop at my ear,
They circle, as with Torahs, round my skull,
In exit and in entrance all day pull
The latches of my heart, descend, and rise –
And there look generations through my eyes.[17]

Paraphrasing the last line, one could say: "and there speak generations through my mouth." "No man is an island," wrote John Donne.[18] No man is a simple being, Klein might have added: each one bears the whole of humanity, multifaceted, prismatic. Each voice is a chorus of voices.

Where do these remarks lead us? To the very core of Klein's oeuvre and to its universal appeal. The celebration of voices and languages is but an aspect of the praise of diversity that is, in my view, the most salient characteristic, and the most appealing, of his works. Klein celebrated differences, singularities, individuals, communities, traditions, beginning with his own community and his own tradition. He was a Jew, proud of it, and would never have considered assimilation as an option: "Now We Will Suffer Loss of Memory" makes this bitterly clear.[19] But for him, belonging to a community never meant the exclusion of others. For instance, he stood for the Jewish cause in the face of anti-Semitism, but he was at times a champion of French Canadians. Read "The Tactics of Race-Hatred," published in December 1944.[20] Klein was fascinated by the then colourful mayor of Montreal, Camillien Houde, without being blind to the mayor's dubious political views, and when Houde proclaimed the French Canadian "a congenital fascist," Klein replied that this was "simply not true" and that by implying that he was "a fascist by blood, ... Houde [was doing] his own self a great injustice."[21] Nor did Klein condone Jewish nationalism when it became exclusive, intolerant, and closed in on itself. This is made perfectly clear in *The Second Scroll* when the narrator criticizes the new Israeli poets:

They were an intractable lot, these Irgun poets, *sabra* poets,
Yemenite poets, who cultivated a hard intransigence, scoffed at
all delusions intellectual, adored only the soil and the gun.... In
their little magazines they invariably referred to themselves as
Anachnu (Us) – unhappy reminiscence of *nous autres, nos otros,*

sinn fein – xenophobic antonym to *Haim* (Them). Not Israelis did they style themselves, but Canaanites – more aboriginal than the aborigines![22]

Interestingly, what Klein's narrator criticizes most in their attitude is their contempt for the Diaspora:

> They hated the ghetto and its melting, paralyzing self-pity; even the unorientated DP's, fabled in their writings as Herr Flotsaum and Doktor Jetsaum, excited only their satire.... And again and again they slipped into their secondary theme – *shlilath hagaluth* – the negation of the Diaspora.[23]

This is a key point, because Klein viewed the Diaspora not only as the story of unspeakable sufferings but also as the site of unparalleled accomplishments. "In Praise of the Diaspora (An Undelivered Memorial Address)," written in 1953, is one of his last major texts.[24] It may even be considered as his spiritual testament. Written along the lines of a medieval, Petrarchan poem, it is a kind of allegorical procession praising the diversification of Judaism as it dispersed in different countries, encountered different civilizations, interacted with them, was enriched by them, and enriched them in turn. Klein does not praise dispersion per se but, rather, diversification, multiplication, fecundity. In the Diaspora thus envisioned, the Jewish people, without ever giving up its identity, becomes the metaphor of humankind's infinite diversity. The Jew becomes the living equivalent of the Medieval Everyman, but this time not in the guise of an allegorical abstraction: he is "Abarbanel? – of the royal court of Spain ... rabbins and cabbalists, pensive, of premeditated gait...the Duke of Naxos ... portly, dignified, men of influence, the *HofJuden* ... my Lord Rothschild ... barons Hungarian, German, French, the touch of the accolade still upon them ... and now in modern dress, the business-suited tycoons ... Nobel Prize winners ... a Polish revolutionary ... artists, writers, scribes exegetes, scientists."[25] He is humanity itself in its infinite diversity.

Thus, when Klein plays with voices, letting his reader hear different ones, he yields to his taste for individuality, singularity, character. He likes to be himself and he likes others to be themselves. He is fascinated by nothing more than the play of differences, the cacophonic yet paradoxically harmonious juxtaposition of differences. His work never becomes more alive than when different voices are heard simultaneously, like in the passage in *The Second Scroll* in which a crowd of refugees speak a flurry of languages simultaneously; or like the double-melodied bilinguefact poem "Montreal," written simultaneously in English and in French. This work points to the importance of spiritual and intellectual values; human differences are not to be deplored but embraced, not to be downplayed or tamed but nurtured and praised. Nothing seems to me more necessary in our age of globalization and the so-called clash of civilizations than this celebration of human diversity. Klein is a writer for our age.

PART TWO

A Targum Leben: The Translator

REBECCA MARGOLIS

Ken men tantsn af tsvey khasenes?
A.M. Klein and Yiddish

As the torch of mainstream North American Jewish literature passed
from Yiddish to English around him, A.M. Klein remained firmly
planted in both languages. His literary career exemplifies the struggle for Jewish continuity in Canada's Eastern European immigrant
community during the first half of the twentieth century. While the
mass migration of roughly 140,000 Yiddish-speakers in the opening
decades of the century was funnelled into English society through
education in its schools, the pre-twentieth-century norm of Jewish
anglicization was no longer automatic.[1] The upheaval of this immigration – with its strong commitments to Eastern European Jewish
tradition – altered the historic connections of the Jewish community
with Anglo-Canada. During the first decades of the twentieth century, a cadre of Jewish activists resisted acculturation by creating a
comprehensive institutional life grounded in Yiddish language and
culture. Klein – poet, writer, activist, and journalist – not only lived
in the two worlds of English and Yiddish, he actively and publicly
attempted to synthesize them.

More than anyone else of his generation in Canada, A.M. Klein
straddled the worlds of English and Yiddish letters in a dynamic give
and take. Yiddish was his mother tongue and the vernacular of his
Jewish immigrant community, and it nourished Klein as a writer. He
was the product of a centuries-old culture of Jewish multilingualism in which Hebrew-Aramaic (*loshn-koydesh*, the Holy Tongue)
co-existed with Jewish vernaculars such as Yiddish:[2] in this vein,
he once referred to himself as an English-language poet who was
"Yiddish-speaking and Hebrew-thinking."[3] He was educated in
English, and it remained his language of creative expression. He

was at the vanguard of a movement to modernize English-language Canadian literature and to introduce innovative content and form. He nurtured friendships with the Yiddish writers of his day and was an avid reader and critic of Yiddish literature; in many ways, the Yiddish literati proved to be his most astute readers. As a Zionist activist committed to Jewish national revival, he upheld Hebrew, not Yiddish, as the language of a collective Jewish future. As a journalist, Klein maintained close professional ties with the Yiddish daily *Der Keneder Adler* (*The Canadian Eagle*); he edited and was a regular contributor to the *Adler*'s sister publication, the *Canadian Jewish Chronicle* (CJC, 1938–55), and he authored the *Adler*'s English page (1938–41). Like so many of his Yiddish counterparts, Klein – the English writer – was able to support his poetic vocation through the Yiddish press.

Despite these apparent contradictions, Klein embodies more than a Yiddish-English binary: he lived a centuries-old polyglot Jewish experience. Klein employed language as a tool to carve out a place for himself as a Canadian-Jewish immigrant writer as Eastern European Jewish communities worldwide were transitioning en masse away from Yiddish. In the final analysis, his attitude towards the role of language – in particular the relative roles of Yiddish, Hebrew, and English – was determined by context rather than dogma and thus appears highly inconsistent. As an ideologue, his language was political; as a popular journalist and activist, his language filled collective needs for community building; as a writer, his language reconciled art with tradition. For this Canadian-English writer, with deep roots in Jewish Eastern Europe, both Yiddish and Hebrew-Aramaic informed his writing and thought.

This chapter focuses on Klein's complex engagement with Yiddish as an activist, journalist, writer and poet, literary critic and translator as well as the reciprocal engagement of the Yiddish community with his writing. It examines two interconnected areas of this interplay: (1) ideology and community, and (2) literature. Scholars have proposed various readings of Klein and Yiddish: Miriam Waddington asserts that Klein's ongoing interest in Yiddish reflects his secular Jewish identity;[4] Adam Fuerstenberg posits that Montreal's Yiddish life nourished Klein's ultimately failed effort to "move from Yiddish to 'Yiddishkeit'" as he "very consciously set out to transfer the essence of Yiddish culture – the folklore, symbols, even terminology

– directly into English as a defence against Jewish assimilation;[5] Zailig Pollock contends that Klein's career reflects an ongoing attempt at synthesizing two modern ideologies – Yiddishkeit and Zionism, which history proved to be a failure;[6] Sherry Simon characterizes Klein as "'the first,' as the liminal figure on the threshold between the Yiddish past and the English present."[7] My focus is the deep ambivalence that marked Klein's active engagement with Yiddish from the outset. I argue that the root of this ambivalence lies in his attempt to synthesize two realms that increasingly acted like oil and water: his multiple identities as a Zionist, critically acclaimed popular Canadian-English writer, and carrier of – and public spokesperson for – Eastern European Jewish tradition.

Ideology and Community

A product of Montreal's Jewish immigrant neighbourhood – "virtually a transplanted Eastern European Yiddish town"[8] – Klein was immersed in multiple languages and cultures: Yiddish, Hebrew, English, Latin, and French. The Klein family's arrival in Canada in 1910 coincided with the country's highpoint of Ashkenazi mass immigration and the development of an all-encompassing Yiddish life that included a vast network of political, social, educational, and literary organizations. Raised Jewishly observant in what he referred to in his poem "Autobiographical" as "the Yiddish slums,"[9] Yiddish was the language of his home,[10] where he was exposed to Yiddish folklore and Hassidic tales. He absorbed the traditional Eastern European mode of Hebrew-Aramaic-Yiddish textual study at the neighbourhood Talmud Torah, where he received his Jewish supplementary education. Moreover, he came of age into an anglicizing Jewish community as Yiddish faced attrition locally as well as internationally. While successive waves of immigrants had bolstered Canada's Yiddish milieu as well as its institutions to promote Jewish continuity through Yiddish – at its height in 1931, 96 percent of Canada's some 155,000 Jews declared Yiddish as their mother tongue, with that number rising to 99 percent in Quebec – the community followed a global shift away from Yiddish.[11] Thus, while he was born in Europe, Klein's family claimed Montreal as his place of birth and he was educated in the local English Protestant schools, where he was exposed to the classics of English literature.

Klein's community activism and journalism would embody all of these strands.

Yiddish and English Youth Cultures

Klein was a member of a new generation of Canadian Anglo-Jewish activists and intellectuals that emerged out of this Yiddish immigrant milieu. Born or raised in Canada, they identified English as their vernacular and as the language of proactive Jewish culture. At McGill University, where he majored in classics, political science, and economics (1926–30), Klein's social circle included Leon Edel, F.R. Scott, and A.J.M. Smith, and he was involved in the fledgling McGill Movement and its venture to forge a modern and cosmopolitan tradition of Canadian English letters. Unlike his Yiddish contemporaries who had immigrated to Canada as adults, Klein filtered his Jewish legacy through an anglicized lens, whereby English served as a versatile literary vehicle to which he could hitch his multifaceted linguistic and cultural heritage.

Despite wider trends away from Yiddish, Klein participated in the vibrant Yiddish cultural life that emerged in the interwar period. From childhood on he was a regular patron of the Jewish Public Library and participated in its Yiddish cultural activities; as an adult he would speak at Yiddish functions and serve on the board alongside local Yiddish activists. In high school, Klein was one of the founders of the "Sholem Aleichem Club," a group of young Jewish intellectuals that gathered to discuss modern Yiddish literature.[12] In his student days, Klein began to establish close personal and professional relationships with leaders of the Montreal Yiddish community – writers, poets, critics, and political figures – including H.M. Caiserman, Moishe Dickstein, Shimshen Dunsky, N.Y. Gotlib, Rokhl Korn, Ida Maze, Melech Ravitch, Sholem Shtern, Shloime Wiseman, Yaacov Zipper, and, most significantly, J.I. Segal.[13] Klein's contacts in the Yiddish world provided him with inspiration and encouragement throughout his literary career. Among the most important of these was Caiserman, editor of *Der Keneder Adler,* and a literary critic, who was an early admirer of Klein. Caiserman's groundbreaking anthology, *Yidishe dikhter in kanade* (*Jewish Poets in Canada,* 1934), refers to Klein as "the most Jewish (*yidishster*) among Canada's Anglo-Jewish poets."[14] Klein was reviewed and praised by

Yiddish critics for his lifelong project to create a Yiddish-English synthesis. Ideologically, however, Klein was never a Yiddishist – a proponent of Yiddish per se as being key to Jewish continuity – and did not participate in the future-oriented and maximalist Yiddish culture that David Roskies has termed "a utopian experiment."[15]

Zionist Activism

In his Zionist activism, with its call for the revitalization of modern Jewish life, Klein expressed a strong stance on the relative place of Yiddish in the modern world. As editor of the *Judaean,* the monthly of Canadian Young Judaea (1928–32), he articulated an ideology of Cultural Zionism that identified Hebrew, not Yiddish, with the collective Jewish future. In a 1928 article, Klein outlines an inevitable post-Haskalah (eighteenth-century Jewish Enlightenment) transition away from Yiddish:

> There came a time, however, when creed was assailed by the incredulous. Then it was that some asserted that the Yiddish language would prove the salvation of cosmopolitan Jewry. Yiddish was to be the Esperanto of the Jews of the whole world – we were to be united in speech. The mother tongue, they believed, would make us all brothers. Uniformity of language, they argued, would produce a national entity; a language was to hold a people; a nation was to live on words.
>
> This, too, proved illusion and fantasy. Statistics show that Yiddish as a spoken language is on the decline. Language alone, the Yiddishist must declare with a defeated bitterness, cannot suffice to preserve a national being – one cannot, if I may be permitted the expression, hold a nation by its tongue.[16]

In an article published in 1929 entitled "Our Language," Klein calls for a revival of Hebrew at the expense of Diaspora languages, notably Yiddish:

> Certainly we must not adopt as our mother tongue the languages of our environment. As for Yiddish, by one to whom that language is dear, a decision can not be made without a pang of anguish – he recognizes the importance of its literature, he

acknowledges the appeal that it has to him, both because of itself and its associations, he basks in its typically national idiom, but he must in the final analysis put it on the same level as Ladino and other languages acquired in the exile years. It is with Hebrew that our past is bound; it is with Hebrew that our future must bind itself.[17]

Moreover, in a 1929 review of *Koheles*, Yehuda Zlotnik's Yiddish translation of the book of Ecclesiastes, Klein further underlines the limitations inherent in Yiddish: the very venture of translating biblical Hebrew into idiomatic Yiddish is fraught with difficulties, with the "high seriousness" of the former being "hardly recognizable in the Jew of the Middle Ages, whose religion is passive resignation, and whose strong and self-asserting Judaism has been beaten into a pulpy impersonality."[18] For Klein, it was in the mouth of this Jew that Yiddish was born – and where it formed its essential character. Thus, early in his journalistic career Klein threw down the gauntlet: Yiddish embodied the past and was dear to him on a personal level, but, as a product of exile, it could not serve as the language of Jewish continuity. While his own stance was unequivocal, as editor Klein did entertain more nuanced discussion on the relative positions of Hebrew and Yiddish.[19] And, despite his rhetoric, Klein did not, in the final analysis, identify modern Hebrew as the new carrier of Jewish literature during his lifetime.[20] For Klein, this Jewish language was a Judaized English.

The Anglo-Jewish Press

Klein's corpus as a journalist in the Anglo-Jewish press – and the position of Yiddish within it – was determined by varying factors beyond Zionist ideology. His audience, current events, and the character of the publications themselves were all key influences. Whereas those who read Klein in the *Judaean* were Canadian Zionists, his readership at the *Canadian Jewish Chronicle* was an anglicizing Jewish community facing increasingly virulent anti-Semitism on the local and world stage. In the years before, during, and after the Second World War – the core of his journalistic career – Klein's international focus in the *Chronicle* was advocacy for the Jews in Nazi Europe and the creation of a Jewish homeland, while his local focus was on education and the building of strong community institutions. Moreover, the *Chronicle* was far from a highbrow publication conducive to the expression of a nuanced ideology on Yiddish or any other topic. Waddington asserts that Klein "conferred on this parochial journal his pithy essays and reviews" on such subjects as English poetry, translations from Hebrew poetry, and Yiddish folklore.[21] Contemporary Jewish culture and the arts account for a relatively small proportion of Klein's journalistic output, and when they are discussed, the focus tends to be on collective rather than on aesthetic considerations.

There is little in Klein's journalistic corpus that points to the efflorescence of modern Yiddish culture that was taking place worldwide during the interwar period. Instead, when Klein discusses Yiddish, he tends to situate it in the mythic past. Klein was writing in English for an acculturating community bound together by a shared Jewish identity, but not necessarily by a shared connection to Yiddish. His relatively few articles on the subject tend towards elements of traditional Jewish folk life. His deep knowledge of Eastern European lore was the subject of a number of columns devoted to the translation and elucidation of Yiddish folklore, which appeared in the *Chronicle* from the 1930s thorough the 1950s[22] and culminated in a six-part study, "The Yiddish Proverb," in 1952.[23] Here Klein characterizes the Yiddish folksong as "a simple and direct utterance" and Yiddish proverbs as unique because of the intrinsic nature of their language: "pathos is the word for Yiddish."[24] In short, Klein echoes the dominant attitudes of the nineteenth-century *maskilim* (proponents of the *Haskalah*) that Yiddish was the language of the *folk*, the popular masses, rather than the high literary language it had become during his lifetime.

His entry into Anglo-Jewish journalism pulled Klein into the local Yiddish milieu. As editor of the *Chronicle*, he shared an office with the *Adler* at 4075 Saint Laurent Boulevard, which put him in regular contact with the *Adler*'s founder and publisher, Hirsch Wolofsky, editor-in-chief Israel Rabinovitch, and literary editor J.I. Segal. In this capacity, Klein covered communal developments and major milestones in the Yiddish world, both in the *Chronicle* and in the *Adler*. For example, he covered the establishment of Montreal's new community art theatre, the YTEG (Yiddish Theatre Group),[25] the developments of the modern secular Yiddish Jewish People's Schools,[26] and visits by Yiddish writers such as H. Leivick

(Leivick Halpern).[27] He noted the birthdays of local Yiddish cultural figures such as historian B.G. Sack and Caiserman,[28] and he eulogized others: Reuben Brainin, co-founder of the Jewish Public Library; Chaim Zhitlovsky, the moving force behind the modern secular Jewish school movement; and Wolofsky and Segal.[29] Moreover, he authored glowing appraisals of works by Canadian Yiddish authors, such as former Montrealer A.A. Roback's *History of Yiddish Literature* (1940), Simkhe Petrushka's *Yidishe folksentsiklopedye (Jewish Popular Encyclopaedia,* 1942), *Mishnayes (Mishna Translation and Commentary in Yiddish,* vol. 1, 1945), and Melech Ravitch's *Mayn leksikon (My Lexicon,* vol. 1, 1945).[30] Klein also reviewed several volumes of poetry by his favourite contemporary Yiddish poet, J.I. Segal.

Despite the *Adler*'s role as a primary forum for new movements in Canadian Yiddish culture – in particular belles-lettres – Klein's engagement with the Yiddish press and its English offshoots remained on a community level. His article marking the *Adler*'s thirty-fifth anniversary in 1942 spotlights the newspaper's inclusive and community-building character.[31] A column celebrating Rabinovitch's fiftieth birthday in 1945 praises the purity of his Yiddish and reflects the values that Klein associated with the language: "his writing, despite the pressure of daily production, remains so purely and authentically Yiddish; its tone, its spirit, is of the folk .... It is a style pure, native, and without those blemishes which the intrusion of alien elements invariably effects."[32] For Klein, writing during the war and postwar period when European Jewish civilization was facing decimation, Yiddish increasingly became an unchanging monument to a lost past.

Ideology and Language Choice

Klein's own decision not to write poetry in Yiddish was rooted both in ideology and circumstance. He was a Jewish writer whose creative language was English and who consciously created what Waddington has called "a personal synthesis of speech" of the multiple languages at his disposal – Yiddish, Hebrew, French, and Latin.[33] In this synthesis Klein faced a paradox: he wrote in English for a general audience, many of whom did not grasp the Jewish dimension of much of his writing. Thus, in 1943 at the request of A.J.M.

Smith, Klein supplied a letter of explanatory notes to his poetry for an upcoming Canadian literary anthology. He expressed hope that these notes not be published and suggested that perhaps Smith had placed too much emphasis on the "Judaica" in his selection.[34] This problem had earlier came to the fore upon publication of Klein's first book of poetry, *Hath Not a Jew ...* (1940), which enjoyed a limited critical response in English circles. A letter, written in Yiddish, by New York Yiddish literary critic Shmuel Niger, spotlighted the issue:

> Won't your English readers need a Yiddish and Hebrew diction-
> ary just as I need an English one? Even more – for me the dic-
> tionary is sufficient; I doubt if it would be enough for them ....
> In order to really penetrate most of your poetry, it isn't enough
> to have the explanation of a particular word or name; it is neces-
> sary to have lived in the atmosphere which nurtures your out-
> look and gives it life. Here no dictionaries will help. One needs
> to have breathed the air of learning Gemara, of Chassidism, of
> Jewish folklore.[35]

Niger's comments resounded with Klein and elicited an explanation, penned in English:

> I have just received your very serious letter and I hasten to reply
> to it because it raises questions not noted by anyone else in rela-
> tionship to my poetry, except yourself – and myself. It is, in a
> word, the problem of synthesis between cultures.
> First, as to the question of language. Today English is my daily
> tongue. I speak it everywhere and always, except to my mother,
> who understands only Yiddish...[36]

Tellingly, Klein finds it necessary to explain why he is not writing in Yiddish: he must defend his choice to write Jewishly in a non-Jewish tongue. He goes on to state, "If I wrote to you in Yiddish you would observe immediately that I think – insofar as sentence structure is concerned – not contents – in English. Naturally, therefore, if I had to write poetry – and the compulsion thereto I shall not now discuss – it had to be in English."[37] Perhaps most central to Klein's relationship with Yiddish is his characterization of the subject matter of his poetry:

What does, what should, a poet write about? Only about what
he feels and what he knows. Borrowed emotions will not do ...
Rilke once made a very pertinent and indeed profound remark
when he said that all poetry is an attempt to recapture one's
youth and even one's childhood. For me that means recaptur-
ing the nostalgia and the beauty of my childhood, which was a
Yiddish-speaking and Hebrew-thinking one, Mitnagid from my
teachers, Chassidic from my father. The theology, I may say, has
vanished but the tradition has remained.[38]

For Klein, writing in English did not entail cultural assimilation
but, rather, a new linguistic synthesis. English had supplanted Yiddish as the new carrier of Jewish creativity; his goal as a writer was
to nurture it until he could form it into a deeply Jewish language.
As Usher Caplan writes, "Klein consciously worked at synthesizing
a style – almost a separate dialect – that would express as faithfully
as possible the content of Jewish civilization in a rich, authentic English."[39] The result was Ludwig Lewisohn's characterization of Klein
in his forward to *Hath Not a Jew* ... as "the most Jewish poet who
has ever used the English tongue."[40]

Whether English could or should supplant a Jewish vernacular
such as Yiddish was a question to which Klein had no answer. This
problematic is epitomized in an encounter with Melech Ravitch,
who repeatedly and unsuccessfully tried to draw Klein into Montreal's Yiddish literary milieu: "When Ravitch once asked him flatly
how he could presume to be a Jewish writer and not write in a Jewish language, Klein seemed to take offense and petulantly walked
away from the conversation – stung as much perhaps by the right-
ness as the wrongness of the question."[41] For Klein, the question was
absurd. He was writing in a Jewish language – a Judaized English. In
a letter to American Jewish writer Karl Shapiro in 1948, Klein discusses the shifting linguistic inventory at the disposal of the Jewish
writer – Hebrew, Aramaic, and Arabic:

Mendelssohn judaized even the German, and as for English, it is
already a vessel prepared. Milton prepared it.
    Now the continuation of our own culture stands before the
Jewish writer as *the* challenge. The hiatus of the Diaspora has
been closed.[42]

Klein drew from the same branch of Eastern European Jewish tradition as did the Yiddish writers, but in English.

Literature

Within the group of Montreal poets that gathered around avant-garde publications such as *Preview*, *First Statement*, and *Northern Review* – P.K. Page, Irving Layton, and Louis Dudek – Klein stands out for weaving his dual Canadian-Jewish heritage into both his themes and language. At heart, Klein was an ambivalent modernist, and his poetry on Jewish themes appears to be anti-modernist in subject matter as well as style.[43] This tension comes to the fore in Klein's relationship with Yiddish, where he draws heavily on Yiddish tradition while downplaying or rejecting overt modernist tendencies in Yiddish literature. Ultimately, Klein related to Yiddish as a mechanism for connecting with collective tradition rather than as a future-oriented creative force that might set the individual apart from his or her community.

Yiddish Folklore

A close familiarity with Yiddish folklore is reflected in Klein's poetry and prose, both in style and content. Fuerstenberg asserts that the Jewishness of Klein's writing transcends easily identifiable religious influences such as language, ritual, and custom; it is "an atmosphere and an attitude" that pervaded every aspect of his being. Moreover, this "Yiddishkeit," which encompasses the "verbal nuances of Yiddish speech" and the "emotional range of Jewish experience," was expressed in particular through Klein's use of folklore.[44] Caplan points to the blend of English nursery rhymes with Yiddish folksong in Klein's children's poems from the 1930s.[45] Waddington identifies numerous poems in *Hath Not a Jew* ... that present aspects of traditional Jewish life lived in Yiddish: customs, anecdotes, folkways, parables, jokes, and typical Yiddish wit. While less prevalently, the *Hitleriad* (1944) includes Yiddish wordplay and puns; the *Second Scroll* combines English, Hebrew, and Yiddish with literal translations of Yiddish idioms.[46] She identifies Klein's use of folk elements – beliefs, dance, figures such as dwarves, proverbs – as well as evidence of his knowledge of the intricacies of the Yiddish language.[47]

Likewise, Hassidic lore – which had expressed itself in the Yiddish vernacular from its beginnings – permeated Klein's writing. Phyllis Gotlieb discusses the ways in which Hasidism's populism is represented in *Hath Not a Jew* ... and how characters from Hasidic lore, in particular Rabbi Nachman of Bratslav, appear in *Poems* (1944) and *The Second Scroll*.[48]

Among Klein's few forays into drama are two works that draw on the legendary Yiddish folk figure Hershel of Ostropol. Klein's verse play by that name, which appeared in the *Chronicle* in 1939,[49] synthesizes English and Yiddish, its style a blend of Elizabethan comedy and Yiddish *purimshpil*.[50] The play reflects Klein's effort to integrate his Yiddish heritage in new ways. G.K. Fischer's study of the play asserts that it reflects "Klein's determination to instill new vitality into Yiddish folklore."[51] According to Fuerstenberg, the play reflects "Klein's ability to transplant Yiddish folklore and the particularities of the Yiddish language into poetry, while serving his own temporary concerns." Situating the play within the context of its publication at the outbreak of the Second World War, he argues that the use of the "quintessential Yiddish folk figure of the *luftmentsh*" – the man who survives by his wits and maintains a sense of confident optimism – serves as editorial commentary that both admonishes the shtetl's passivity and praises its resilience in the face of impending danger.[52] In the postwar period, Hershel of Ostropol featured in a script for musical comedy entitled *Worse Visitors We Shouldn't Have*, which Klein completed in 1952.[53]

The Problem of Yiddish Modernism

Despite the prominent Yiddish influences in his writing, Klein distanced himself from the modernist movement in Yiddish literature. As a journalist, Klein commented on international Yiddish literary culture with relative infrequency. During and after the Second World War, he wrote essays on the popular folk poet Itzik Manger and on Yehoash's translation of the Bible into Yiddish, but these were few and far between.[54] He translated poetry by New York poets Yankev Glatshteyn and Mani Leib into English.[55] However, rather than present the Yiddish avant-garde, his wartime and postwar translations of works such as Glatshteyn's "Smoke" served to memorialize the losses of the Holocaust. As Zailig Pollock points out, "Klein tended to dismiss the many Yiddish poets whose work reflected the spirit of modernism." This was particularly true for modernist poet Moyshe Leib Halpern, whom he asserted in a letter to Shmuel Niger was "not a particularly Yiddish poet; he was essentially European and twentieth century."[56] Near the beginning of his poetic career, Klein translated Halpern into English; these translations, which appeared in the *Chronicle* in 1932 as a tribute following the author's death,[57] exemplify Klein's ambivalence about Yiddish modernism. As Linda Rozmovits contends, Klein radically altered and subverted both the text and subtext of the original Yiddish.[58] A member of New York's *Di Yunge* (Young Ones) group of poets, Halpern presented the grit of the urban, immigrant experience in direct, edgy verse, which, according to Rozmovits, Klein rendered into a "virtually unrecognizable, thoroughly demodernized form."[59] She characterizes Klein's translations of six poems from Halpern's avant-garde volume, *In nyu york* (*In New York*, 1919), as "radically unfaithful."[60] Klein decontextualizes the poems, elevates Halpern's diction, adds detail, and reworks narrative lines, which strips the poetry of its power. For example, here is the second stanza of *"Mayn portret"* ("My Portrait"):

In the original Yiddish (transliterated):
Breyte noz un teyvlbremen

tseyn un lipn volfish vild
ober oygn hob ikh bloye,
oygn bloye, gut un mild.

In my own English translation:
Broad nose and devil's eyebrows,
teeth and lips wolfish wild,
but I do have blue eyes
blue eyes, good and mild.

Consider Klein's version:

Platyrhine nose and devil's brow.
My lips are lupine in intent;
Howbeit those my eyes are blue,
Are blue and most benevolent.[61]

Rozmovits suggests that Klein's "unsympathetic treatment of Halpern's poems" reflects the problem of Jewish artistic modernism that lay at the heart of both his and Halpern's work.[62] With modernism advocating individual innovation over collective tradition, Jewish modernists faced an ongoing struggle of two diametrically opposed forces: that of their art and that of their community. Halpern's aloofness from his Jewish community represented a source of tension for Klein. Klein dealt with this problem paradoxically; for example, he was a modernist poet who critiqued modernism's elitist tendencies, in particular in Jewish writers, whom he accused of shunning their identities.[63]

At the same time, Klein's translations of Halpern embody the poet's early struggle to create Jewish poetic discourse in English. Esther Frank posits that Halpern represented a means for Klein to work out his own poetics, for example by employing Elizabethan diction.[64] This experiment is akin to Klein's Hebrew-English translations of Bialik's poetry in the 1930s, which Lawrence Kaplan characterizes as "subject to the failures of poeticisms, overwrought archaic Elizabethan rhetoric, elevated diction, and the like."[65] Although Klein rejected Halpern as embodying the true spirit of Yiddish, he drew on him to push the boundaries of his own poetics.

Klein and J.I. Segal

Ultimately, Klein favoured writing that offered a positive portrayal of Jewishness, and he responded affirmatively and often sentimentally to Yiddish writing of this vein. Both Rozmovits and Pollock suggest that this explains his fondness for the poetry of J.I. Segal, with its warm depictions of traditional Jewish life.[66] Segal appears as Klein's favourite among contemporary Yiddish writers. Klein translated his verse into English,[67] and he enthusiastically reviewed his books of poetry.[68] The two poets were friends who mutually admired each other's work and shared a common ideal – to transplant and preserve Eastern European Jewish tradition in Canada. Each experimented with Jewish-Canadian literary modernism, Segal in Yiddish and Klein in English. Fuerstenberg asserts that Segal was "one of his main inspirations for his attempt to adapt the folk culture and idiom of Eastern European Yiddish tradition to the English language."[69]

There is a deliberate selectiveness behind the aspects of Segal's literary career that Klein chose as inspiration. Segal was the moving force behind Canada's Yiddish modernist movement: he cultivated a close affinity with the *Di Yunge* – he lived and wrote among them in New York between 1923 and 1928 – and served as founder and editor of avant-garde Canadian literary journals. However, Klein does not discuss Segal's role as Canada's pioneering Yiddish modernist; rather, he spotlights the poet's link with a Jewish past as epitomized by the idyllic Hassidic milieu of Segal's youth in the shtetl of Koretz. In his review of Segal's *Lyrik* (1930), he writes: "the main characteristic of the book is its elemental simplicity, its primitive naiveté. It is poetry unadulterated by literariness."[70] Klein's reviews of Segal's *Lider un loybn* (*Poetry and Praise*, 1945) emphasizes Segal's role as "the last of the Mohicans" and elegist of a vanished world.[71] He juxtaposes Segal with his modernist contemporaries:

> No other contemporary poet has developed so authentically Yiddish a muse – it is not the muse of Mani Leib, which is essentially Slavic, nor that of the late Moishe Leib Halpern, which was much worldlier, nor of the Russian Yiddish poets, who show perhaps a wider scope, but certainly a thinner intensity. It is rather the poetry which might have been that of the Bratzlaver, if the Bratzlaver had spoken verse instead of prose.[72]

At Segal's death in 1954, Klein wrote: "Poetry for him, the faithful guardian of an antique tradition, was not only a calling to be followed; it was a call to be answered. That call came to him across the generations by way of an unbroken sacred legacy."[73] For Klein, Segal's Yiddish poetry, with its simple vernacular and Hassidic spirit, came to encapsulate the losses of the Holocaust, of "a world passed by."[74] It is perhaps more than coincidental that Klein's own decline into silence coincided with Segal's death.[75]

The Hitleriad

The permeability of the threshold between English and Yiddish comes to the fore in Klein's mock epic poem *The Hitleriad*. Its twenty-seven stanzas employ the declamatory style of Augustan verse to offer biting criticism of Hitler and his henchmen. Writing in the mode of the moralizing public poet, Klein anticipated a broad readership for the work and a corresponding galvanization of public opinion against the Nazis. Composed in 1942–43, *The Hitleriad* was published in 1944 to disappointing critical reception, virtual silence from American-Jewish critics, allegations of failure by Canadian critics, and limited popular success.[76] While less damning than other reviews, fellow Anglo-Jewish writer Irving Layton praised the technical mastery of the work but strongly questioned Klein's choice of satire in the face of Nazi brutality.[77] More recently, Michael Greenstein opened his chapter entitled, "Canadian Poetry after Auschwitz" with a reference to Klein:

> Before writing *The Second Scroll*, A.M. Klein published *The Hitleriad*, a mock-epic poem contravening Theodor Adorno's famous injunction, "No poetry after Auschwitz." But *The Hitleriad* lacked the necessary historical distance for coping with the enormity of the Holocaust: satiric, Augustan rhyming couplets proved inadequate to this unparalleled tragedy, and by the time Klein had grasped the historical perspective, he succumbed to silence, as if in obeisance to Adorno's prophetic caveat."[78]

Needless to say, few people "grasped the historical perspective" better than Klein; rather, *The Hitleriad* has been badly misunderstood, in large part because of the missed Yiddish connection. After all, *The Hitleriad* appears to be a work composed from a deliberately universal stance and stripped of a Jewish voice. Even Klein wrote that "the only thing Hebraic about it" was "perhaps its indignation and compassion."[79]

Melech Ravitch offered the most insightful reading of the work in a review in the *Adler*, in which he unravelled some of the apparent incongruities of *The Hitleriad*. Identifying Klein as one of the leading Anglo-Jewish poets to bring his Jewishness to the fore, he points to the conflict inherent in authoring Jewish literature in non-Jewish languages. However, Ravitch praises both the skill and content of the *Hitleriad*: it "gives courage" and "takes the bull by the horns" by tackling burning issues while still maintaining its poetic integrity and not becoming "Jewish–hysterical." He concludes that it is "a refreshing Jewish work, although penned in English," and calls for a Yiddish translation of the full text.[80] The following week, J.I. Segal obliged by publishing a Yiddish translation of poem XXVI of *The Hitleriad* in the *Adler*. This poem, arguably the most "Jewish" in content, refers explicitly to the Nazi genocide. Here is the first stanza in the original English:

Let them come forth, those witnesses who stand
Beyond the taunt of perjury, those ghosts
In wagons sealed in a forgotten land,
Murdered; those phantoms the war-tidings boast,
Those skeletons still charred with the gestapo brand![81]

This poem would have had great personal resonance for a reader of
the *Adler,* who would have been well informed about the atrocities
described. It is also among the most simple in its use of vocabulary.
Here is Segal's translation:

zoln zey aroyskumen di eydes, shoyn derleyzt, bafrayt,
fun hinter der farshverung in zeyer loyterkayt.
in vegener farziglte in a fargesn land
derharget; fantomen vos dertseyln nokhanand.
di meysim glien nokh unter shtomp fun der geshtapo hant.[82]

This translation has stripped Klein's poem of its Augustan verse – it
appears in the more familiar rhyming couplets – and in the process
effectively removes the moralizing distance between the poem and
the events it is describing. This radical change in tone is akin to
Klein's own translations from Yiddish to English; or, the rewriting
of poetry to suit the aesthetic considerations of a very different poet
and the expectations of a very different audience.

From a Yiddish perspective, *The Hitleriad* fits into the corpus of
Jewish literature. Ravitch makes a case for the essential Jewishness
of the work in the satiric mode that English readers found so problematic. As Caplan points out, the work emerged from an author
"steeped in a tradition that did, in fact, allow him to make even
Hitler the butt of satire."[83] Klein was writing through the lens of an
age-old Jewish tradition of lampooning the enemy. Among Ashkenazi Jewry, the annual dramatization of the Book of Esther, in the
Yiddish *purimshpil,* had long served as a venue for laughter and the
breaking of communal taboos. Caplan writes: "Strange as the results
of this aesthetic may now seem in certain parts of *The Hitleriad,*
it must be said that Klein's weakness for black humour and melo-
drama, the mingling of laughter and tears, was profoundly Jewish
and a hallmark of his Yiddish mentality."[84]

Translations of Yiddish Books

The synthesis of Yiddish and English is evidenced most directly in Klein's translations of books by Montreal Yiddish writers. Klein authored an English rendition of *Adler* publisher Hirsch Wolofsky's memoirs, *Mayn lebns rayze*, which appeared in 1945, a year before the Yiddish original.[85] As Pierre Anctil has shown, Klein's *Journey of My Life: A Book of Memoirs* omitted and altered the original content to render it universally accessible, elevating Wolofsky's folksy, popular, and idiomatic Yiddish to a high, literary English.[86]

Klein's review of Israel Rabinovitch's study of Jewish music, *Muzik bay yidn* (*Music Among Jews*, 1940) stressed the need for translation: "It is regrettable that as yet the book appears only in Yiddish; an English translation would be a consummation greatly to be desired."[87] Klein undertook this project in 1952 and produced an abridged version of the original text. True to his word, *Of Jewish Music, Ancient and Modern* did reach a wider audience and received praise for the quality of its language.[88] In transformation through translation, both works served to universalize and elevate the Yiddish originals.

Conclusion

Even with the profoundly Yiddish character underlying Klein's writing, his relationship with Yiddish evinces a deliberate distance. During the interwar period and even more so during and after the Holocaust, Klein presents Yiddish as a folk language and as a source of respite in the past. This relationship stands in direct contrast to the generation of Yiddish literati that, in Canada as well as in the United States, was active in creating a vibrant Yiddish culture. Anita Norich has documented the wartime Yiddish writers and critics who were engaged in pushing the boundaries of literary modernism as well as the very concepts of modernity.[89] Klein's attentiveness to Yiddish was motivated by a collective Jewish home vanishing and then vanished. This can be seen in his "In Praise of the Diaspora (An Undelivered Memorial Address)" (1953), which serves both as a eulogy for the lost culture of the Yiddish Diaspora and as a call for its ongoing affirmation. Klein extols the linguistic versatility of Jewish culture, from Aramaic to Arabic, and "now, with a deeper love, with memories the years have not yet dimmed, it is in Yiddish that it speaks." However, "the Diaspora is dead."[90] In danger as well was the particular brand of Diaspora synthesis to which Klein had devoted his literary career. The entry into seclusion that marked the end of his writing can be understood as an expression of this death.

With linguistic loyalties rooted in his diverse roles as a public poet, journalist, and activist, Klein was trapped between the cultures he sought to synthesize. His steady descent into silence in the mid-1950s can be understood as a response to twin insurmountable challenges to his synthesis: the demise of the Yiddish heartland in Europe and the attrition of a readership steeped in Yiddish. It is telling that among the last visitors that Klein agreed to see after the onset of what his son has called "non-physical suicide" was Israeli Yiddish poet Avrom Sutzkever.[91] In a visit to Montreal in 1959 as part of a North American speaking tour, Sutzkever specifically requested a meeting with Klein, the poet he had heard so much about from Ravitch and Segal. Klein, he had been told, was one of the few writers who took Yiddish seriously and had completed translations of Yiddish poetry into English. During the meeting at Klein's home, the two poets talked at length about Yiddish literature and other topics. However, after the meeting Sutzkever had tears in his eyes: "Did you see his desk?" he asked Ruth Wisse, who had accompanied him on the visit: "There wasn't anything on it. Nothing. Not a pencil, not a pen, not a book, not a shred of paper. It was empty. When that happens to a writer, he's finished."[92]

Perhaps most telling was Klein's funeral in August of 1972, held in the most simple and traditional Eastern European fashion. No mention was made of his career as a poet; rather, Klein's friend Rabbi Pinchas Hirschprung delivered "a pious eulogy entirely in Yiddish."[93] In the end, Klein was born and died in Yiddish; however, he lived struggling to forge a synthesis of Yiddish and English into a language that was authentically Jewish.

IRA ROBINSON

Some Hebrew and Yiddish *Vorlage* in the Poetry of A.M. Klein

Usher Caplan remarked about A.M. Klein that "his goal, in a sense, was to affect a modern 'translation' of Judaism into English."[1] This reflects a reasonable consensus among students of A.M. Klein's oeuvre that it is impossible to understand Klein without taking his Jewishness into serious consideration.[2] It is also fairly universally accepted that, in particular, the poetry of A.M. Klein was affected in an important way by his Jewish heritage. This is certainly the opinion of one of his earliest serious readers, Ludwig Lewisohn. Writing in the 1930s, Lewisohn commented that Klein's was authentic Jewish poetry in the English language. He thought that Klein was

> the first contributor of authentic Jewish poetry to the English language. He knows the Talmudic sages, great and small ... and into his English poetic style, even to the wild wit and sparkle of his rhymes, he has transfused their ardors, their dreams, their exquisite goodness, their storming of the very courts of God.[3]

These views are echoed by the contemporary critic, Zailig Pollock, who stated in the 1990s that a "turning away from modernism to Jewishness ... marks the real beginning of Klein's career as a poet."[4] Yet another sure sign that Klein is a *Jewish* writer is the presence of a commentary, in which Solomon J. Spiro attempts, with much success, to ferret out Judaic references in Klein's works. Spiro's work serves as a sort of Rashi commentary to Klein's scripture.[5] It is further widely known that Klein had full access to both the Hebrew and Yiddish languages and literatures, and that he utilized them in the creation of his poems. However, to my knowledge, there has been no systematic attempt to examine the Hebraic and Yiddish sources of Klein's poetry as *vorlage*. In particular, it would be of some importance to know whether Klein, in his frequent references to the Hebrew Bible, had a Hebrew or an English text on his desk or in his mind's eye. This chapter attempts to illustrate both the possibilities and the advantages of this knowledge.

The term *vorlage*, adapted from academic biblical studies, denotes the text that a translator has in front of him/her as s/he translated, which can be reconstructed by working backward from the translation.[6] In biblical studies, in which meanings of words and phrases are often unclear, the close study of ancient translations of the Hebrew Bible, like those of the Greek Septuagint or the Aramaic Targum, can often give important clues to the nature and meaning of the text in question. Given that Klein's linguistic formulations are often biblical in origin, it would be of significance to be able to better discern his ur-text.

I begin with the assumption that Klein's critics have, I think correctly, understood that his ultimate goal was a translation of Judaism (though perhaps *yiddishkeit* is a better, more all-embracing, term for the sort of Jewish civilization he sought to evoke)[7] into an English idiom.[8] If this idea is correct, then it follows that Klein's poetic translations of actual or purported Hebrew and Yiddish originals will reward a careful investigation.

It need hardly be said in this context that Klein was himself a sensitive and talented translator, especially of the Hebrew poetry of Chaim Nachman Bialik, who was himself a (some would say *the*) major poet of the twentieth century and one who engaged actively in the creation of a modern secular Jewish culture on the basis of a translation of the best of the old Jewish culture into a new idiom.[9] Moreover, translation of the ideas of traditional Judaism in order to be au courant in a particular time and place was demonstrably an idea current in A.M. Klein's Montreal. Hirsch Wolofsky, for instance, was the publisher of Montreal's Jewish newspapers in both Yiddish and English. Klein not only knew him well but also translated his autobiography from Yiddish to English.[10] In 1928–29, Wolofsky published a series of columns in the Montreal Yiddish-language newspaper, *Der Keneder Adler*, which amounted to a sort of contemporary commentary on the Torah.[11]

In his introduction to this commentary, Wolofsky began by seeking to position his work in the tradition of the premodern *midrashic* and *homiletic* literatures of Judaism. Just as these premodern works explained contemporary problems in terms of the Torah, utilizing literary embellishments in order to reach an audience, so Wolofsky hoped to write a twentieth-century commentary "according to the American version [*nusakh*]." For him, North America presented a situation in which the original "text" of Jewish life had largely been forgotten, and contemporary Jews lived their lives, as it were, in "transition" – that is, at a remove from the original (*targum-lebn*). Thus, contemporary North American Jews lived in a world where practically nothing was "original" and all was "translation" [*targum*]. For Jews living in such a world, Wolofsky proposed to present a series of homilies that might, indeed, be more *targum* than original but that were conceived by him to be in the spirit of the original.[12] Klein, I believe, had a similar sense of both the realities and the possibilities of such a "translation."

The beginnings of the insight that a possible contribution to the ongoing discussion and appreciation of Klein's Jewish poetry might emerge from an examination of the *vorlage* of his poems emerged from an ongoing project of mine to translate selected A.M. Klein poems into Hebrew and Yiddish.[13] As I read his poems – presented to the reader, of course, in English – I nonetheless sensed what the Yiddish literary critic Shmuel Niger noted in his well-known letter to Klein:

> Won't your English readers need a Yiddish and Hebrew dictionary, just as I need an English one? Even more – for me the dictionary is sufficient; I doubt if it would be enough for them ... In order to really penetrate most of your poetry, it isn't enough to have the explanation of a particular word or name; it is necessary to have lived in the atmosphere which nurtures your outlook and gives it life. Here no dictionaries will help. One needs to have breathed the air of learning Gemara, of Chassidism, of Jewish folklore.[14]

What can an examination of Klein's *vorlage* do for us? Let us examine some poems in this light. In doing so, we will observe two important things: first and most obvious, we will see where

Klein straightforwardly reflects his source, which thus enhances our understanding; second, and even more important, we will see numerous instances in which Klein is consciously at odds with his source.[15] Examples of the advantages of considering Klein's *vorlage* come readily to the surface in even a brief examination of his work.

Thus, in Klein's poem "To the Jewish Poet,"[16] he addresses the ambivalence of the Zionist effort to build a new Jewish homeland.

> You cherished them as ancient gems, those tears
> of Jeremiah...
> But now forget them! Spurn them! The dawn nears!
> The Dawn arises, tinted white and blue,
> Upon a land, lean to the parvenu, –
> Make fat that land with sweat, and not with tears...

The Jewish poet is exhorted to forget and to spurn the hitherto precious tears of Jeremiah's lamentations and to "Make fat that land with sweat, and not with tears." In using the phrase "make fat," Klein clearly evokes the words of the prophet Isaiah:

> Make the heart of this people fat,
> And Make their eyes heavy,
> And Shut their eyes;
> Lest they, seeing with their eyes,
> And hearing with their ears,
> And understanding with their heart, Return and be healed[17]

Through a contextual appreciation of the verse in Isaiah, Klein's *vorlage*, we can gain an additional nuance concerning the poet's concern that the Zionists are ignoring much that is precious in their tradition as they attempt to build a new Palestine.

Klein's "Concerning Four Strange Sons"[18] makes obvious reference to the four sons mentioned in the narrative of the Passover *Seder*. However, Klein changes the classical order of the Haggadah in his poem. The order of the four sons in the Haggadah, Klein's *vorlage*, is: first the *Hakham* (wise), then the *Rasha* (wicked), then the *Tam* (simple), and, finally, *She-eyno yodea le-sh'ol* (one who does not know how to ask). In his poem Klein changes this order:

> Concerning four strange sons, the Torah wrote:
> The sage, the simpleton, the knavish lout,
> And the poor yokel, whence no speech will out.

Paying attention to Klein's *vorlage* in this poem thus requires us to pay close attention to the stanzas describing the "poor yokel" and the "knavish lout," whose order has been reversed.

Yet another of Klein's translations of the Passover Haggadah is his poem "Chad Gadya."[19] This poem is correctly designated as a free rendering of the song that concludes the Passover *Seder* with its story of the consequences of the one kid goat, bought for two *zuzim*, which leads to God's slaying of the Angel of Death.[20] What is significant in this poem in terms of our examination of Klein's *vorlage* concerns those places where the poem departs from its source. Thus, in line 5, the cat (*shunra* in the original Aramaic) is rendered as *Graymalkin*. This unusual word for cat is certainly a Shakespearian allusion, where the word is used for the demonic companion of the first of the three weird sisters in the first scene of *Macbeth*. This complex allusion thus refers us to the sinister nature of the cat in the traditional interpretation of the *vorlage*, which tends to think of the various beasts as symbols of the nations that oppressed Israel: Assyria, Babylon, Greece, and Rome. Indeed, it is possible that Klein, by his use of the rare term *Graymalkin*, might have wished to evoke the classical four nations (*malkhuyot*) of that oppression.

Moreover, understanding the *vorlage* of the Haggadah's "Chad Gadya" enables us to have a more profound understanding of those elements in the poem that do not appear in the *vorlage*, including its penultimate stanza:

> In that strange portal whence
> All things come, they re-enter;
> Of all things God is centre,
> God is circumference.

This passage attempts to tie together the disparate elements of "Chad Gadya" and to foreground God's presence and direction of the action, which is not evident other than in the last verse of the original.

In Klein's lengthy poem on Spinoza, "Out of the Pulver and Polished Lens,"[21] there is an interesting and unusual alliteration, "Ah, what theology there is in spatted spittle." The passage may well evoke Numbers 12:14: "If her father had but spit [*yarok yarak*] in her face," in which Moses speaks of Miriam's punishment of banishment from the camp of Israel through an analogy of her being shamed by her father spitting in her face. The verse centres on an alliterative use of the word for spit. This device may be there to turn our attention towards the treatment of Spinoza by his Jewish contemporaries, who moved to shame him and thus to remove him from their environs.

The poem "Bestiary"[22] commences with a wish that God breathe a blessing on the small bones of the child who seeks the biblical beasts.

God breathe a blessing on
His small bones, every one!

This expression, unusual in English, is a natural translation of the Yiddish expression of health for children: *a gezundt oyf zayne bayndelekh* (literally, health to his small bones).

Another possible instance of somewhat awkward expressions in English explained through the use of a putative Yiddish *vorlage* is to be found in the poem "Scholar."[23] In line 5, the phrase "Hot for wisdom," which seemingly has little meaning in English, may in fact be a rendition of the equivalent Yiddish expression *heys far khokhme*. Since the "scholar" is a goat, the use of a Yiddish *vorlage* may indicate that the author is pursuing an ironic image, since the language of a true Judaic scholar would have been Hebrew, not Yiddish.

The Hebrew *vorlage* also seems to be the source of a number of Klein's interesting expressions. Thus in the first line of his "Psalm XVIII,"[24] "She has laved her body in living water," living water is a literal rendering of the biblical phrase, *mayim chayim*,[25] which appears in the Hebrew Bible in the context of a purification ritual. In the context of the poem, the bride undergoes a purification after her menstruation through bathing in the "living waters" of the *mikveh* (ritual pool), after which she may have sexual relations with her husband.

The first line of "Psalm XXIV"[26] also contains a phrase that may be explained with reference to Klein's *vorlage*. "O incognito god, anonymous lord" seems to me to be a fairly direct translation of the Hebrew *adon olam* (hidden Lord) and a play on *Adon Olam* (Lord of the World / Eternal Lord), the initial words of a popular Hebrew liturgical hymn.

In "Psalm XXVI,"[27] Klein alludes to the "alluvium of Nilus." While it is certain that the River Nile's Latin name was familiar to Klein from his classical studies, it is yet possible to understand Nilus, within the Jewish context of the poem, as the medieval Hebrew rendering of the river's name, which Klein would have easily encountered in Rashi's commentary on the Torah (which he had undoubtedly learned prior to his exposure to Latin in school).[28]

The play on words in "Address to the Choirboys,"[29] "pass away … come to pass," seems to derive directly from the Hebrew original *vorlage* of the High Holiday liturgy, which itself involves a play on words. In a centrally important part of the High Holidays liturgy, the worshipper reflects on what will come in the new year: *kama ya'avrun ve-kama yibarayun* (how many shall pass away, and how many shall be created).

Jewish liturgical allusions are also to be found in "Benedictions,"[30] which is based on a series of blessings Jews make as part of their morning prayers. In that poem, however, we find, when looking at Klein's *vorlage*, that he decided to play off, rather than to reflect, his source. Thus, in the first line, he wrote: "For that he gave to a stone understanding to understand direction." This allusion to the lodestone does not reflect the original, in which the rooster (*sekhvi*) is given the understanding "to discern between day and night." This theme of playing off the original is continued in the next line: "For that he made no slave for me," which gives an opposite sense than is found in the *vorlage*, which states: "Who made me not a slave" (*she-lo assani aved*). The irony of the next line: "For that he clothes the naked with the nudities of beasts" is greatly strengthened by reference to the *vorlage*, which states simply "Who clothes the naked" (*malbish arumim*). The final line of the poem, "For that he smites me each dawn with a planet," can only be properly understood in relation to the *vorlage*: "Who establishes the earth on the waters" (*roka' ha-aretz al ha-mayim*), where the sense of the verb *roka'* (literally, to hammer, or flatten out) is transposed into a stunning image.

Klein attempted yet another interpretation of this morning benediction when he wrote in his "Stance of the Amidah": "who hast given to the bee its knowledge."[31] Without any reference to the *vorlage*, the line lacks meaning, since bees do not figure in the Judaic liturgy. It is only with reference to the *vorlage, la-sekhvi*, that we realize that Klein is attempting a bilingual play on words.

There is no doubt that some of the individual examples I have cited in this chapter, with respect to the understanding we can gain by paying attention to A.M. Klein's *vorlage* in studying his poetry, are simply the result of my own subjectivity. I contend, however, that in their aggregate they give us yet another path through which to gain a more profound understanding of Klein's poetry.

Thus, in the case of his poetry, we have seen that it is of some importance to work backward from the poems to their source material and to take note of the ways in which, for Klein, the cadence of verses from the Hebrew Bible, Talmudic phrases in Aramaic, and Yiddish conversational patterns constitute crucial compositional factors. That Klein seems to use more Hebrew than Yiddish *vorlage* in his poetry indicates a preference for the classic Jewish language – Hebrew – over the vernacular Yiddish, which is often used in an ironic sense. Understanding Klein's Hebrew and Yiddish *vorlage* serves to open a new, intertextual dimension of his poetry and to enrich our understanding of his literary creativity.

PIERRE ANCTIL

Wolofsky *ibergesetst,* or How Does A.M. Klein Translate?

Many readers know that A.M. Klein was at home in the Yiddish language and maintained close ties with the Yiddish intelligentsia of Montreal throughout his life. Given the date of immigration of his parents to Canada, at the height of the mass migration of Eastern European Jews, and the fact that Yiddish was the language of his home, it is no exaggeration to state that Yiddish was the poet's *mame loshen,* or mother tongue. Born in Ratno, Ukraine, in 1909, Klein arrived in Canada in 1910, at a time when the Montreal Yiddish community had established itself near the port and, later, on the Plateau Mont-Royal. In 1907, the number of city residents that could speak and read the language fluently was such that a Yiddish daily paper, *Der Keneder Adler* (*The Canadian Eagle*), was founded by Hirsch Wolofsky and survived a number of initial crises in the interwar period. In 1910, the first Yiddish book published in Montreal appeared, entitled *Kinder ertsyung ba Yidn, a historishe nakhforshung* (*The Education of Children among Jews, a Historical Research*), which described how Jewish schools could be organized around modern principles without losing their religious significance. More significantly, in 1918, Jewish Montreal witnessed the publication of a first book of poetry in Yiddish, *Foun mayn velt* (*From My World*), written by another Ukrainian, Jacob Isaac Segal, who immigrated in 1911. These were the beginnings of a literary movement that appeared in Montreal and elsewhere in Canada early in the twentieth century and that, by the 1930s, gave birth to a distinct Yiddish culture surprisingly rich in scope and creativity.

Although Klein was indeed immersed in the Yiddish language at home and in the neighbourhood where his parents initially settled, he attended the city's Protestant school system where he quickly learned the ways of his new country and its dominant language, English. His enrolment in 1914 at the Mount-Royal Elementary School, on the Corner of Rachel and Clark streets on the Plateau Mont-Royal, was not necessarily the choice of his parents, but, rather, the product of a compromise reached a few years earlier between the francophone Roman Catholic, the anglophone Protestant, and the established Jewish elites of the city. Translated into provincial law in 1903, touching the Jewish pupils of Montreal and Outremont attending the public school system of Quebec, this agreement stated unequivocally that Jews would be considered Protestants for educational purposes. In a sense, this set of historical circumstances transformed A.M. Klein, like many Jews of his generation, into a bicultural individual able to move adeptly between the Eastern European atmosphere and intimacy of his home and the wider Anglo-Canadian imperial values that were common to all those who were educated in the Protestant institutions of the city. This particular reality can be easily traced in A.M. Klein's chef-d'oeuvre, *The Second Scroll*, written at the end of his literary career. In this work, the narrator, Klein's alter ego, is raised in a family that has retained strong connections to the Old World, where an uncle named Melech Davidson maintains a link with his family, recently settled in Montreal:

> I never saw my uncle Melech, but reports of his Talmudic exploits kept sounding in our house and there made a legend of his name. To Montreal, to our modest address on the Avenue de l'Hôtel de Ville, there came from Volhynia letter after letter, penned in the strange script of eastern Europe – all the sevens wore collars – letters twittering the praises of the young man who at age twenty had already astounded with his erudition the most learned rabbis of the Continent. Dubbed *the Ilui* – the prodigy of Ratno – it was in these epistles written of him, amidst a clucking of exclamation-marks, that he had completely weathered the ocean of the Talmud, knew all its bays and inlets, had succeeded in quelling some of its most tempestuous commentators.[1]

This complex cultural identity was further deepened when A.M. Klein entered Baron Byng High School in 1922, and then McGill

University in 1926. Despite Klein's intimate acquaintance with the Yiddish language and the *weltanshauung* of traditional Eastern European Jewry, as a young writer he adopted the language he'd learned in school, and which offered the promise of a wider audience beyond the immediate confines of Montreal's Yiddish immigrant milieu. No doubt, the idiom of Shakespeare and the British Empire signified to the poet a possible entry into the broad edifice of English-Canadian literature and even beyond; whereas Yiddish, the language of Sholem Aleichem and the proletarian writers in the United States, meant confinement in an ethnic domain unlikely to bring wider fame and influence. Yiddish, as a literary medium, could have an appeal only to those who had come to the country in the period of the great migration as young adults and never fully mastered the official languages of Canada, such as Jacob Isaac Segal, Ida Maze, Sholem Shtern, and Noah Isaac Gotlib. Authors like Rokhl Korn and Melekh Ravitch, who had already gained a literary reputation in Poland or Russia between the two wars and settled in Montreal after the Holocaust, also considered Yiddish a kind of *oytser*, a language to be cherished. For them English remained a foreign tongue, all the more so since they felt that they had an obligation in their literary works to use an idiom that had been obliterated from Eastern Europe by the Nazi campaigns of mass murder, and would otherwise forever remain mute. Having been raised in Canada, Klein felt no kinship to either group of writers, although he knew most of them well and understood their reasons for clinging to Yiddish.

In fact, Klein maintained very good relations throughout his career with the Yiddish littérateurs who had arrived in Canada early in the twentieth century and belonged to his generation. Although English was his literary medium, he undoubtedly felt part of the same cultural élan, as is evidenced early on from his choice of themes and from the strong Judaic content of his poetry. In "Heirloom," written in the early 1930s, Klein exemplifies his attachment to the piety and religious devotion of his father, although he saw himself as a modern Jew indifferent in everyday life to the injunctions and precepts of the Torah:

My father bequeathed me no wide estates;
No keys and ledgers were my heritage;

Only some holy books with *yahrzeit* dates
Writ mournfully upon a blank front page –

Books of the Baal Shem Tov, and of his wonders;
Pamphlets upon the devil and his crew;
Prayers against road demons, witches, thunders;
And sundry other tomes for a good Jew.[2]

This osmosis between Yiddish letters in Montreal and the early anglophone Jewish writing of the 1930s is nowhere more evident than in the book of literary criticism published by H.M. Caiserman in 1934 entitled *Yidishe dikhter in Kanade* (*Jewish Poets in Canada*). In his enthusiastic essay, Caiserman considers the flowering of Yiddish literary talent in Montreal and elsewhere in the country, generously interspersing his own prose with excerpts from poetry already published in Canada. He then goes on to include in his list the Jewish writers who had begun their career in English, including a certain Abraham M. Klein, then only twenty-four years old. Room was also left in Caiserman's essay for the English-language poetry of Hyman Edelstein, Frida Miron, Regina Leonora Schulman, Vera Black, Rose Appelbaum, Shulamis Borodensky (Shulamis Yelin), Nemy Lenin, Ruby Friedman, and Phyllis Cohen, a complement of ten anglophones out of a total of forty-three poets and writers found in *Yidishe dikhter in Kanade*. In 1934, for Klein, Caiserman had prepared the following short biography, which attests to the precocity of his talent: "*Zayn ersht lid iz dershinen in* Menorah Journal, *1927. Dernokh zikh gedrukt in farshidene kanader un amerikaner journaln. Hot fartik tsum druk a groysn band lider.*"[3] A number of these early English-language poets came from families deeply rooted in the world of Eastern European Jewry.

Despite having clearly chosen English as his literary medium, Klein nonetheless maintained throughout most of his life, and certainly during the period when Yiddish writing was at its peak in Montreal, some form of cultural link with the idiom of his forebears. This included substantial effort directed at translations. In the late 1940s and early 1950s, at a time when Yiddish volumes were still being published in Canada in considerable number, he undertook to prepare an English-language version of three full-length Yiddish texts authored by individuals whom he knew well and who were related in one way or another to the Montreal Yiddish-language daily *Der Keneder Adler*. These were: Israel Rabinovitch's study *Muzik ba Yid oun andere esayn oyf muzikalishe temes*; Hirsch Wolofsky's memoirs *Mayn lebens rayze, zikhroynes foun iber a halb yorhundert Yidish lebn in der alter oun nayer velt;* and Moishe Dickstein's *Fun Palestine biz Eretz-Israel* (published in instalments in 1950 in *Der Keneder Adler*). Klein's translations appeared successively under the titles *Of Jewish Music, Ancient and Modern*; *Journey of My Life: A Book of Memories*; and *From Palestine to Israel*. Rabinovitch, who was an amateur musicologist, took the position of editor at *Der Keneder Adler* in 1924; Wolofsky founded the Montreal Yiddish paper in 1907; and Dickstein was one of the early collaborators of Reuben Brainin when, in 1912, he took the helm of *Der Keneder Adler*. All three were born in the former Russian Empire and became accomplished journalists in Montreal.

Klein's emotional and literary attachment to Yiddish also extended to the translation of short poems, often traditional in form and carrying a certain folkloric coloration. His fonds at Library and Archives Canada contain roughly fifty examples of Yiddish songs and anonymous texts, which reflect the religious character of the Hasidic world of his father in Eastern Europe. Many of these translations were not published and may simply have served to deepen his connection to a language and culture that was an intimate part of his upbringing. Certainly, they reminded Klein how far he had travelled as an individual when he crossed the highly visible boundary between the familiar Yiddish world of his parents and the high-culture English language sphere of McGill's academic discourse. Still, Klein understood all along that, while moving from one world to the other, a cultural loss had been incurred that could never be compensated no matter how brilliant his literary career in the wider confines of Anglo-Canadian circles. An acute awareness of this displacement is visible in some of the remarks and annotations that accompany Klein's translations of traditional folkloric material, such as this short reflection written in 1940: "One of the most striking of the qualities of the Yiddish proverb is its realism, the view of life that it presents, a view that penetrates through the hypocritical and the sham and emerges with wisdom hard, matter of fact, almost cynical." Certainly, as Klein was well aware, the sense of marginality felt by Eastern European Jews, and the suffering that it implied at times, had forged an approach to language that bore little resemblance to the elevated prose of the Elizabethan age. Klein also contributed translations of classic Yiddish short stories, notably one by Isaac Leib Peretz entitled *"Ne'ilah in Gehenna"*[4] (A Yom Kippur Service in Hell). He also rendered into English a number of poems by Jacob Isaac Segal, three of which appeared in 1940 in the *Canadian Jewish Chronicle.*

Many of these literary transpositions offer a unique glimpse into the perceptions that Klein had developed of his Yiddish origins, but none more effectively than his English-language version of Hirsch Wolofsky's memoirs, *Mayn lebens rayze, zikhroynes foun iber a halb yorhundert Yidish lebn in der alter oun nayer velt*, published in 1945. Klein's relationship to this text implied more than a literary exercise or a re-enactment of his Eastern European origins. Wolofsky was the poet's mentor in many ways and had offered him the prospect of a safe-conduct between the Yiddish idiom of his childhood and the English sphere in which he had begun to earn his living and to practise his trade as a creative writer. Born in the Polish town of Shidlovtse in 1877, Wolofsky immigrated to Montreal in 1900. He was one of the foremost representatives of a Yiddish culture successfully transplanted onto Canadian soil at the beginning of the twentieth century. After having founded *Der Keneder Adler* in 1907, Wolofsky managed in 1914 to convince the Montreal Jewish magnate, Sir Mortimer B. Davis, to finance the creation of an English-language periodical. For this purpose, Wolofsky used the argument that newly arrived Jews needed a publication to help them adapt more readily to the new socio-economic conditions in which they found themselves. The *Canadian Jewish Chronicle* would be Wolofsky's modest offering to the small English-language Jewish readership that was gradually developing in the city at that time. While *Der Keneder Adler* was perceived upon its inception as the voice of the Montreal Yiddish-speaking community, and an active supporter of the literary movement that flowered almost immediately in the downtown immigrant core, the monthly *Canadian Jewish Chronicle* focused upon a more cultured elite whose mode of expression was several degrees more reserved.

Hirsch Wolofsky was most probably the greatest community leader to emerge from Yiddish Montreal. Not only was he a towering figure in the domain of journalism and in the sphere of Canadian Yiddish letters, he involved himself during several decades in building a network of institutions that would deeply influence the cultural identity of his co-religionists. Although he remained somewhat aloof from the city's radical political circles, led by people with strong anarchist, socialist, unionist, or leftist Zionist convictions, Wolofsky nonetheless contributed an inordinate amount of energy to building organizations or consolidating existing ones that were devoted to the maintenance of a vibrant Yiddish culture. Since he had arrived in Canada at the very beginning of the mass migration, when almost no institutions existed to assist immigrants (with the exception of the Baron de Hirsch Institute), and since he himself understood better than most the trials and tribulations of his fellow Eastern Europeans, Wolofsky sought to put into place associations that could come to their help. Seeing that the Jewish downtown neighbourhood was in a state of disarray and unable to exercise leadership in key issues such as philanthropy, religious governance, and Jewish education, he used *Der Keneder Adler* to rally the will of various and often opposed Jewish political factions, and to move them in the direction of a unified community administration. Thanks to the efforts of Wolofsky, the United Talmud Torahs was put into place in 1916, relief destined to Jewish war refugees in Europe was organized, the Canadian Jewish Congress emerged in 1919, and, finally, in 1923, after protracted negotiations, the *Va'ad Ha'ir* was founded to orchestrate the certification and distribution of kosher food in the city, not to mention a host of lesser institutions such as orphanages, homes for the elderly, and Zionist associations.

In 1938, Wolofsky decided to offer A.M. Klein, who was then pursuing a separate career as a young lawyer, the position of editor, editorialist, and columnist at the *Canadian Jewish Chronicle*. Since the English-language Jewish monthly shared offices at 4075 boulevard Saint-Laurent with the more influential *Keneder Adler*, this kept the poet in contact with the Yiddish intelligentsia of Montreal, notably Jacob Isaac Segal, Israel Rabinovitch, Mordecai Ginzburg, Benjamin Sack, Chaim Kruger, Rabbi Yehuda Leib Zlotnick, Melekh Ravitch, and Israel Medresh. Unlike Samuel Bronfman, the wealthy distillery owner who was a dominant presence in A.M. Klein's public life, and who was an assimilationist at heart, Wolofsky kept the poet in constant contact with his Eastern European roots while offering him unlimited space to express himself in a true literary vein. Anglophone Jewish readers, unlike their Yiddish-speaking counterparts at *Der Keneder Adler*, did not count on the *Chronicle* as a source of fresh news of the world or for information about their immediate Montreal environment. For this, there existed mainstream English-language newspapers. Rather, for them, the *Chronicle* was a window onto a more personal and intimate form of identity, and, as such, it was acceptable that it limited itself to publishing literary texts and broad reflections on Jewish themes. To Klein, this was an extraordinary occasion to be his own man, and he remained at the helm of Wolofsky's English-language monthly for more than fifteen years, until 1955. As Usher Caplan remarks:

> Over the years the *Chronicle* was to become his most important creative outlet. Besides writing on current events, he published in its pages a large number of poems, stories, book reviews, literary essays, and translations. As editor, he was free to write almost anything at all for the paper.[5]

Wolofsky, whose mastery of the English literary tradition was approximate, was probably glad not to interfere with Klein's handling of editorial matters. His young associate, in his late twenties when he took over at the paper, attracted a serious readership, paid great attention to the quality of the texts he published (whether his or those of collaborators), and exhibited sound judgement in political matters. Leaving the *Chronicle* in the hands of a serious if still young poet was in keeping with Wolofsky's managerial choices, exemplified earlier in the century by the hiring of Reuben Brainin and other such luminaries to lead *Der Keneder Adler* out of a provincial state of mind and to instil in its pages some of the brilliance of learned European Jewry.

While Bronfman was a demanding and at times domineering personality, prone to exact as much out of A.M. Klein's literary talent as he possibly could, Wolofsky appears to have been a benevolent figure in Klein's life. Furthermore, the owner of the *Chronicle* had no immediate expectations for himself when he welcomed Klein into his circle of close contributors. Wolofsky was rarely featured in the English-language monthly directed by Klein, nor did he figure prominently among its writers or columnists. By the time he attracted the young poet to his team of talented literati, Wolofsky's career as a journalist/publicist had come to an end. In 1938, he was close to sixty-two years old and he had other projects in mind, one of which was to prepare his memoirs as a community leader.

There are indications that Wolofsky began to write the story of his long and productive life early in the 1940s. In a chapter of his memoirs entitled "My New Life in Warsaw," before touching upon the subject at hand, he digresses to mention how he is emotionally affected by the mass murder of Jews in his country of origin:

Ober baym onhoyben tsu dertsaylen mayne zikhroynes vegen Varshe, gefin ikh zikh shoyn in Montreal dem tsvayten vinter, vou es is kalt oun forn kayn Florida gloust zikh shoyn nit. Vi ken men foren zikh varimen in a tsayt ven milyonen foun oundzere brider geyen op mit blut, veren poshet oysgeshokhten vi di shof durkh dem roshe Hitler mit zayne blut-hint![6]

Before beginning this chapter of my life which took place in Warsaw, let me state that I am now in Montreal for the second winter, where the climate is much colder and have no intention of going to Florida. How could one think of spending time in warm countries when millions of our brothers are suffering the worst torments and are sent to their deaths like sheep, under the leadership of criminals like Hitler and his blood-thirsty henchmen![7]

The owner of *Der Keneder Adler* wasn't a sophisticated writer even in Yiddish; rather, he used a vernacular version of the language that served his taste for action and conflict, such as in the passages of his memoirs relating to the kosher butchers' strikes or in describing his eventful trips to Poland and Palestine. His literary style was not akin to the elevated poetry published in the city and did not lend itself to an abstract contemplation of beauty. Wolofsky was a *journaliste de combat*, a man devoted to the Zionist cause and the defence of Diaspora Jewry whether in Eastern Europe or in North America. An immigrant to a new land, in *Mayn lebns rayze* he often marvels at the freedom that Canadian Jews enjoy, as well as at their material comfort in Montreal after having been there for only a few years. More interestingly, from an anthropological point of view, Wolofsky describes in a folkloric vein his childhood in Shidlovtse, and his early adulthood in Warsaw and Lodz, at a time when a national-ist Poland had emerged out of the First World War and tended to severely repress Jewish aspirations. Quite clearly, *Mayn lebns rayze* is written as a testimonial to an existence lived between two worlds: that of traditional Judaism in its Eastern European form before the advent of modernity and that of the Diaspora in a progressive lib-eral country like Canada. In accord with his religious upbringing, Wolofsky's memoirs mirror certain Talmudic strategies in that the information they contain is offered without any specific order or chronology. Chapters are often disjointed, the narration suffers from an abuse of secondary material, and important or halakhic passages dealing with matter of the utmost political and cultural significance are abruptly interrupted by haggadic anecdotes that do not add to the flow of the text. In short, the memoirs leave an impression of pleasant disorder, and the reader is often rushed from one context to the other as though Wolofsky had lived the various episodes of his existence all at once. In a passage centred on the months he spent in Lodz when he was an eighteen-year-old, the author makes no effort to conceal his limitations as a memorialist:

Ikh batsvek do nit in mayne zikhroynes tsu shilderen dos yidishe leben foun fuftsik yor tsurik in Varshe oder in Poylen, vayl ikh pretendirt nit tsu zayn kayn historiker. Ikh dertsaylt nor dos, vos hot zikh opgedrukt in mayne zikhroynes.[8]

As I do not pretend to be a historian, I have no intention in these memoirs of describing in detail Jewish life in Warsaw or in Poland forty or fifty years ago. Rather I will tell only that which has impressed itself in my memory.[9]

By the early 1940s, Wolofsky knew that many Canadian-born Jews could not read his prose. He was well aware that if he wanted to leave his mark on the community's record, he would need to have his memoirs translated into English. In 1939, Samuel Bronfman had been elected to the presidency of Canadian Jewish Congress, while in the 1930s his brothers had taken control of key Montreal Jewish organizations and philanthropic agencies. Mr Sam, as he was some-times called, surrounded himself with people who were anglophone

Jews and who had little patience with Yiddish, save for Hannaniah Meir Caiserman, who belonged to an earlier age and became the Congress's first secretary general in 1919. Similarly, in many sectors of Canadian-Jewish life, English was about to replace Yiddish. Faced with such a prospect, Wolofsky turned to Klein, the only true anglophone writer he employed and whom he understood to be a respected person in the community. There were important differences between the two men. While Wolofsky was an activist and the mouth-piece of many immigrant lobby groups and *landsmanshaftn*, an individual continually trying to influence government officials in favour of Jewish refugees, Klein remained a modest and unassuming figure who concentrated mostly on his literary career. More important, the owner of the *Canadian Jewish Chronicle* was a man who had been forced to leave Eastern Europe in a context of political repression and who had remained attached to Yiddish-speaking Poland, while its editor viewed Montreal as his true home and the English language as his only professional idiom.

One can hypothesize that cooperation between Wolofsky and Klein probably began in earnest quite early, since the English version of *Mayn lebns rayze* appeared a few months before the Yiddish version. This can be read as a sign that the translator had the manuscript in his hands even before it was finalized by the ailing author. Perhaps because of this unique situation, once completed and published, the two texts can be read as two separate strands and not as mirror images of each other. Klein did not exactly translate *Mayn lebns rayze*; rather, he wrote a new and different book from the material that his employer had supplied. All in all, it is as though the narrative created by Wolofsky from his own Yiddish Polish background and the succession of events that he himself had experienced had been reinterpreted by Klein to fit a new cultural pattern and to conform to a different Jewish identity. Few, at the time, realized how wide an abyss separated the two versions. The degree of variance between *Mayn lebns rayze* and *Journey of My Life* is in many ways an indictor of the cultural gap that, immediately after the Second World War, had opened between the immigrant generation and Canadian-born Jews. Klein not only propelled Wolofsky's prose to a level of perfection and formal complexity that the Yiddish text did not possess, but also transformed Wolofsky into a well-read and learned anglophone, which he most certainly was not.

Save for the first few chapters, which describe Wolofsky's upbringing in his native town, *Mayn lebns rayze* is essentially written as
detailed journalistic reportage, interspersed with random reflections on Judaism and Jewish politics (when events are conducive
to such asides). Under Klein's guidance the text appears rather like
a detached narrative, written from a distance and long after the
fact. Furthermore, the English version is the product of a meticulous
and systematic mind, impervious to the travails of everyday life. In
this language, the book is structured almost as though the story is
being told in the third person, at a distance from the uncertainties
and exhaustion of travel – this at a time when the means of long-
distance travel were limited to trains and ocean liners. While
Wolofsky recalls many circumstances of the past in minute detail
and enters into long digressions, Klein summarizes and reorders
this material. Because the translator uses a language that is more
universal than Yiddish and does not offer the same level of complexity or intensity with regard to describing Jewish culture and
religious practice, he tends to simplify passages that he thinks will
not appeal to English-language readers beyond the pale of the local
community. Clearly, Klein has the same literary reflex in managing
the translation of *Mayn lebns rayze* as he has in his own career as a
Canadian anglophone writer: he retains a certain Judaic sensibility
without forcing the issue to the point where the text becomes inaccessible to a wider non-Jewish readership. Of what use is it to assert
oneself as a Jew in the Canadian landscape, either through the use
of images or specific terms, if it becomes a barrier that most anglophones cannot surmount?

A few examples taken from Wolofsky's original text, in parallel
with Klein's translation, clearly show the extent to which the English version is a reinterpretation of Yiddish culture and an attempt
to present the world of Montreal's Eastern European immigrants,
circa 1945, in a different light than in the Yiddish version. For reasons other than Klein's, in 1998 I undertook, at the request of Jack
Wolofsky, the grandson of the founder of *Der Keneder Adler*, a
French-language translation of *Mayn lebns rayze* (published under
that title in 2000 by les Éditions du Septentrion). This translation
was made directly from the Yiddish text without consulting the
1945 Klein version. My purpose was to make available to the francophone public a glimpse of Wolofsky's life as a community leader

and to provide an illustration of the climate that prevailed in the Montreal Jewish community in the first third of the twentieth century. For this reason, I felt that I had to stay as close as possible to the Yiddish text as the French language would allow and, thus, not stand in the way of a reasonable understanding of Montreal's Yiddish culture. Later, when I compared my work to that produced by Klein some fifty years earlier, I was astounded to see how different the two versions were and how much the poet had modified Wolofsky's vision of himself and his universe. The following passages underline the gap between the author of *Mayn lebns rayze* and his first translator. In these few lines, the author recalls under what circumstances *Der Keneder Adler* appeared, followed by my translation and then Klein's:

> *Mit etlekhe vokhn far der dersheynung foun "Keneder Adler" hot a higer druker ongehoybn aroysgeben a vekhntlike tsaytung in der form foun a tsirkular oun dokh hot es der oylem tsukhapt.*[10]

A few weeks before the launching of the *Keneder Adler*, a local printer had put a Yiddish weekly for sale, which resembled in form that of a publicity sheet, and which had been well received by the public.[11]

But the thing did not come off as a result of mere longing. The early trials and difficulties of the paper, amusing in retrospect, seemed almost insurmountable at the time. But I persisted. As a matter of fact, a few weeks prior to the publication of The Eagle, a local printer issued a weekly paper in the form of a circular, and its issues sold like hot cakes.[12]

In this instance, the poet adds to the original text a commentary that reflects his generational view of the travails experienced by the immigrants. Wolofsky could not have reflected in so detached a manner on his early journalistic career in pre-First World War Montreal. In the following quotation, Wolofsky recalls how the paper went through a series of financial crises before it could be viable and earn the support of a wider readership. In fact, in 1907, the number of Yiddish-speaking immigrants in the city was probably barely large enough to afford *Der Keneder Adler* a stable audience, a situation that continued migration in the years leading up to the First World War would alter dramatically. While Wolofsky's text is factual and recounts precise events in his life, Klein adds a dramatic touch to impress upon the reader a historical perspective that reflects the point of view of Canadianized Jews:

In a frimorgen hot di gaz-kompanye oundz opgeshniten di gaz oun elektrik far nit batsolen dem bil in tsayt. Mir hoben dan nit gehat kayn dolar in bank.[13]

One morning, as we were not in a position to honour our bills, the utility company came to our offices and cut our gas and electricity. We were then completely without financial resources.[14]

The beginnings were beset by difficulties, at once amusing and heartbreaking. Hardly had I got into the swing of things, when in five days I discovered that our plant was without gas or electricity; the company had discontinued the service for non-payment. Nor was there a dollar in our bank account to meet the emergency.[15]

At other times, and these were probably the most frequent in terms of textual manipulation, Klein simply omits entire passages from Wolofsky's text, particularly those dealing with the folkloric or ethnic aspects of Jewish life in Poland, Israel, or Montreal. As if he felt that they would bring needless insistence on the Yiddish and Eastern European roots of Canadian Jewry, Klein left out sections as long as several pages. No doubt the translator felt that this would be an element in the narration that the anglophone reader could find tiresome, particularly if *Mayn lebns rayze* found itself in non-Jewish hands. And thus, much of the colour and cultural value of Wolofsky's memoirs tended to evaporate or to be greatly reduced in value in the 1945 English version, an editorial choice on the part of Klein that was in contradiction with my objective in creating a French-language translation. To me, an anthropologist situated outside the Jewish cultural realm, Wolofsky's text conveyed the values espoused by the early immigrants, describing their emotions as they adapted to the New World.

When translating *Mayn lebns rayze*, I wanted the francophone readership and, primarily, myself to gain access to Wolofsky's cultural identity as a recent immigrant and an entrepreneur in the Yiddish-speaking community. I also recognized that, starting with my publisher, Denis Vaugeois, it would be largely non-Jews who would set eyes on the French-language version. For this reason, and to help contextualize Wolofsky's memoirs, several hundred footnotes were added to the text, including short biographies of personalities mentioned by the author who did not belong to the realm of Quebec history or Catholicism. Likewise, a glossary of Judaic terms and an index of names appear at the end of the French version to guide the reader unfamiliar with terms and notions that were commonly used in Yiddish, mostly in the religious sphere. These appendices help underscore the cultural distance between *Mayn lebns rayze* and the contemporary francophone reader.

There are many omissions in Klein's *Journey of My Life* when one compares it with the original Yiddish text. They reflect the cultural *parti-pris* that Klein sought to impose on Wolofsky's memoirs. One of the most striking is the author's own admission, made at the beginning of a chapter entitled *Zikhroynes foun Lodzsh* (Memories from Lodz), that he intended to describe only what he remembered personally of his life in Eastern Europe, Israel, and Montreal. Still, Wolofsky did not intend to distance himself from international and national events that took place several decades earlier, as they affected him in his career and as a journalist-editor. Clearly, he felt that his text should unravel freely, as his memory and emotions allowed, and not be constrained by the narrow confines of history and documentary evidence.

It is worthwhile considering what motivated Klein in his translating method. If he had been faithful to the original, its author would have revealed an understanding of the world that was at variance with what Anglo-Canadians held to be of paramount importance, notably the pre-eminence of the British Empire in world affairs. Furthermore, a close translation of the Yiddish text would reveal forms of argumentation that were foreign to a person belonging to the mainstream of Canadian society, not to mention folkloric notions and customs that, seen from the outside, bordered on the incomprehensible. Today, in an age of multiculturalism, these differences of perception and outlook seem innocuous, but in 1945, in the aftermath of the Holocaust, it may have seemed quite otherwise to Klein. Furthermore, the translator was also acutely aware that, in the 1930s, Montreal Jews had experienced a surge of anti-Semitism in their own city.

A notable instance in which Klein suppresses a passage that reveals the internal logic of the Eastern European Jewish mind is a case in which he omits the opening of a chapter. Entitled "My First Trip to Europe and Eretz-Israel," Wolofsky's chapter opens with a discussion that took place in 1921 between Rabbi Zvi Cohen and Wolofsky on the merits of trying to sell complete editions of a Talmud printed in Montreal in 1919, and known as the *Montrealer Shas*, in Europe. The logic in the Yiddish original is as follows:

"*Oyb azoy, azoy iz dokh der inyen an inyen,*" says Rabbi Cohen.

"*Mayle di zakh iz a zakh, iz memayle der inyen an inyen,*" says the Talmudic student (*yeshive bokher*) to a father marrying his daughter.

"*Mayle, az di zakh iz nit kayn zakh, iz der inyen nit kayn inyen,*" retorts the father of the bride.

"*Iz do di zakh a zakh, oun memayle iz der inyen an inyen,*" further repeats the Talmudic student.

"*Az di zakh iz kayn zakh nit, iz der inyen kayn inyen nit,*" retorts the Talmudic student after a counter argument received from the father.

"*Di zakh iz take kayn zakh nit, ober der inyen iz yo an inyen,*"[16] concludes Wolofsky himself.

If so, then the matter is settled.
If the question is such, then the matter is settled.
If the matter is not settled, then it is better to abstain.
If the issue is decided, then it is best to move forward.
If the issue is still undecided, then it is better to remove oneself.

The effort is not worth it, but I am still happy I have taken the decision to go to Europe.[17]

In other circumstances Klein takes away from Wolofsky's memoirs what might be seen as politically embarrassing material. Any issues that could be seen as related to the Gouzenko affair were removed. This affair erupted in 1945 when a Russian embassy worker in Ottawa revealed that a Communist spy ring existed in Canada and that it relied on the sympathy of the local left. Jews – notably Fred Rose, a member of Parliament for Montreal-Cartier since 1943 – were prominent among those who favoured strong ties with the Stalinist state. At the time of Rose's election, cooperation with the Red Army seemed a natural reflex on the part of Canadians calling for the military defeat of Hitler. It was quite another matter at the beginning of the Cold War. In his book, Wolofsky describes his sojourn in Soviet Russia in 1934, long before Canada entered into an alliance with the Western democracies to defeat Nazism. One of the author's sons had strong Communist sympathies and was already in the Soviet Union when Wolofsky arrived in Minsk to convince him to follow him back to Canada. In describing his peregrinations in Russia, the editor of *Der Keneder Adler* makes several positive comments on the Soviet system of government, which Klein toned down in the English translation:

> *In ovent hob ikh gemakht a bazukh in shtadishen park, vos ruft zikh der «kultur park», oun vos ikh hob dort gezen hot mikh beemes shtark farinteresirt, vayl dos hot shoyn tsu ton mit der groyser makht vos Soviet-Rusland hot aroysgevizen in der milk-home oun foun vanen es hoben zikh genoumen di koykhes bay di Sovieten tsu kenen baykumen di shtarke militarishe mashin foun di natsis oun derlangen Hitler'n zayne gut fardinte klep.*[18]

In the evening I took a walk in the municipal park, which was called the "Park of Culture." What I have seen there interested me enormously because it had to do with the might which Soviet Russia would later show during the war. Thanks to such strength, the Soviets were able to overcome the powerful military machine of the Nazis and give Hitler the fatal blow which he deserved.[19]

Klein's simplified version reads:

> When I visited the Park of Culture, I had occasion to see some-
> thing which throws light upon the marvellous resistance which
> the Soviets are putting up against the Nazi aggressors.[20]

Wolofsky knew that irony and humour made for good reading in
popular newspapers, especially when the readership was composed
of recent immigrants from Eastern Europe who did not hold Russia
in high esteem. His memoirs were no exception to the rule, and there
are numerous uncharitable allusions in the text to pre-Soviet days.
At one point Wolofsky visits the Kremlin and, upon being shown
the riches of the Romanoff dynasty by his official guide, cannot stop
himself from sitting on the throne of Nicolas II, the very same one
upon which the young Czar had been crowned emperor in 1895. "It
was a sort of Jewish revenge for all the agony which our people had
suffered under his regime,"[21] adds Klein as an explanation to excuse
the author's chutzpah in such circumstances. The narration then
becomes more pointed when Wolofsky contemplates the symbols of
Czarism now in Soviet hands, objects that, for centuries, instilled
fear in the hearts of Russian Jews:

> *Ven me hot mir gevizen di farshidene klayder foun di tsaritses*
> *vos ze hoben getrogen bay zayre koronatsyes, hob ikh a trakht*
> *geton: ven hot a yid gehat di meglekhkayt aher arayntsukumen*
> *oun iberhoypt tsu veren azoy haymish tsu konen makhen a shpas*
> *foun alemen ? Oun ikh hob dan gefilt tsu zogen a dank dem*
> *bolshevism.*[22]

> When we were shown the various dresses which the tsarinas
> had worn during the crowning ceremonies, I had this thought:
> how often in the past had Jews a chance to come in such a place
> and most of all to look upon such wealth with familiarity, to the
> point of making a joke of it? I felt I owed a debt of gratitude to
> the Bolshevists.[23]

> As I looked upon the gorgeous dress of the departed Tzarinas,
> I reflected: When before did a Jew have the opportunity of
> entering these sacred precincts? Although a cat might look at a

queen, not so a Jew. He couldn't even dwell in this city, without special permission. The Soviet Regime had changed all that. It had in truth proclaimed the equality of all races.[24]

Klein also felt compelled to modify descriptions of events and scenes that might appear too detailed or too emotional for the mainstream Canadian reader, and, in his English language poems, the transition from Yiddish to English must have been particularly arduous at times. In *Mayn lebns rayze*, Wolofsky's Jewish protagonists are surrounded by their own familiar idiom and use the Yiddish language in circumstances of great intimacy. When they communicated in Yiddish, whether in Canada or in Poland, East European Jews referred to a set of values and notions that were not necessarily known outside their circle and that related to a cultural grammar all their own. Klein wasn't interested in modifying the text to enhance Wolofsky's ethnographic study of his generation. Quite the opposite, Klein aimed to break the barriers erected around minority culture; he aimed at a broader consensus not found in Wolofsky's memoirs. A good example of this tendency is provided at the beginning of a chapter when Wolofsky finds himself leaving Canada in 1934 for his third and last trip to Europe and Palestine. Almost as soon as he arrives in Poland he makes plans to travel to Soviet Russia. The trip across the border is not easy to organize since the two countries barely have diplomatic relations. A proper visa is needed to cross the border into the Communist neighbour, and Wolofsky must plead his case to the Russian consul in Warsaw, accompanied by an employee of the Polish navigation company, a certain Tenenbaum. The three men meet and try to communicate in several languages, until they realize that they are all Jews. It turns out that the consul had been in Montreal and had been interviewed by Wolofsky years earlier, his picture having appeared in the pages of *Der Keneder Adler*. Instantly, the context changes and emotions deepen. Wolofsky is literally swept off his feet:

Bekitser, mir hoben zikh tseredt in a faynem yidish oun es lozt zikh oys, az Tenenboym is a zun foun a bavouster rov oun az der Rusisher konsul oykh a rov's a zun. Der geshprekh iz gevorn alts varimer. M'hot zikh afile dertselt fayne idishe vitsen. M'hot servirt te, oun mir zaynen ale gevorn zer haymish.[25]

Finally we conversed for a while in an elevated Yiddish and it was revealed that Tenenbaum was the son of a well-known rabbi and likewise with the Russian consul. Our chat became very intimate and we even exchanged fine Jewish jokes. Tea was served and we all felt as if we were among old friends.[26]

It also appeared that Tannenbaum was the son of a rabbi; as was the Consul. My application for a visa turned into a very friendly social visit. We exchanged Jewish jokes; we drank tea together.[27]

Klein's translations offer at once continuity and rupture vis-à-vis Montreal's Yiddish heritage. Undoubtedly, the poet understood very well the language and culture of Eastern European immigrants and even, at times, was a participant in the city's Yiddish institutions, such as the Jewish Public Library or the editorial offices of *Der Keneder Adler*. When he translated Yiddish prose, Klein went in directions that reveal his refined aesthetic penchants, his taste for high literature, and his sense of universal culture, all elements that ran against a Yiddish canon favouring intimate familiarity between individuals and folkloric modes of expression. Nowhere is this tension more visible than in Klein's work on Wolofsky's memoirs in the mid-1940s. Because the owner of *Der Keneder Adler* was a respected community figure and represented Polish Yiddish culture in Montreal, Klein's translation of *Mayn lebns rayze* reveals strong undercurrents of resistance to the original text. More broadly, the comparison of the Yiddish and English versions of Wolofsky's memoirs brings to light a crucial moment in the history of Jewish literature in Canada, when a transition was effected between the parlance of the immigrants and the dominant language of the country. This change bears further study, in part because Yiddish is rarely within the grasp of researchers in the field of Jewish-Canadian literature and is fundamental to our understanding of Jewish literary creativity in Montreal. One could even argue that, precisely because Canadian-born Jewish writers in English were so successful after the Second World War (notably, Klein himself), the difficult road that led from one idiom to the other was quickly forgotten.

Clearly, the Yiddish literary heritage is still perceptible in Klein's oeuvre, particularly in his poetry, where many of the images used before him by Jacob Isaac Segal, Noah Isaac Gotlib, and Sholem

Shtern resurface in the form of allegoric descriptions of Montreal. Klein's intense emotional outpourings, his visceral attachment to Judaism as a central metaphor of life, and his allusions to elevated forms of mysticism also point to a strong Yiddish connection. At the same time, the poet's use of literary English, peppered in *The Rocking Chair* with references to Medieval French, do not allow the unique rhythm and resonance of the Yiddish language to break through. To casual English-language readers, a text by Klein is a familiar landscape with unusual cultural references. For most of them, it wouldn't readily come to mind to perceive in the deeper strata of his poetic works the influence of a language common among Eastern European Jews before the Holocaust. In achieving such a synthesis of two seemingly unrelated cultures, Klein must have experienced a level of creative tension common in Jewish literature throughout history. The daunting task to which the poet attached himself early in his career must also have been exhausting. Klein may have recognized early on that the long negotiations required to bridge the two worlds would eventually lead to an impasse, which could only be resolved by abandoning one heritage in favour of another. Perhaps in such an instance Klein was reminded of I.L. Peretz's famous short story *"Tsvishn tsvey berg"* (Between Two Peaks), when the teachings of the Hassidic *rebbe* of Biala clash with the misnagdic doctrine of the *Brisker rov*. The two figures know each other well, as the *rebbe* had been a student in the *rov*'s yeshiva in Brisk for many years. Although they are from the same world, differences of accent in their understanding of the holy texts and a specific sensitivity to nuances in the practice of Judaism profoundly set them apart. Ultimately, the *Bialer rebbe* and the *rov* of Brisk meet on a highly emotional occasion, but they cannot enter into a dialogue and they maintain a distance:

They came to no agreement. When he returned to Brisk, the rov still was hostile, as he had been before.

But the meeting had one positive result. After this the Brisker Rov stopped his persecution of Hasidim.[28]

PART THREE

Montreal and Beyond

LIANNE MOYES

Reading A.M. Klein's "The Mountain" Alongside the Montreal Poems of J.I. Segal[1]

Mount Royal in the Literary Geography of Yiddish Montreal

That Mount Royal was important to A.M. Klein is clear from the number of times it figures in his writings, both published and unpublished. Among English-language poets of mid-century Montreal, Klein is the only one to have devoted three poems specifically to the mountain. The poems "Winter Night, Mount Royal," "Lookout: Mount Royal," and "The Mountain," published in *The Rocking Chair and Other Poems*, give us a sense not only of what the mountain meant to Klein but also of how it was lived by Montrealers residing in the neighbourhoods adjacent to it. Klein's poems of Mount Royal, like other poems in *The Rocking Chair*, are clearly inscribed within the field of English-language writing of 1940s Montreal. But Klein's mountain poems also bear the traces of Montreal writing in Yiddish (Fuerstenberg, "From Yiddish," 66–7), a field in which the figure of Mount Royal holds a particularly important place. The mountain, Pierre Anctil explains, reminded Yiddish-speaking immigrants of the hills around Jerusalem as described in the Talmud. It rendered the Montreal landscape spiritually significant in a way that allowed them to adopt the city as their own (Anctil, "À la découverte de la littérature yiddish montréalaise" 24–5). Klein, we remember, calls the mountain "[his] spirit's mother" in "Montreal," the poem that comes immediately before the Mount Royal poems in *The Rocking Chair*. Anctil also recounts how, in 1919, a small socialist-Zionist cooperative that participated in the first General Assembly of the Canadian Jewish Congress called itself *Tur Malka* ("mountain of the king" in Aramaic), the name in the Talmud of a mountainous, fortified site in Palestine (Anctil, *Tur Malka*, 16). Sherry Simon observes in her reading of Anctil that, "by naming the mountain in their own language, the Jews were appropriating the geography of the city, adding their own history to a site marked by previous histories" (Simon, *Translating Montreal*, 114).

Yiddish-language journals and memoirs of the 1920s, 1930s, and 1940s make repeated references to Mount Royal. Consider an entry dated 2 May 1926 in the journal of Yaacov Zipper, a writer who had arrived in Montreal the previous year: "A warm, delightful day. We took the children to the playing field at the foot of the mountain. And I myself became somewhat child-like" (Garfinkle and Butovsky 66). In the literary memoir of Zipper's brother, Sholem Shtern,[2] the New York writers who visited Montreal in the 1930s and 1940s are presented as awe-struck at the sight of the mountain. As Shtern reports during the visit of Zishe Weinper, translated here by Anctil:[3]

> Tout juste au-dessus de nous un soleil aux reflets aveuglants descendait sur la cime boisée de la montagne. Dressée sur les hauteurs verdoyantes maintenant envahies d'une teinte dorée, la croix donnait l'impression d'être entourée de flammes puissantes. Les rayons cernaient de part en part les troncs des arbres et leurs branches baingaient dans l'intensité lumineuse du crépuscule. (Shtern 66–7)

This scene recurs throughout Shtern's memoir, often described from the perspective of two men, waiting for a tram on St Laurent or du Parc, or walking on de l'Esplanade, an avenue that runs along Parc Jeanne-Mance (then Fletcher's Field), across from the lower, eastern slope of Mount Royal. If we remember that de l'Esplanade was the site of the Jewish Public Library of the period as well as of Ida Maze's salon,[4] we begin to realize how considerable a presence the mountain was in the literary geography of Yiddish-speaking Montreal. As David Shtern notes in his Preface (Shtern 24–6) and as Anctil observes in his essay on Shtern (Anctil, "Sholem Shtern," 316, 322), the latter's memoirs are extraordinarily attentive to the topography of Montreal as well as to the inscription of the community within the city: "Le marché de fruits, les petits commerces de volaille et de poison, les conversations en yiddish, l'atmosphère des lieux, voilà qui constituait en quelque sorte un nouveau mode de vie juif au pied de la montagne" (Shtern 67). Another New York visitor featured in Shtern's memoir, Fishl Bimko, attributes great literary potential to this situation at the foot of the mountain: "'quelle beauté! Quelle vision exceptionelle! Vraiment, pour un poète, ce lieu est béni entre tous. Ici un écrivain devrait pouvoir écrire les oeuvres les plus magnifiques'" (Shtern 119).

Shtern's memoirs document the first impressions and celebratory statements of visiting writers. But how did Yiddish-speaking writers who lived in Montreal, writers such as Noah Isaac Gotlib,[5] Moyshe Leib Halpern,[6] Jacob Isaac Segal,[7] or Shtern himself portray the mountain? And how do those portraits compare to Klein's? Segal is the writer I focus on in this chapter, in part because Klein knew Segal and wrote reviews of his work in the *Canadian Jewish Chronicle*,[8] and in part because a number of Segal's poems are available in translation. When I read Klein's Mount Royal poems alongside Segal's poems on Montreal (those available in French or English translation), I hear echoes – not many echoes, but enough to give me pause and make me want to read more carefully. In particular, there are lines from Klein's "The Mountain" (1948)[9] that resonate with lines from Segal's "Montreal" (1934), "M.L. Halpern" (1937), and "Late Summer in Montreal" (1950). These resonances are interesting not only for the continuities and discontinuities they bring into focus but also for what they suggest about the significance of the mountain in the lives of Yiddish-speaking immigrants and their children. Reading the poems of Klein and Segal beside one another gives some sense of the landmarks, spaces, sight-lines, and modes of circulation, both on the mountain and off, that mattered to or troubled those living beside it. The cross that stands on Mount Royal appears, for example, in Segal's "Montreal" and "M.L. Halpern" as well as in Klein's "The Mountain"; the streetcars that ran throughout the city until the late 1950s appear both in Segal's "Late Summer in Montreal" and in Klein's "The Mountain." We do not know which of the latter two poems was written first,[10] but the question of who influenced whom interests me less than does the fact that these writers were clearly reading each other (and many others) at the same time that they were mapping the space of Montreal. My aim is not so much to compare Klein and Segal as to highlight the specificities of each and, especially, to gain perspective on Klein's "The Mountain" through its intertexts, both historical and literary.

"The Famous Cross"

If, as Brian Trehearne argues, Klein's "The Mountain" is one in a series of poems that inventory the characteristics of "various objects, buildings and locations" specific to Quebec and especially to Montreal (Trehearne 145), then it is worth noting that the poem begins with the cross, the huge metal structure erected in 1924 by the Société Saint-Jean-Baptiste and lighted at night by scores of light bulbs:

> Who knows it only by the famous cross which bleeds
> into the fifty miles of night its light
> knows a night-scene; (Klein, *Rocking Chair*, 35)

Yet, having begun with the cross, Klein's poem immediately moves to diminish the significance of knowing the mountain by the cross. Why set the cross up as a dramatic source of light and, at the same time, reduce it to a mere "night-scene"? In what follows, I trace this gesture to the field of Yiddish-language writing and specifically to the poetry of Segal. Throughout the 1930s and 1940s, in literature in Yiddish and in memoirs about the period, references to the mountain are often accompanied by references to the cross. A poem written by Gotlib following his arrival at the train station in 1930, for example, speaks of downtown streets and squares "bathed" in the light of a summer morning and of the city "vibrating" with activity and noise. What particularly surprises Gotlib's speaker and holds his attention is the mountain, "[c]ouronné d'une croix très haute" and "[r]evêtu d'un manteau de verdure" (qtd. in Anctil, "Sholem Shtern, écrivain Montréalais," 319; Gotlib 7).[11]

In Segal's poems, the cross is not consistently evoked along with the mountain, but when it is – notably in poems of the 1930s – it is stripped of its specifically Christian symbolism and described in terms of light shining into the night. By emphasizing light, the poems foreground an aspect of the Mount Royal cross that has powerful symbolic value within Judaism. Segal's 1934 poem "Montreal" opens with the speaker addressing God. Resigned to the fact that God will not redeem him and that he must live as a stranger in his own city, the speaker struggles to deserve the earthly beauty he finds around him. He describes the mountain as rising proud behind the bustling markets on St Laurent and, in winter, as "resplendissante dans la lumière crue de la neige" (Segal, *Poèmes Yiddish*, 138; Segal, *Mayn nigun*, 284).[12] Whereas the mountain, associated with royalty and the majesty of wildlife, is presented in daylight, in brilliant sunshine, the cross is presented at night: "Toute la nuit rayonne la croix / *qui sait*, pour l'éternité?" (Segal, *Poèmes Yiddish*, 138; Segal, *Mayn nigun*, 284; my emphasis).[13] I hear in this line a genuine question on the part of the speaker about how long the cross will be there, on top of the mountain. Segal, after all, had arrived in Montreal in 1911 and had known a time, prior to 1924, when there was no cross on Mount Royal. In addition to questioning the "eternal" character of the cross's light, Segal's "Montreal" presents that light as covering a vast terrain but becoming paler and weaker the further one is from the source: "Sur de grandes distances, elle jette sa lueur / même pâle et blafarde" (Segal, *Poèmes Yiddish*, 138; Segal, *Mayn nigun*, 284).[14] The poem makes a distinction between the light reflected by snow on the mountain and the light of the cross; the latter is less intense, less able to illuminate the world around it.

Segal's "Montreal" simultaneously features the cross as part of the city's landscape and diminishes its strength. The light of the cross is presented as covering a vast terrain but growing weaker the further one is from the source. This gesture is not unlike that of the opening lines of Klein's "The Mountain," except that Klein's poem is more explicit than is Segal's regarding the need to look beyond the cross to other histories. The attitude of Segal's speaker towards the cross and its light, both here and in the poem "M.L. Halpern" discussed below, is ambivalent, even troubled. Klein's speaker strikes me as less troubled by the Christian symbolism of the cross. However, like Segal's speaker, he is interested in and inspired more by the mountain than by the cross. In this sense, the opening gesture of Klein's "The Mountain" is both continuous with and discontinuous with the portrait of the mountain offered by Segal's poems, a point to which I return below.

The Cross Made Strange

In Shtern's memoir, visiting writers are generally impressed by the sight of the mountain and its cross. Yet the cross also has negative associations. Consider what Halpern is reported to have said to

Shtern as they walked under the trees along Fletcher's Field at the
beginning of the 1930s:

> Montréal ne ressemble à aucune autre ville. La communauté
> juive s'y trouve plus accueillante et plus yiddishisante qu'en
> d'autres localités. Même les gens qui réussissent dans la vie
> n'hésitent pas à rester dans la ville, à l'ombre même de la croix
> qui trône au sommet de la montagne. Cette croix me rap-
> pelle d'ailleurs ma bourgade natale, Zlotshev, où les chrétiens
> s'amusaient à lâcher des chiens sur nous, jeunes écoliers juifs qui
> nous nous rendions au *kheyder*. Malgré cela, je ressens encore de
> la nostalgie pour Zlotshev, mais pas pour la croix qui s'y élevait
> ou pour ses chiens. (Shtern 104)

This conversation reportedly took place on the way back to
Halpern's hotel after an evening at the Jewish Public Library in celebration of Halpern's poetry. The evening had begun, Shtern recalls,
with Segal reading an essay on Halpern's work (Shtern 99). Klein,
too, was well acquainted with Halpern's poetry and, in 1932, one
week after Halpern's death, published English translations of six of
his poems in the *Canadian Jewish Chronicle* (Rozmovits 1). In 1937,
Segal published a poem entitled "M.L. Halpern,"[15] which is arguably as much about Segal as it is about Halpern. This poem, like
"Montreal" discussed above, is of interest here insofar as its presentation of the cross anticipates that found in Klein's "The Mountain."
Segal's "M.L. Halpern" begins by characterizing Montreal as simultaneously "beautiful" and "accursed," and it ends with the lines:

> They remodelled my entire wardrobe,
> So I should not fall starving on their hard threshold
> A fallen one who dragged himself over here
> *Who knows* from what distance, and strange
> On the high mountain the great cross lights up
> the whole night. (qtd. in Friedman 30; Segal *Di drite sude*, 271;
> my emphasis)

Segal would not have had access to Shtern's account of Halpern's
response to the cross, published in 1982. It is possible the story of

Halpern's views circulated at the time of his visit; but it is also likely Segal shared Halpern's complicated relationship to the cross.

Segal's poem, like Halpern's discourse, is marked by movement, the movement of the immigrant who has "dragged himself over here / Who knows from what distance" and the movement created by words such as "distance" and "strange," whose function in the poem's syntax is loose enough to allow them to refer forward (to the light of the cross) and backward (to the process of emigration). The cross, in both Segal and Halpern, is presented in the context of this movement. The cross reminds Halpern of his village; it makes him nostalgic and, at the same time, takes him back to the "Catholic-inspired anti-Semitism" (Simon 114) he had fled. Segal's poem is more circumspect in its treatment of the cross. For Segal's speaker, the cross is simply "strange." How "strange," too, for the speaker to find himself living, once again, beneath a cross after "dragging himself" all that distance. The word "strange" is relatively common in Segal's poems,[16] and it frequently expresses the speaker's sense of alienation from Christianity. In "Old Montreal," for example, a poem published in the same 1937 collection as "M.L. Halpern," the speaker identifies his own neighbourhood around St Urbain and René Lévèsque (then Dorchester) with the adjoining Chinese quarter (Segal, *Poèmes Yiddish*, 120–1; Segal, *Di drite sude*, 46–7).[17] In using Chinatown as a figure of his own difference from the Christian majority, Segal's speaker tends to orientalize it. But Chinatown is also a place in which he feels at ease – indeed, it is the one place in the city where, on a Sunday, the "strange church bells" (qtd. in Friedman 41; Segal, *Di drite sude*, 47) are not ringing. The poem closes with the bells passing over the rooftops of the speaker's neighbourhood "tel un vol d'oiseaux sauvages / dans un ciel gris" (Segal, *Poèmes Yiddish*, 122; Segal, *Di drite sude*, 47).[18]

Klein's Personal Inventory of the Mountain

As I suggested earlier, the first lines of Klein's "The Mountain" echo lines from Segal's poems "Montreal" and "M.L. Halpern." This is especially true of the fragment "Who knows" and the image of the cross lit at night. However, if Klein's poem begins by emphasizing its continuities with the poems of Segal, it also marks its departures.

Whereas Segal's poems focus on distance and strangeness, "The Mountain" favours proximity and familiarity. What is more, Klein's cross, unlike Segal's, "*bleeds* light," a trope that evokes Christian iconography and, specifically, the Passion of Christ. But Klein's poem refuses to reduce the mountain to "the famous cross," in the same way that it refuses to reduce the mountain, in lines four through six, to an image on a postcard: "The buffalo straggled of the laurentian herd" is another of the poem's memorable images (Klein, *Rocking Chair*, 35). Seen from the southeast, Mount Royal resembles the hump of a buffalo. What is more, if the Laurentian Mountains to the north of Montreal can be imagined as a "herd," then hills such as Mount Royal and Mont-Sainte-Hilaire are easily imagined as "stragglers." Yet the cross and the straggled buffalo, however memorable, are not privileged images within the poem. They are not the images through which Klein's speaker "knows" or "remembers" the mountain. Klein is not interested in the mountain as a landmark or symbol;[19] nor is he interested in it as a sacred place, a place associated with the mountains in Hebrew scripture (Pollock, *A.M. Klein*, 193). His is a personal inventory of the mountain based upon his own history, upon his own acquaintance with Mount Royal as a secular space. I suggested at the outset that the mountain rendered the Montreal landscape spiritually significant for Jewish Montrealers. But the mountain does not need to be a sacred space to feed Klein's spirit. Klein's "Montreal" characterizes Mount Royal in distinctly material as well as in distinctly spiritual terms, as "my spirit's mother / Almative, poitrinate" (Klein, *Rocking Chair*, 30). These words suggest not just the shape of the mountain but also the meanings the poet lends that shape. Klein's morphology of the mountain is one of attachment, of infant to mother and of child to familiar ground. His mountain is experienced up close rather than at a distance, on the hill rather than in the streets below.

In "The Mountain," Mount Royal inhabits the speaker as much as he inhabits it. Both Robert Melançon and Trehearne make a similar argument about the speaker's relationship to the city in "Montreal" (Melançon 27; Trehearne 164). Citing the stanza of "Montreal" in which Mount Royal is mentioned, a stanza that begins "You are a part of me, O all your quartiers," Trehearne notes the "blurring" of "the distinction between [the speaker] and his surroundings" (163). I find the same blurring in "The Mountain" in the speaker's account of riding around the mountain in a streetcar:

In layers of mountains the history of mankind,
and in Mount Royal
which daily in a streetcar I surround
my youth, my childhood (Klein, *Rocking Chair*, 35)

In 1947, the year Klein wrote the Mount Royal poems, he was a lecturer at McGill. Given that he was living on Hutchison near St Joseph (Caplan, *Like One That Dreamed*, 135) and using his law office on St Jacques (then St James) to prepare classes and to write (129), the de Bleury–du Parc tramway, which ran from Van Horne to Craig, would have been a likely choice and would have given him the sense of "surrounding" the mountain (Compagnie des Tramways de Montréal). Within the terms of the poem, the speaker's gesture of surrounding the mountain is tantamount to surrounding or embracing his former or remembered self. Indeed, it is possible to read the mountain as the embodiment of his youth, his childhood,[20] and to read the poem as another "portrait of the poet as landscape."

For Klein's speaker, Mount Royal also holds within it "the history of" his youth, his childhood. That history is written on the mountain, "marked and spotted," for example, on the adder's tongue and the trilliums, "threaded with earth, and rooted / beside the blood-roots" (Klein, *Rocking Chair*, 35). In Klein's own history, the April rituals of his childhood were repeated with his children as, year after year, Klein took his children to Mount Royal after the thaw (Caplan, *Like One That Dreamed*, 136). "My father," Colman Klein remembers, "knew certain special places where trilliums grew, adder's tongue, bloodroot. He was fascinated, would show us every year how the bloodroot yielded its bit of dye" (qtd. in Caplan, *Like One That Dreamed*, 136). As Pollock suggests, bloodroots are a powerful image for Klein, one associated in his unpublished novel "The Inverted Tree" both with the annual trips to Mount Royal to pick wildflowers and with the darker story of a hereditary weakness in the lungs and heart (Pollock, *A.M. Klein: The Story of the Poet*, 138). This darker story – figured elsewhere as "A prowler in the mansion of [his] blood" (Klein, *Selected Poems*, 73) – was written out of the poems in *The Rocking Chair*. But, as Trehearne's chapter on the latter collection shows, the darker story haunts a number of them nonetheless. Indeed, Colman's troubled response to the "bleeding roots" in "The Inverted Tree" (Klein, *Notebooks*, 41), and Pollock's interpretation of a cryptic note by Klein about Dante in the Forest

of Suicides (Pollock, *A.M. Klein: The Story of the Poet*, 138) give
us insight into the emotional landscape that had to be bracketed in
order for Klein to construct "The Mountain" as a retreat into a kind
of childhood paradise (see Bentley, "Klein, Montreal, and Mankind,"
48–51; Brenner, "A.M. Klein's *The Rocking Chair*," 95–6; Pollock,
A.M. Klein: The Story of the Poet, 193–5).

"Our huge village city"

Segal, too, writes a poem in the latter half of the 1940s in which the
speaker rides a streetcar. Consider the opening lines of "Late Summer in Montreal," translated by Miriam Waddington:

> Mount Royal, our mountain king,
> our forest legend, our huge village
> city, today grows soft and mild,
> the streetcars run peacefully
> on polished wire strings, relax
> on quiet tracks; today is Sunday. (Segal, "Late Summer," 56;
> Segal, *Seyfer yidish*, 461)

Segal lived on Clark near the intersection with Mount Royal. Given
that the speaker in "Late Summer in Montreal" mentions the pov-
erty he sees on St Dominique, it is likely the poem refers to trams on
Mount Royal or perhaps on another street that crosses St Laurent
and St Dominique. As in many of Segal's Montreal poems, it is Sunday. However, in the lines that follow those cited above, the speaker
is less alienated than he is in poems of the 1920s and 1930s. When he
hears Sunday morning religious broadcasts and Mendelssohn's organ
music, he recognizes in them his own prayers and his own Psalms.
In this way, his poem suggests the Jewish roots both of the Mendelssohn family and of Christian prayer (Friedman 47). Segal's speaker
marks his difference from the majority yet he does so in a way that
emphasizes radical continuities between Judaism and Christianity.

In spite of the shared reference to streetcars, Klein's and Segal's
poems are quite different. Whereas Segal's "Late Summer in Montreal" uses Mount Royal as a landmark to identify the city in which
the speaker circulates, Klein's "The Mountain" remembers everyday
practices of the mountain that make it meaningful to him and to

many Montrealers. Hence, the emphasis on the word "daily" in the second stanza of "The Mountain," in contrast with the "night-scene" of the first stanza. Whereas Segal's poem expresses the meditations and epiphanies of a specific day – "today is Sunday" – Klein's poem captures the repeated action of his daily journey around the mountain and of his ritual visits in specific seasons. "The Mountain," then, layers moments in time; "Late Summer in Montreal," in contrast, layers place (as well as certain religious texts). In Segal's poem, Montreal is read in relation to the village of Korets, the shtetl that Segal left at the age of fifteen. The two places are superimposed as well as juxtaposed in the image "our huge village / city."[21] In Klein's poem, the city in question is Montreal. The reference to the role of mountains in the "history of mankind" speaks, in part, to the significance of the mountains of ancient Palestine in the imaginary of the Montreal Yiddish-speaking community (Anctil, *Tur Malka*, 15–18), but the poem turns immediately to and remains on Mount Royal. Klein's "Autobiographical," written earlier in the 1940s, makes a gesture similar to that of Segal's poem, especially in lines such as "Out of the ghetto streets where a Jewboy / Dreamed pavement into pleasant bible-land" (Klein, *Selected Poems*, 86–9; Melançon 33–4). Indeed, the "elsewhere" of a poem such as "Autobiographical" is both the shtetl and Jerusalem. In "The Mountain," however, the focus is the speaker's relationship to Montreal.

There is nothing specific in "The Mountain" to say that the speaker is Jewish, and nothing to say he is not. Klein's speaker approaches the question of self-identification obliquely. This is perhaps the most significant difference between Klein's poems of Montreal and those of Segal. In his discussion of Klein's *The Rocking Chair and Other Poems*, Trehearne remarks upon the near-complete erasure of Judaism (136, 162). At the same time, Trehearne identifies a number of "countering forces" at work in "Montreal," which, in his view, "reinstate the centrality of Jewish culture in the city by figuring the poem's speaker as its metaphoric body" (162–3). As Trehearne points out, for this reading to work, "we must know that our speaker is Jewish" (166). A similar argument might be made for "The Mountain" insofar as corporeal metaphors identify the speaker with the mountain and inscribe one upon the other. Think, for example, of the buttercups that throw rounds of yellow upon the speaker's heart, or of all the speaker's "Aprils" marked upon and rooted beside the wildflowers. At the same time, this poet-mountain metaphor is not nearly as sustained as is the poet-city metaphor. The speaker of "The Mountain" does not "take in" or "incorporate" the mountain the way the speaker of "Montreal" takes in or incorporates the city (162–4). What is more, the speaker is not alone on the mountain; he remembers himself there with others, and, in this sense, there is little possibility of a one-to-one identification with the mountain.

In each of Klein's Mount Royal poems, the mountain is a shared space in which Jewish culture has an important place. In "Winter Night: Mount Royal," the speaker registers the passing of a sleigh whose runners are described as "scrolling it into the mist" (Klein, *Rocking Chair*, 32). The figure of the scroll is a recurring one in Klein's oeuvre (Pollock, *A.M. Klein: The Story of the Poet*, 3–9). In some poems from *The Rocking Chair* – "Portrait of the Poet as Landscape" and "Montreal," for example – the "scroll" is virtually the only reference to Judaism (Trehearne 136). In "Lookout: Mount Royal," the speaker locates himself, albeit indirectly, as one kid among "other kids of other slums and races" (Klein, *Rocking Chair*, 33). And in "The Mountain," the perspective is of someone who has grown up in and raised their children in the neighbourhoods adjacent to the mountain; someone for whom Olmsted's park has served the role of backyard and country place as well as public park; someone who has played baseball on Fletcher's Field, heard concerts at the bandstand on the grassy slope near the Cartier monument (Weintraub, *City Unique*, 187), and walked up the mountain with a lover. Klein's speaker locates himself within this relatively heterogeneous collectivity. His Jewishness, which may be legible to some readers and not to others, is part of the heterogeneity. What Segal's and Klein's "streetcar poems" share, in spite of their significant differences, is a certain ease with the city, a sense on the part of the speaker of his own belonging, however conflicted that belonging might be. Because this ease, this sense of "our huge village city," is fairly rare in Segal's poetry (Friedman 47), it makes me think that Segal had read poems such as "Montreal" (composed in 1944) and "The Mountain" when he wrote "Late Summer in Montreal." Or, perhaps, he had read "Montreal" and written "Late Summer in Montreal," which, in turn, inspired Klein's use of the streetcar device in "The Mountain."

Counternarratives

Mount Royal is an originary site in the history of Montreal, a point of reference and a material ground for the elaboration of many of the city's narratives. Among the most pervasive of these is the narrative of de Maisonneuve's planting a cross on Mount Royal in 1643. The 1924 gesture of erecting a permanent metal cross on the mountain can be read as a reinscription of that history. But there are other histories and other ways of imagining the mountain – as Shtern's account of "un nouveau mode de vie juif au pied de la montagne" (Shtern 67), Segal's and Klein's portraits of Mount Royal, and names such as *Tur Malka* (Anctil, *Tur Malka*, 1997) demonstrate. In Simon's terms, the mountain is palimpsestic, "a site marked by previous histories" (Simon 114). This sense of layered history informs Klein's "The Mountain," especially the line "In layers of mountains the history of mankind" (Klein, *Rocking Chair*, 35). In order to open a space for alternative histories, for counternarratives to that of de Maisonneuve, Klein's poem turns away from iconic images such as the cross, whose place at the summit would seem to give it a monopoly on the meanings of the entire space. "The Mountain" simultaneously features and downplays the cross. It does so in order not to explore the symbolism of the mountain within the context of Jewish religious tradition (Pollock, *A.M. Klein: The Story of the Poet*, 193) but to construct Mount Royal as a worldly, or *secular*, space.[22] In other words, rather than substitute Judaism for Christianity – and rather than struggle with the relationship between the two in the way that Segal's poems do – Klein's mountain poems shift ground, away from religion. The mountain, in Klein's poems, is not a place for making claims in the name of one set of beliefs or another but, rather, a space (one among many) for elaborating a secular history of life in Montreal. Klein's strategy for writing such a history was to focus on personal rather than on collective meanings and narratives, and to allow a portrait of the mountain, its many layers, to emerge by way of fragments from his own life history.

SHERRY SIMON

Montreal, Dublin, Prague, Jerusalem, and the Others: A.M. Klein's Cities

A.M. Klein's best-known work, his 1951 novel *The Second Scroll*, is a saga that takes the narrator from Montreal to Jerusalem through a series of stopovers, including Casablanca and Rome. Though the novel is based on Klein's own voyage to Israel in 1949, it adopts an itinerary that is slightly different from the one Klein himself took. Klein flew directly to Lydda in the new state of Israel. It was only on the return flight that he made stopovers in Paris and Rome, as one was inclined to do in the days when air travel was still a luxury and visits to the great capitals of European culture de rigueur (Klein, *Second Scroll*, n127)

Why did Klein reverse the order so that the stopovers came first? The change is minor and might seem insignificant, but it reflects the essence of what happened when the travel journal was transformed into a novel. When Klein turned his own experiences into the intricately shaped multilayered prose poem that is *The Second Scroll*, he converted the raw material of his journey into an elaborate allegory whose scope far exceeded that of Klein's personal voyage. The novel is no longer the story of one individual's long-awaited opportunity to visit the Holy Land; rather, it is the history of an entire people, the historical voyage over centuries that took the Jews of the Diaspora back to the Promised Land. In this iteration of the voyage, Jerusalem had to be the logical endpoint.

The stopover cities stand in for episodes in Jewish history. Each city – Montreal, Rome, Casablanca, Jerusalem – represents a specific configuration in the relations of Jews and non-Jews in the course of many centuries: Montreal was the North American city in which Klein and many other emigrants from the *shtetl* created a new brand of diasporic Judaism; Rome was the city of apostasy, in which forms of Christian beauty exercised their strongest temptations; Casablanca was an important home to Sephardic Judaism and of Jewish conversation with Islam; Jerusalem was the capital of the new state of Israel, where, in 1948, both a political and a religious dream were realized. There is something of an ironic parallel between the "stopover" of the tourist and the sojourn of Jewish communities in cities that they were sometimes forced to abandon – cities that, at their height, might have aspired to become a "new Jerusalem" and that might later have been emptied of their Jewish populations. (Though he would not have anticipated it, this would be the case for Casablanca, which Jews were forced to flee in the 1950s and 1960s.) As markers of diasporic history, as sites of fusion between languages, as ciphers of the imagination, cities play a special role in Klein's understanding of Jewish history, and it is not surprising that, for his most accomplished work, *The Second Scroll*, Klein would adopt an episodic structure that used cities as structural elements.

"Whispers of the four corners of the world"

As a Jewish writer deeply aware of history, Klein understood his time and his place as part of a series echoing the events of the past, the moments of tension and fusion that are the experience of the Jewish Diaspora. Klein experienced his home city Montreal in resonance with the other great cities of historical Jewish culture, reflecting back onto Montreal the imaginative worlds he had gathered elsewhere. A short entry in his notebooks describing a man carrying a *lulav* during Sukkot indicates this strong consciousness of historical coexistence:

> Along the ghetto-street shuffles my unclejew, bearing palms.
>   Palmleaf of Asia, caftan of Europe, macadam American.
>   With every step, the palm leaf sibilates above his head,
> whispers of the four corners of the world, of glories past and
> gone, of ease in Zion, lore in Babylon. (Klein, *Notebooks*, 22)

These whispers from the four corners of the world are the echoes of other cities and times in the streets of today. In "A Psalm Touching Genealogy," Klein famously proclaims that the poet is born in a "residence" that attaches him to the history of his people: "Not sole was I born, but entire genesis: / For to the fathers that begat me, this / Body is residence" (*Complete Poems*, 2:624, lines 1–3). This dwelling-place is both metaphorically and historically situated. The continuity of history allows the poet to connect with experience across the realms of Jewish experience, enabling identification here with the "sodality" of Talmudic scholars, there with the "noble lineage" of Hasidism or the "halidom" of the kabbalistic city of Safed.[1] But it also allows an imaginative leap to faraway places: "Your halidom is mine. / Your streets, terraced and curved and narrow, I climbed in my youth, attending on your sages" (1:143, lines 25–7).

And again in his poem "And in That Drowning Instant" Klein conveys this identification with different moments of Jewish history, to end finally at "Jerusalem-gate and Temple-door":

> the image of myself intent
> on several freedoms
>   fading to
> myself in yellowed Basle-print
> vanishing
>   into ghetto-Jew
> ...
> to show me in old Amsterdam
> which topples
>   into a new scene
> Cordova where an Abraham
> faces inquisitors (2:608–9, lines 5–17).

And therefore it can be said, as Noreen Golfman suggests, that "the central persona of Klein's written work ... assumes the stance of God, who from some propitious vantage point chronicles all the aspects of Jewish culture in an effort to remind his readers of all the archetypes in the collective cultural memory; so that the Jew who walked through eastern Europe in the middle ages ... is the same Jew who walks the streets of the urban ghetto in contemporary Montreal" (Golfman 189).

Among these different moments, a few cities stand as especially emblematic moments of fusion with Jewish experience. Prague held a special place in his imagination and was to have played a large role in the novel Klein began on the golem. In the extensive notes he prepared for "The Golem" Klein devoted a great deal of energy to researching the city, its geography, its physical aspect, its architecture, and its views. A view of the city as it first appears to the narrator indicates the symbolic weight this setting is meant to bear:

Prague – sloping huddled roofs
[...] the first as it were a city wearing alchemist's hats,
a city besotted and staggering, with drunken gables, gasping dormers, and roofs awry.
loutish, indifferent, smugly hunched, roofs tilted as though they were hats worn to shut out the world (Klein, *Notebooks*, 164).

The city takes on the character of mystery and degradation to be explored in the story.

Dublin finds itself on the map of Jewish history as the city of Leopold Bloom, creation of James Joyce. For much of his life, and at times with great passion, Klein was a reader of Joyce, and this reading intensely refracted his relationship with Montreal. Both Klein and Joyce were products of a parochial education, a heritage they were able to redirect towards new readers. In his extensive studies of Joyce, Klein applied himself to Dublin's geography as he applied himself to the text of *Ulysses*. Joyce's itinerary through Dublin was also a pathway into ancient Greece, and Klein was understandably drawn to this narrative in which times and places were collapsed. "Vico, Dalkey, is indeed Vico – The Key," is the concluding phrase in his long chapter on the Vico motif, the last in a series of allegorical readings of Joyce (Klein, *Literary Essays,* 366). Klein's special attachment to *Ulysses* took the form of detailed notes for interpretations of specific chapters, including "Oxen of the Sun." Usher Caplan, in his biography *Like One That Dreamed*, tells us that Klein dreamed of turning Montreal into a model of Joyce's Dublin, a city of exuberant linguistic fictions. He "often thought of writing a monumental poem or novel that would capture the Montreal of his youth just as *Ulysses* had memorialized Joyce's Dublin ... In the forties he made several starts ... drawing up elaborate schematic outlines in clear imitation of Joyce .... In the end he was daunted by the challenge and abandoned the idea of writing the Canadian *Ulysses*" (Caplan, *Like One That Dreamed*, 53). He did visit Ireland on a return trip from Jerusalem but left no notes of this visit.[2] Like Joyce, Klein was passionately attached to city life and to the music it produced. Both were aware that cities are soundscapes and that they provide a particular music to ears that can recognize it.

Soundscapes

Together, these many cities trace a map of Klein's intellectual and poetic universe and its connections to Jewish history. That the city often comes to frame and represent moments in the commonality of Jewish experience emerges out of the reality of Klein's own life as a resident of Montreal. As a modernist, he was part of the ongoing effort to "write" the city, to imagine its forms and represent its movement. Like the novelists and poets of the modern city – from Virginia Woolf to Dos Passos, from T.S. Eliot to the Yiddish poets of New York – he understood that the city is a powerful presence and a fertile site for experiments in narrative forms and lexical syncretism. But for Klein, the city was especially resonant as a layered construction of new and old, relics and innovations, as a palimpsest of memory, and as a structure of sound. As an enthusiastic city-dweller, Klein loved imagining the soundscapes of these cities. The great cities of the earth, says Klein, enter one's life in childhood as sounds:

> London, two slow drumbeats; Paris, the drawing of a bow over a violin; Bagdad, a flute of assonance; Rome, the single cello string plucked vibrating – the name Jerusalem always called to me, short long, short long, like the blast of a silver trumpet. (Klein, *Notebooks*, 185)

The poet reads the "parchemin roll" of the city, but he is, to paraphrase Klein, the chief auditor of its soundscape (*Complete Poems*, 2:622–3, line 58).

Montreal was Klein's city, and affection for this city runs through all of Klein's work. Though Klein was aware of anti-Semitism and of the negative aspects of Quebec nationalism, he most often depicted Montreal as a site of productive and enriching fusions. Klein's childhood (he arrived in the city with his parents in 1910) was spent in the largely Yiddish-speaking streets of the Jewish neighbourhood. Like

most of his generation of immigrants, Klein looked to the English
side of town for his education (at McGill) and for his cultural life.
Unusually, however, Klein was also familiar with French-speaking
Montreal. He studied law at the Université de Montréal and spent
a year in northern Quebec, in Rouyn, as a beginning lawyer. This
experience, and perhaps also his early student job as a tour guide
around Montreal, provided the familiarity with east-end Montreal
that became the basis for Klein's popular *Rocking Chair* poems. As
a "spieler" on sightseeing buses, Klein would lead tours that started
from Dominion Square to visit not only such sites as Notre Dame
Cathedral, City Hall, Lafontaine Park, and the nearby French neighbourhoods, but also such sites as Westmount, Sherbrooke Street,
Mount Royal "with its new steel girder cross, the southern lookout
from the mountaintop, and St. Joseph's Oratory with its massive
dome still under construction. One of the longer trips out of the
city went to the Indian reservation at Caughnawaga" (Caplan, *Like
One That Dreamed*, 54). This early student experience would have
given Klein a panoramic view of his city, and indeed many of Klein's
poems, especially those which use the focus of Mount Royal, gather
up the entire expanse of the city in their single embrace.

   Klein's keen ear for the soundscape of Montreal is evident in the
poems of *The Rocking Chair* – most famously in his mixed-language
poem "Montreal,"[3] but also in many other of his portraits of Montreal, as in "Dominion Square":

Our dialects: the bronze of Bobby Burns
beloved of the businessman his once a year,
the calèche at the curb, rolled from old France
and the hotel-door's foreign eloquence
converge, as in a radio sound-room, here.
But do not linger; but are bruited hence
by streetcar through the angular city, by
tunnel through mountain to the suburbs, by
the trains that whistle from this terminus
into the flat, the high, the dark, the sunlit distances.
(*Complete Poems*, 2:672, lines 13–22)

The park, "a sudden meadow dropped amongst brick," is a "minia-
ture" of the "composite land." Dominion Square, says Klein, reflects

through its architecture (the Sun Life building on the one hand, the "roofed apostles" of the cathedral on the other) its flora and the "criss-cross paths" (the shape of our flag), the mixtures that make up the land. This mix is social too, including "the men on benches who only rise to beg." But the park is also the site of the fleeting convergence of idioms, local and foreign. Languages mingle in the leisurely swirl of the park, coming together for a moment. Then the encounter is swiftly dissolved as the languages and their speakers are whisked away to their further destinations – by streetcar or by the train that carries the more privileged under the mountain to the suburbs. Carried away on sound, "bruited hence," the languages are transported to the furthest corners of the city. Dominion Square, like Mount Royal, offers the image of momentary reconciliation, the criss-cross and convergence of styles and languages.

Most of the poems in *The Rocking Chair* are, like "Dominion Square," urban poems – and they shape a kind of travelogue of the city, from the bookstores and hospitals to landmarks like St Joseph's Oratory or noisy political meetings. In light of this emphasis on the city, the choice of the title of the collection is puzzling. Why was "The Rocking Chair" highlighted and its title given to the whole collection? This poem emphasizes the stasis of Quebec rural life and hardly reflects the spirit of most of the other poems. But this ambivalence does reflect the slow change in the self-perception of francophones in Montreal in the 1940s. Though the population was increasingly urban, French-Canadians had not yet become full citizens of their city, and the cultural forms that were to express this citizenship had not yet emerged. And so, though the title is misleading and plays into stereotypes of traditional rural life, the collection as a whole accurately evokes a moment of change in Montreal's urban imagination.

The Polyglot City

The keenness of Klein's ear was a result not only of his gifts as a poet but also of the very special circumstances in which he grew up in Montreal. Miriam Waddington's perceptive and pioneering 1970 study of Klein explains that Klein was brought up in a situation in which the languages he learned were attached to discrete, absolutely separate milieux: English and Latin at school, Yiddish at home, and

Hebrew at religious school. "The culture which each of the three languages represented was kept separate from the others, complete in and for itself" (Waddington, *A.M. Klein*, 9). The fact that all of these languages were transmitted to him in a strong and culturally vibrant form was crucial. The English that Klein learned at Baron Byng school was a colonial, hypercorrect language, enriched by the poetic heritage of nineteenth-century Victorianism. Similarly, the Yiddish of his parents was vigorous and self-confident, and Hebrew was part of a solid tradition. Consequently:

> The earliest linguistic influences which shaped his speech were
> therefore pure and uncorrupted, and the culture which each
> of the three languages represented was kept separate from the
> others, complete in and for itself. Love and family belonged
> with Yiddish, while Jewish religious tradition with its strong
> moral emphasis and its formal academic expression came to him
> through Hebrew. English was the language of the great secular
> poets. (Waddington, *A.M. Klein*, 9)

The separate anchoring of his languages, in strong and vibrant cultural milieux, distinguishes Klein from other polyglot poets of his time. The example of Eugene Jolas, a poet and later editor of James Joyce, is relevant here. One might consider Jolas's poem about New York:

> We listened to the choral voices of Manhattan
> All the languages were melting one into the other
> Toutes les langues fêtaient des épousailles
> We saw the dance of the words of corbyantic names
> A storm of words organized catitatas over the city
> Antique rune-words wed French syllables
> Anglo-Saxon sounds mingled with Yiddish vocables
> Dutch vowels embraced the Spanish verbs
> A Flemish word fled into Italian nouns
> The lexicon of Hell's Kitchen melted into Portuguese
> White Chapel cockney united with Broadway double talk
> A Luxembourg dialect fused into Louisiana French
> Paris argot joined the slanguage of the Rialto
> All the vers of the world flowed gently into each other

In a miraculous music of incantations.
(Jolas qtd. in Apter, 117)

This poems sounds something like Klein's "Montreal" – a hymn to
the mixture of languages that make up the city. Klein's description
of "lexicons uncargo'd at your quays," however, is constructed in
the form of a palimpsest of languages, one superimposed on the
other (*Complete Poems* 2:622, line 26). In "Montreal," as in other
poems, Klein superimposes the form of one language onto the other
to form new words such as "escaliered," "sonnant," "bilinguefact,"
"hebdomad," or "sanct." Jolas, here as elsewhere, lists the various
languages, insisting on the accumulation of idioms, one next to the
other.[4] The differences between Klein and Jolas in their city-hymns
are significant, not only of a difference between the cities themselves
(Montreal and New York), but also of the personal trajectories of the
poets. Jolas was born in Alsace but spent many years in the United
States. He observes the city from the standpoint of the immigrant
and explains that he came to writing multilingual poetry as a way
of expressing not only the singularity of New York but also his own
singular position as an outsider:

> Language became a neurosis. I used three of the basic world lan-
> guages in conversation, in poetry and in my newspaper work. I
> was never able to decide which of them I preferred. An almost
> inextricable chaos ensued, and sometimes I sought a facile escape
> by intermingling all three. I dreamed a new language, a super-
> tongue for intercontinental expression, but it did not solve my
> problem. I felt that the great Atlantic community to which I
> belonged demanded an Atlantic language. Yet I was alone, quite
> alone, and I found no understanding comrades who might have
> helped me in my linguistic jungle. (Jolas, *Man from Babel*, qtd. in
> Perloff n.p.)

Multilingualism for Klein, as we have seen, suggested a completely
different form of experience – a mixture of Yiddish, Hebrew, English, and French that made absolute sense in the context of Montreal
and represented an ordered interface rather than a chaos. There is
a striking contrast between Jolas's formulation of his own singular problem of multilingualism – "I was alone, quite alone" – and

Klein's multilingualism as an expression of the Jewish Diaspora in a specific place, Montreal. In a detailed study of Jolas's multilingual poetry, Marjorie Perloff concludes that these poems are driven by an "additive" technique that is, finally, simplistic: "The notion of interjecting 'all the other languages spoken today' into the fabric of English is still a bit Utopian"; rather, "multilingualism functions, not by mere addition, but by the infusion into one's own language of the cultures that are changing its base" (Perloff n.p.). *Finnegans Wake* does this by retaining English syntax, and it exploits not only Joyce's knowledge of numerous foreign languages but also his virtuosic grasp of English itself. Similarly, in *The Second Scroll* and other writings, Klein participates in the polyglot aesthetics of fragmentation that are characteristic of modernism. Indeed, Klein shows prescience in establishing a striking match between the experience of Montreal as a historically fragmented city and the emotions we associate with the modernist sensibility – the sense of inner dividedness, of estrangement amid the familiar, of the precarious and unsettled grounds of language.

Klein is not a representative of the modernist as wanderer or exile. Unlike Jolas, unlike the emblematic figures of Beckett or Nabokov or Gertrude Stein, Klein did not feel obliged to leave his home in order to stage a confrontation between his sensibility and an alien environment. Klein's modernism takes shape within the multiple languages of a "home" city. His situation is therefore similar to that of two familiar, canonical Jewish writers who were also shaped by the divisions of their cities – Kafka in German-Czech Prague and Italo Svevo in German-Italian Trieste. These are writers who are at home in a space of competing idioms, in a place of permanent dislocation. But there is also a vertical dimension to Klein's experience of home. Not only is the city the site of a confrontation between competing language powers, but it is also a space that recedes infinitely into the past, a "mise-en-abîme" of diasporic histories.

Finally, Jerusalem

The competing languages of Montreal are for Klein a powerful aspect of its identity as a city of the Jewish Diaspora. An essay left unpublished at Klein's death, "In Praise of the Diaspora," vaunts the "polyglot library" accumulated during the course of the "long secular journey" of the Diaspora. Tracking an itinerary that in some ways recalls the voyage of *The Second Scroll*, Klein chronicles the voyage of Jewish tradition not from place to place but from language to language.

> Recording the works enduring a single culture, it shifts from language to language; now as it holds up with pride, indeed, with veneration, the great corpus of Talmudic learning, it speaks Aramaic; now, as it leaps forward from Babylon and in a later day conjures up the name of Maimonides and his school, Arabic are its accents; and now, with a deeper love, with memories the years have not dimmed, it is in Yiddish that it speaks.
>   Nor do these three exhaust the versatility of its utterance. Upon all the tongues of Europe the Jewish genius played as upon instruments orchestral ...
>   The catalogue seems endless. All the languages are mustered to its roll. (Klein, *Beyond Sambation*, 473–4)

It is within the context of Klein's "praise of the diaspora" that one can understand his depiction of Jerusalem. Jerusalem is the endpoint of the narrator's quest in *The Second Scroll*. But, surprisingly, Jerusalem has little physical presence in the novel. It is only evoked as a city in a few rapid sentences. It is true that the narrator is on the trail of Uncle Melech, and the rhythm of the chase picks up as the narrator feels he is closing in on his goal.

> My sojourn in Israel was a continual going to and fro, an unremitting excitement. I wanted to take in the whole country, all at once. If a plane had been available I should have loved to have risen in it so that I might look at Dan and Beersheba simultaneously. If I could only stretch out my arms and make them the land's frontiers! (Klein, *Second Scroll*, 47)

This kind of Olympian perspective produces a panorama lacking in detail. It is as if the Holy Land, and Jerusalem in particular, has the same blurry contours as Uncle Melech. The true reality of this place is unrepresentable. And indeed, Jerusalem is more often compared to the fabled pages of the Bible than to any real place. Klein had described the Giudecca of Venice in much the same terms as he would Jerusalem:

Here, I dreamed conjurations of far-off places; and, because I learned Venice while I learned my Bible, these dreams seemed always to float down the reaches of the sea always to settle at last over the hills of Palestine.

It was a city out of the Scriptures, this Venice, a commentary on all that in the Scriptures pertains to the sea; it evoked for me, as I watched the unburdening of the strange cargoes of its galleasses, the apes and peacocks of Holy Writ; its mighty traffic and great navigation, its captains and its pilots ... this was Tyre restored again. (Klein, *Notebooks*, 149)

Only Old Jerusalem is evoked as a neighbourhood of labyrinths, its "winding, chaffering streets, its ancient courtyards, in the shabby rooms of charity-supported academies" (Klein, *Second Scroll*, 48). But Klein's narrator is not so much seeing Jerusalem as "re-visioning it," seeing it again as a reflection of some memory, some episode of reading.

For there wasn't a place, disguised though it might be under a latter-day name, that didn't speak to me out of my personal past. Even as I arrived in Lydda, there came to me the memory of those winter evenings in Montreal when, as a boy of thirteen, I had gone through the tractate *Baba Bathra*, pausing in young wonder at the mathematical ingenuity of the famous merchants of Lud, whose shrewd manipulation of percentages had caused so much concern to the sages of the Talmud. It was the same, it was intenser, in the case of the other cities of Israel – Carmelcrowning Haifa, idyllic Tiberias, Jerusalem ineffable. (Klein, *Second Scroll*, 47)

The "renewed Zion" of today remains as mythical as the one imagined, in yet again the same dream-like fashion, for the character in Klein's golem story:

When as a young boy, the consolations and prophecies of Isaiah before me, I dreamed in the dingy Hebrew school the apocalyptic dream of a renewed Zion, always I imagined it as coming to pass thus:.... The cloud then began to scatter, to be diminished, to subside, until revealed there shone the glory of a burnished dome – Hierosolyma the golden! (Klein, *Second Scroll*, 13)

"The fabled city" is not in fact a place of streets and shops but, rather, turns out to be less a place than a soundscape, the poetry of everyday language and speech (Waddington, *A.M. Klein*, 123). The Hebrew language was in a feverish process of renewal in 1949; they were responding to and reflecting all the new experiences of the people who were then arriving in Israel. The figurative language of advertisements and daily transactions constituted the real miracle for Klein. What Klein recognizes and is able to describe in Jerusalem is the language – on this he waxes eloquent. It is the sounds of the city that he evokes – not the sights: "In the streets, in the shops, everywhere about me. I had looked, but had not seen. It was all there all the time – the fashioning folk, anonymous and unobserved, creating word by word, phrase by phrase, the total work that when completed would stand as epic revealed!" (Klein, *Second Scroll*, 55). Jerusalem turns out, then, to be not the city of triumphant trumpet blasts but, rather, the city of myriad stitching cells, putting together a language that had for centuries been isolated from the streets and that was – through this process of renewal – turning into a new kind of urban poetry.

It is curious that Klein focuses only on the birth of modern Hebrew, neglecting what must have been a polyglot brouhaha in the Jerusalem of the late 1940s. The end of the Second World War and the newly declared independence of Israel would have meant that Jerusalem was a city filled with languages and accents. Klein does give the texture of this kind of language confusion in an earlier chapter, evoking the many voices that clamour for help at the offices of the Jewish relief organization in Italy. Perhaps it is because of the narrator's task of preparing an anthology of Hebrew poetry that he remains attentive only to the sounds of the nascent language of Hebrew. But we are also led to understand, as the narrator leaves Jerusalem for home, that some of what he has seen and heard in that city has been a disappointment. And that Jerusalem cannot take over as the only soundscape of modern Jewry.

And so, though Jerusalem remains the fabled eternal goal of his voyage in *The Second Scroll*, Klein reserves his highest, and final, praise for the diasporic urban soundscape. The "stations" of the diasporic voyage are momentary manifestations of Jewish history, fascinating in their diversity, troubling in their fragility.

Looking for A.M. Klein in Winnipeg's Anglo-Jewish Press

In the late 1940s and early 1950s, A.M. Klein travelled frequently to the Canadian west on behalf of the Canadian Jewish Congress and the United Jewish Relief Agency. In announcing his 1949 speaking tour to Moose Jaw, Weyburn, Estevan, Dauphin, Melville, and Humboldt[1] – towns and small cities on the Canadian Prairie where today there are few, if any, Jews – the *Jewish Post* of Winnipeg refers to him as "a famous Canadian orator" and proclaims, "it is well known that Mr. Klein is one of the outstanding Canadian poets, but it is less well known that he is one of the foremost experts in Hebrew literature and civilization on this continent."[2] As I was to find out, however, references to Klein's literary and scholarly talents were exceptional in the western Canadian Jewish English-language press. Indeed, Klein's presence in western Canada during his lifetime, and what was known about him, were the issues that guided my recent research at the Jewish Heritage Centre of Western Canada archive in Winnipeg.

Winnipeg, Canada's third-largest city and the economic and cultural capital of western Canada in the first half of the twentieth century, was also arguably the second most important centre of Canadian Jewry. It was not a surprise, then, to discover that, for a good part of the twentieth century, ties between Winnipeg and Montreal's Jewish communities were close and direct. When Klein came to western Canada in 1949, he brought with him not only literary credentials but also those he had earned as the former editor of Montreal's *Canadian Jewish Chronicle*, the paper closely associated with the Canadian Jewish Congress and its president from 1939 to 1962, the former Manitoban Samuel Bronfman. The

Bronfman family plot at the Shaarey Zedek cemetery in Winnipeg is a curious and even melancholy sight: large enough for several generations, it bears only three headstones – those of patriarch Ekiel, wife Minnie, and baby Minette – a testament to the eastward migration that many other Winnipeg Jews would follow, including the educator Jacob Zipper, writer Miriam Waddington, and Rabbi Solomon Frank. Rabbi Frank was a mainstay of the *Jewish Post*'s editorial page (and, for a period, its editor) until he moved to Montreal in 1947, where he succeeded Klein as editor of the *Chronicle*. Nor was the migration a one-way street; for example, Abraham Arnold, born in Montreal in 1922 and a graduate of fabled Baron Byng High School, also attended by Klein and, perhaps most notoriously, Mordecai Richler, settled in Winnipeg in 1965. Arnold became regional director of the Canadian Jewish Congress, a regular columnist for the Winnipeg Jewish press, and a major force in the Jewish Historical Society of Western Canada (the society was amalgamated into the newly created Jewish Heritage Centre of Western Canada in 1999). Arnold safeguarded the Winnipeg Jewish community's Yiddishist and leftist culture, long after most of its members had moved into the political centre and lost their ability to speak, or even understand, Yiddish.

This story reflects my own. As a child, I attended the Hebrew Talmud Torah, where, from time to time, and seemingly on a whim, the school's cranky choirmaster, celebrated for hitting recalcitrant students with his tuning fork, would show up in our classroom to teach us Yiddish.[3] This spotty apprenticeship has necessarily affected the scope of my research. Specifically, I have been able to *dépouiller*, as we say in French, the Winnipeg English-language Jewish press but not the Yiddish press.[4] This press dates back to 1910, when *Der Courier* was founded. It changed its name to *Dos Yiddishe Vort* in 1917, and English did not appear in its pages at all until 1938. Coincidentally, but perhaps significantly, this was the same year that Klein became editor of the English-language *Canadian Jewish Chronicle*.[5] In other words, Klein's decision to address his community through its English media, and the *Vort*'s decision to gesture in this direction, flowed from the same realities of the increasing cultural and economic integration of Jews into Canadian society. In the meantime, not one, but two English-language Jewish weeklies had been founded in Winnipeg: the *Jewish Post* in 1925 and the

Western Jewish News in 1926. Their appearance and longevity led Lewis Levendel to ask the obvious question: how, he wonders, "did three independently owned Jewish weekly newspapers survive for more than six decades in a city with a Jewish population that did not exceed 20,000 during that time?"[6] True, twenty thousand in the 1920s represented 8 percent of Winnipeg's total population – today, the Jewish community only accounts for 2 percent, with around thirteen thousand members. Levendel points to savvy commercial and advertising strategies on the part of the various owners, but he also quotes Anthony Astrachan on the legendary vigour of the community, nourished as it was by five traditions: "political activism, radicalism, a vital Yiddish culture mixed with universal Jewish devotion to education, a prairie mystique, and a geographic isolation that has made Winnipeg the centre of its own diaspora."[7] He also cites A.B. Bennett, who characterized western Canadian Jewry as "a venturesome pioneering population – the most consciously Jewish and aggressively active" in the Dominion.[8]

Klein's exchanges with this community, particularly in Winnipeg, would not be primarily literary in nature. With a single exception – a 1951 appearance at the Winnipeg Festival of Jewish Culture – I have found no record of literary events in which he participated, despite the effervescence of Jewish cultural life in Winnipeg.[9] For the most part, Klein's presence in western Canada was a political and humanitarian one, primarily in the service of the Canadian Jewish Congress and the Zionist movement.

Klein and Birobidjan: A Homeland Terminated

In January 1937, the *Jewish Post* reported on Klein's imminent arrival under the headline: "Abraham Klein on Extended Visit to Many Western Points." Here, Klein is referred to as "the assistant executive director of the Zionist organization."[10] The timing of Klein's visit was almost certainly coincidental, but only a week earlier, the following ad had appeared in the *Post* under the banner headline: "A GREATER PROMISE: BIROBIDJAN":

A momentous drama of immigrant life in the autonomous Jewish Republic Birobidjan that will thrill people of all races and creeds. Actually produced in Birobidjan. Russian songs and music that

will thrill you! Russian dialogue with English titles. Russia's
Greatest Masterpiece. First Canadian showing. Direct from
"Soviet Russia." Regent Theatre, One week only starting Friday,
Jan. 4th.[11]

The ad caught my attention not so much for its content as for
the venue. My grandfather managed the Regent Theatre throughout
my childhood and until his death in the early 1970s. As a child,
I went there just about every Saturday afternoon to munch pop-
corn and enjoy a triple-bill – usually a Western, a Japanese monster
movie, and a historical epic. I remember crawling out the window
of my *zeyda*'s upstairs office to sit atop the canopy that protected
the theatre's entrance to watch the Royal Visit of Queen Elizabeth
II in 1959; but, until discovering this ad, it had never occurred to
me that the theatre he managed had once hosted pro-Soviet films
(there had been more than one, I discovered). Even more curious,
if Birobidjan loomed at the beginning of my research, it was also
present at the end: one of the last articles by Klein to appear in the
Jewish Post addressed the very same question. Entitled "The Place
That Wasn't There," the 1951 article proceeds with typical Kleinian
wit and cadence to mark the Soviet regime's decision to terminate
this homeland: "With the establishment of the State of Israel – now
a fait accompli – there no longer remains any reason to keep Biro-
Bidjan [sic] extant even on paper. Hence the last mesmeric touch of
the week: a declaration declaring that that shall henceforth cease
which hitherto did not exist!"[12]

Almost fifteen years earlier, at the time of his 1937 visit, Klein
was in effect the representative of a Zionist movement in compe-
tition with the Organization for Jewish Colonization in Russia,
known by its acronym ICOR, and the Canadian Birobidjan Committee, founded in 1934, the same year that the Soviet government
declared Birobidjan a Jewish *oblast*, or autonomous region. In 1937,
more than twenty-five thousand Jews were living in the oblast, and,
as early as 1926, the Winnipeg branch of ICOR had conducted a
fundraising campaign to buy tractors for it and had undertaken to
establish twenty-five families there in a sort of red *aliyah*.[13] In January 1935, a public meeting in support of Birobidjan at Winnipeg's
I.L. Peretz School "was such a success that hundreds of people had
to be turned away."[14] In other words, whatever existence the Biro-

bidjan project actually had in 1937, it was certainly more than on paper. Even after the Second World War, when Klein returned to western Canada on behalf of the Canadian Jewish Congress and the United Jewish Relief Agencies, the dream of Birobidjan had not yet receded into the obscurity it knows today. In November 1945, the Canadian Birobidjan Committee held a meeting at the Montefiore Club in Montreal – about as far from a labour temple as one can imagine – to launch a campaign to settle war orphans and to open vocational schools. In 1947, the committee supported the United Nations resolution calling for the partition of Palestine and the establishment of the Jewish state, thus following not only Soviet foreign policy but also a logic developed by Chaim Zhitlovsky, one of the leading Yiddishist intellectuals of the age. Winnipeg, Henry Srebrnik tells us, "was a Zhitlovsky fortress," a city he visited frequently.[15] In the *Vokhenblatt*, he wrote: "Our Jewish people now has two countries in which a new Jewish life is being built, a normal life.... They ought not to be seen as antagonistic alternatives."[16] By the time Klein returned to the west in 1949, it was the beginning of the end of what Srebrnik terms the "apogee" for Canadian Jewish Communists. If, as Srebrnik puts it, "the Soviet Union had fathered one Jewish state, Birobidzhan, and ... had been midwife to the birth of a second one, Israel,"[17] by 1949, word was emerging of the anti-Semitic purges unleashed by Stalin in the Union of Soviet Socialist Republics and related events in the people's democracies of Eastern Europe. Over the next few years, Birobidjan would be exposed as "largely fraudulent and a failure. All the stories and statistics had been, simply put, mainly fantasy."[18] Klein's 1951 article, triumphant in tone, is perhaps best regarded as a fine example of the adage "revenge is a dish best served cold."

Klein and the Anglo-Jewish Press

The republishing of several of Klein's *Chronicle* editorials in the *Jewish Post*, as well as the occasional appearance of his translations into English of Hebrew poems by Chaim Nachman Bialik, "the Jewish national poet of our generation,"[19] raises an interesting question: if Winnipeg Jewish culture was largely Yiddishist, and Yiddish culture was associated with secularism and political radicalism, what impact did Klein have by appearing in the Anglo-Jewish press?

The prejudice against the English-language Jewish press should not be underestimated. Levendal reports how Leona Lasker, a Winnipeg educator, "remembered that the two Anglo-Jewish newspapers were not as respected as the *Israelite Press* [the English name of the *Vort*], and were often referred to as 'the local rags.' As a researcher of this press in her student years, she found that they appealed primarily to the establishment, "'Waspish' Jews."[20] And as a child growing up in Winnipeg who sat down every evening to a portrait of I.L. Peretz over her dining room table, Miriam Waddington believed that

> everyone who didn't know Yiddish had assimilated and was doomed and lost to Judaism. I couldn't imagine why the services in the Reform synagogue were in English, or why anyone needed an Anglo-Jewish press. It seemed to me they were all imitating the English, but like all imitations, they were never as good as the original.[21]

True, the Anglo-Jewish newspapers did not reflect the radical culture of Jewish Winnipeg to the same degree as did the Yiddish press, but it would be a mistake to see them as complacent "rags" that spoke only of social teas hosted by wealthy Jewish homemakers, newly opened summer resorts, and the joys of cross-border shopping. The study circles of the *Arbeiter-Ring*, visits by cultural figures from the Soviet Union, and literary events associated with Bundists and left-wing Zionists were all routinely advertised and reported on in the *Jewish Post* throughout the 1920s and 1930s. The three holiday supplements of the *Post* – Rosh Hashanah, Chanukah, and Pesach – approached some two hundred pages and contained long essays by leading Jewish intellectuals of the period on topics philosophical, literary, and political. Klein's literary endeavours from this period were given no attention by the Winnipeg Jewish press, but Miriam Waddington, who left Winnipeg in 1930, would later write eloquently – and as a fellow Montrealer – about Klein's radical poems from the 1930s.[22]

Would poems that addressed social injustice have been out of place in the western Canadian Jewish press at the time? In the 1930s and early 1940s, the papers regularly included eye-witness, usually anonymous, accounts of life in Nazi Germany and Nazi-occupied Europe, especially of the persecution of Jews. The *Post* also published Thomas Mann's anti-Nazi polemics,[23] and, in the same 1937 issue as the ad for the film on Birobidjan, a front-page article on the civil war in Spain took a decidedly Popular Frontist line. In a regular column entitled "Off My Chest," Pierre Van Paassen wrote that "the Spanish people are giving the French and the Germans and the Austrians an object lesson in how Fascism must be combated. For the first time bourgeois liberals have understood that they must stand together with the working-class organizations if the road to the marauders of humanity is to be barred."[24] The other lead story? – "Palestine Arabs Yielding on Boycott of Royal Commission."[25] In other words, this front page can tell us much about the orientation of the Anglo-Jewish press – at least until the end of the Second World War and the establishment of the State of Israel – interested as it was in questions of democracy and fascism, pro-Zionist, and supra-class in its defence of Jewish issues, which were regarded as part of a larger struggle for social justice. In these respects, Klein's political interventions fit well enough into the *Jewish Post*.

In fact, the *Posts*'s own political views aligned with Klein's when, in 1935, along with the *Yiddishe Vort*, it endorsed CCF candidate A.A. Heaps's run for Parliament. According to Henry Trachtenberg, this was uncharacteristic behaviour for the *Post*. He points out that, while the *Yiddishe Vort* routinely endorsed left-wing candidates, including Communists in municipal elections, the *Jewish Post* "shrank from any frank discussion, let alone endorsation, of Jewish class voting."[26] The attraction the CCF held for Jewish intellectuals in Montreal and Winnipeg is worth considering since, in most discussions, attention is usually directed almost exclusively towards the considerable Jewish support for the Communist Party. However, as Nelson Wiseman has observed, "Immigrants to Canada from many states carried the social democratic banner [and] those from Britain had a pride of place."[27] Among these social democratic immigrants from Britain were Jews, including some who played a prominent role in the 1919 Winnipeg General Strike. Wiseman points out that, unlike the Communist Party, whose membership was largely Jewish and Ukrainian but ran mainly Anglo-British candidates in elections to ward off charges of acting in the service of an alien ideology, the CCF was heir to, and built upon, the social-democratic immigration from Great Britain. While CCF publications engaged in negative cultural stereotyping of Ukrainians, "no such ethnic stereotyping of

Jews is to be found in the CCF papers. Indeed, in the 1940s Monty Israels served as the CCF's provincial (Manitoba) chariman."[28] In Klein's case, social democratic politics – namely, his interactions with pro-CCF anglophone intellectuals around the Montreal Writer's Group, not to mention his own CCF candidacy in 1944 in Montreal-Cartier (Klein withdrew before the 1945 federal election) – and his advocacy of a viable Jewish intellectual and literary life in English went hand in hand. It was not until relatively late in Klein's literary career, however, that the Jewish press in western Canada would provide its readers with any sense of the complexity of his political and literary engagements.

Klein and the State of Jewish Culture

Occasionally, an article by Klein that dealt with broader issues of Jewish culture did appear in the *Jewish Post*. Perhaps the most substantial of Klein's pieces to be published before or during the war was "The Thirteenth Apostle," a response to the furor created by Sholem Asch's interview with the *Christian Herald* in 1944, in which he admits to having always been attracted by the personality of Jesus. Apparently, the confession caused quite a stir, but it was one that Klein felt was overblown, calling it "a tempest in a baptismal font."[29] More to the point, Klein didn't find Asch's treatment of biblical themes very interesting and claimed that "in the writing of Asch, one will look in vain for those creative insights which characterize biblical works of Thomas Mann.... One finds merely a detailed scenario of incidents already revealed in the gospels, the whole ornamented with picturesque prose erected in the best Hollywood manner."[30] What stands out in Klein's critique is not so much the dismissal of Asch himself but, rather, the implicit defence of Jews who have lost the ability to read or live in Yiddish: Asch's pro-Christian remarks appear first in English translation, "but we do not tremble at the possibility that those Jews who read him are but a step away from conversion.... Nor is there any likelihood that the Jewish soul of Asch himself was at any time in spiritual jeopardy."[31]

While spending Succoth in Winnipeg during his 1949 eighteen-city tour, Klein gave an enlightening interview to the *Jewish Post*. The interview would be noteworthy if only because, this time, Klein was speaking *directly* to a western Canadian Jewish readership and not through a reprint from the *Chronicle*. But the interview stands out especially for what Klein has to say about the state of contemporary Jewish culture and his own literary projects. Under the headline "American Jewry Practice 1 out of 613 Mitzvot," Klein complains that "only Z'dokoh – charity – is left for American Jewry."[32] According to the *Post*, "while touring the west, Mr. Klein took time out to deliver some clever, barbed shafts at the shallowness of mass Jewish culture honoured here." Noting that most of Klein's own contributions to contemporary Jewish culture are in English, the *Post* reported how "the poet asserted that our view of 'Jewish culture' must be broadened to include many languages besides Hebrew and Yiddish ... and he referred to Maimonides' great works in Arabic as precedents. 'Works devoted to broad human values, above and beyond sectarian Jewish themes, are also Jewish achievements,' he said."[33] The reference to Hebrew, not just Yiddish, is telling, because apparently Klein was not impressed with the quality of contemporary Israeli literature. Nor did he appreciate what he called the tendency in Israel to "write off Diaspora Jewry as a lost cause: 'The destruction of the Galut preached over there must be combatted,' he claimed, not least of all because Israel in 1949 'cannot spare time for cultural refinements and the literary wider horizons that come only with stability, and the close of the frontier era.'"[34] Klein was a committed Zionist, but he continued to insist upon a dynamic life for Diaspora Jewry, a cultural, intellectual, and political life in dialogue with the broader community.

In the interview, Klein also discussed his work on Joyce's *Ulysses*. The *Post* reports how he "enthusiastically described his affinity for Joyce's techniques because [they] emulated the intellectual brilliance and playful delight in legalistic pranks and wiles found in so much of Jewish halachic literature."[35] Similarly, Klein "traced his interest in *Ulysses* and his penchant for French poetry to early exposure to Catholic influences in his native Quebec: 'After all, the Talmudic system and the Jesuitical system are just reverse sides of the same coin,'" he concludes.[36]

This interview follows fast upon the first time Klein received any serious literary attention in the Winnipeg Jewish press. Under the banner "High Praise for Klein's Verse,"[37] the *Jewish Post* reviewed an article by Wilfred Eggleston that had appeared a few days earlier on the editorial page of the *Winnipeg Free Press*.[38] The occasion was

Klein's Governor General's Award for *The Rocking Chair and Other Poems*.[39] In fact, the *Post*'s review consists almost entirely of citations from Eggleston's article – it might as well have been a reprint – that praise Klein for moving beyond his "elected" role as "a lyric voice for Canadian Jewry."[40] Conceding that this had already won for Klein "a unique position in Canadian letters," Eggleston enthuses that "now he turns to a broader field, that of his native province of Quebec, and essays a series of witty felicitous sketches of French Canada together with more general themes such as his 'Portrait of the Poet as Landscape.'"[41] However, Eggleston's remarks go beyond the thematic; for example, he praises Klein for overcoming "a quandary which has baffled a good many versifiers of his generation: how to be modern and yet intelligible," comparing his writing to the musical idioms of Bartok, Prokofiev, and Gershwin. Eggleston concludes that "this is a very clever book, almost too clever for Klein's audience. Canadians are not too fond of the elaborate exquisitely-fashioned pun, or erudite double meaning; and *The Rocking Chair* is full of astonishingly clever puns."[42]

This article would prove to be the most sustained literary treatment Klein received in the western Canadian Jewish press – until his death in 1972, that is. This is altogether remarkable considering that the holiday supplements of the *Jewish Post* continued to publish substantial pieces of literary criticism on other writers. But these came mainly from American wire services and other syndicated arrangements, in which no one seemed to have either the time or the inclination to write about Klein.[43] Indeed, the *Jewish Post* obituary, appearing under the title "A.M. Klein: Canadian Poet," confirms what our survey suggests: it begins by noting how "the world of 'anglo-Jewish' literature has suffered a number of irreparable losses in recent months," including Maurice Samuel, Judd Teller, Paul Goodman, and Klein. The author, noted American-Jewish scholar and poet Stanley F. Chyet, laments that "it is, one supposes, something of a commentary on the quality of North American Jewish intellectual life that the poet Klein was the least known [of them]."[44] In "The Death of a Poet," an unsigned obituary in the *Yiddish Press*, the English-language overleaf complement to *Dos Yiddishe Vort*, Klein is referred to as "the most Jewish poet who has ever used the English tongue, [the] only Jew who has ever contributed a new note of style, of expression, of creative enlargement to the poetry of that tongue."[45] The quote is not from Eggleston but, rather, from Ludwig Lewisohn, who was exceptional in his support for Klein, but was countered in the same obituary by Roy Daniells, once the head of the English department at the University of British Columbia: "He is a Jew, and his sensibility is saturated with the sweet oil of orthodoxy.... Klein's range includes moods of rage against tyranny, frustration over injustice, solicitousness over the suffering of the dispossessed and shrewd appraisal of the mundane world. But the centre from which all radiates is the love of one tradition."[46] These arguments over the universal and the specific – I hesitate to use the term "particular" for its pejorative connotations – are familiar to any practitioner of letters in a minority situation. The same debate has raged over Quebec writing's relation to France and Canada's to its British and American counterparts. That Klein should become caught up in them after his death in venues that paid scant attention to his literary contributions while he was alive is perhaps more than a little cruel. I like to imagine that he would have found the dispute absurd and would have responded to it with his customary wit – the kind of wit in evidence, for example, on the sole occasion upon which Klein turned it directly on Winnipeg. The issue at hand was precisely the curious way that the city's Jewish community remembered its dearly departed. As Levendel reports: "a prime feature of Winnipeg's Jewish newspapers [was] the *in memoriam* ads with pictures of the deceased on the anniversary week of death.... This unique practice brought out the satirical pens of a few fellow editors down east."[47]

A.M. Klein was among them. Here is what the editor of the *Canadian Jewish Chronicle* had to say on the matter in 1942, in an article entitled "Your Picture in the Paper":

Now, we ask what macabre morbidity it is that prompts editors to accept these unearthed cadavers, to display them ... upon the weekly galleys. We mean no disrespect to the dead; some of our best friends are corpses of long-standing – if that is the word. But why should it not be enough merely to mention the fact of the anniversary, together with the appropriate verses and call it a day of filial piety. Why the touching addition of a photograph dressed in the latest style of 1909 – of a man or woman who has departed this life and all its vanities, full many a year agone.[48]

Did readers in Winnipeg ever know of this playful lambasting of their strange ways? For the most part, probably not. But it's never too late to repay a favour: in the spirit of a new appreciation of Klein's life and work, perhaps a *Yahrzeit* photo of him in the *Jewish Post* wouldn't be such a bad idea after all.

PART FOUR

The Literary Offspring:
Richler, Cohen, and Michaels

REINHOLD KRAMER

Richler, Son of Klein

If A.M. Klein opened a way for Montreal's Jewish writers to enter the English mainstream, we might speak of several literary sons: Irving Layton, Leonard Cohen, and Mordecai Richler. From Layton – who, of the three, knew Klein best – one gets a fairly objective poetic assessment in "Requiem for A.M. Klein":

Your scholar's mind neat as your hair

... your psychological obtuseness

And the sentimentality each clever Jew
Misconstrues for sensitivity ...

You were a medieval troubadour
Who somehow wandered into a lawyer's office
And could not find your way back again (28)

These are astute comments, except the last lines, which seem to hint that Klein's mental illness was an ideological mistake: if only he hadn't taken up law. In any case, "Requiem for A.M. Klein" reminds us that Layton brushed Klein aside as inconsequential. Not Layton's boorish persona, not his poetic style, not his Nietzschean pronouncements: none of these owes anything to Klein. Layton was not, finally, a son.

As for Cohen and Richler, it's tempting to believe that their filial relations to Klein were as they claimed: one the honoured son, the other the prodigal. Cohen was far less deferential to Klein than his tribute poem would suggest. The Klein in Cohen's "To a Teacher" is a saint, a god-priest. One can't imagine Klein sympathizing with the self-divided *Death of a Lady's Man* or with the psychic experiments of F in *Beautiful Losers*. Yet Cohen, in "To a Teacher," imagines the mentally ill Klein as a close relative of F: "Did you confuse the Messiah in a mirror, / And rest because he had finally come?" "To a Teacher" is an affecting poem, but, like Layton, Cohen confuses literary/philosophical issues with medical concerns. Certain philosophical preoccupations may be intensified by mental illness, but it is highly doubtful that a condition such as Klein's depression was the *result* of the intransigent philosophical problems into which he ran headlong.[1] Cohen is not a son.

That brings us to Richler. Richler ignored the deference usually given to the wounded and instead treated Klein as a significant force to be fought against. I would argue, nevertheless, that Richler owed a great deal to Klein, that Richler's stylistic and philosophical antipathy to Klein hid a profound indebtedness, and that the reluctance to properly credit Klein had to do with Richler's insecurities about writing, money, and metaphysics.

Stylistically, of course, all three younger writers hurried away from Klein into popular speech. Often Klein's "method" was the search for the "hapaxlegomenon" – a word of which only one instance of use is known – which supplied not only a chapter title for Klein's partially completed untitled novel[2] but also the metaphor for the novel's hero, Pimontel, and, by extension, for Klein himself: the word, the person like no other. In this matter, Klein was not able to fully digest modernism. He read Joyce and immediately wanted to become him. Like Klein, Richler was initially beguiled by modernism. His first published novel, *The Acrobats*, was a pastiche of Hemingway and Lowry, but because he was of a different generation and personality than Klein, and because his nearer models included Céline and Henry Miller – at once more ambiguous and more easily discarded influences – Richler shucked modernism with little pain. Whereas Klein's too-academic thesaurus makes it difficult for one to hear voices other than his own in his work, Richler learned (first with help from Céline, then by listening to his father Moe) how to capture the inflections of those around him. The movement away from modernism was already in process in *The Acrobats*, though the acquisition of Yiddish-inflected speech patterns came more slowly and was not accomplished until *The Apprenticeship of Duddy Kravitz*, Richler's fourth published novel.

Klein's clear artifice made his style unique, brilliantly so, and, ultimately, he owed very little to other writers, not even to Joyce. Conversely, the danger of Richler's style was that it could turn into reportage: he quoted others directly, to the point that in *Barney's Version* his editor Louise Dennys gave particularly high praise to Izzy Panofsky's dialogue,[3] much of which Richler had taken verbatim from comments by Detective Inspector Ben Greenberg in an article that Richler had written twenty-five years earlier for *Saturday Night* magazine. It would be Klein's gift of structure, as we will see shortly, that allowed Richler to move *St. Urbain's Horseman* far beyond reportage.

A second obvious way in which Richler departs from Klein is in his understanding of the writer as someone who must be fiercely independent of every attempt to control or direct his speech. In *Solomon Gursky Was Here*, Shloime Bishinsky's verdict on the L.B. Berger/Gursky relationship is Richler's commentary on the Klein/Bronfman relationship: "a poet they should never be able to afford."[4] When people speak of Richler's antipathy towards Klein, they generally refer to *Solomon Gursky Was Here*, published in 1989. But Richler had been on Klein's case long before that, at least as early as 1954. *Son of a Smaller Hero* briefly mentions the poet David Lerner, who writes speeches to be read "by philanthropic millionaires at Zionist banquets." Lerner, to the delight of his wallet, discovers that, among Canadian Jews, his ode to the apparent Torah-rescuer Wolf Adler circulates much better than did his *Ode to Sacco and Vanzetti*.[5] This lampoon of Klein was written at a time when few people knew about Klein's suicide attempts earlier that same year. In 1954, Richler was not speaking ill of the dead or mocking someone who had struggled with mental illness. In 1954, to those who did not know him well, Klein was still a successful writer who had a Governor General's Award, a community leader who edited the *Canadian Jewish Chronicle*, and a bourgeois making a good wage writing Sam Bronfman's speeches.

Richler was at that time barely able to keep himself alive, writing in Montreal and London, relying, in large part, on his first wife Cathy Boudreau's income. Richler had left Habonim and Zionism behind a few years earlier, and one detects in his attitude the emotions of a young writer who feels himself unjustly neglected and who sees an older writer gain acceptance by curtailing his social criticism and kowtowing to community politics. In repudiating Klein, Richler was repudiating certain aspects of modernist style, perhaps also socialism, and certainly Zionism. And Richler was right about Klein's lack of independence. Two deleted stanzas from "Portrait of the Poet as Landscape" show Klein lamenting his status:

> However, for bread and the occasional show,
> He finds him, kindler of copy, daily at desk.
> For mongers and martmen he swinks it, writing
> their war-whoops, hailing their heroes ...
> ... he butters his bosses, he jumps at their jests.[6]

Richler never softened in his belief that the writer must be fiercely independent, so much so that he dared to satirize the Bronfmans, trying to fashion himself as the inverse of Klein. Yet in *Solomon Gursky Was Here*,[7] and in his unflattering portrait of Klein in the article "Mr. Sam,"[8] the question of the writer's independence was more vexed than a cursory look at L.B. Berger shows. True, neither Mr Sam nor any Zionist organization could claim Richler as a lapdog, yet in some ways his independence was less than complete. Throughout his career he had been highly ambivalent about writing schlock for films, fearing that he might be compromising his independence in order to achieve big paydays. As well, for a couple of cases of Macallan, he gave Macallan product-placement throughout *Solomon Gursky Was Here*. With respect to sellouts, as in other matters, Richler's fiction was more nuanced than was his non-fiction. In the non-fictional "Mr. Sam," Richler simply denounced Klein for grovelling. One might say that Richler's lampoon of Klein was a way of defining "sellout" so that Richler himself couldn't be accused of it. Selling out wasn't ultimately a question of economics, Richler implied, but, rather, a question of whether one grovelled before the boss or the racial group. And Richler never grovelled.

Despite Richler's repudiation of Klein, Bill Weintraub claims that Richler *did* like A.M. Klein's work.[9] We could add that, in *Solomon Gursky Was Here*, Richler acknowledged his filial relationship to Klein by making L.B. Berger the father of Moses Berger. Rachel

Brenner provides the crucial piece in the puzzle, noticing that Jake's search for Joey Hersh, the Horseman in *St. Urbain's Horseman*, echoes the narrator's search for Melech Davidson in *The Second Scroll*.[10] Although Richler lampooned Klein mercilessly, the evidence suggests that Brenner is correct: both Klein and Richler set their protagonists the simultaneous tasks of coming to terms with Judaism and with the Holocaust; both writers set up a search in which a mysterious relative seems to hold the key to these issues; both use the narrators as a surrogate for the author; both have the narrator follow the mysterious relative to sites that are philosophically or historically crucial to the Jews; both make the mysterious relative potentially superhuman (Klein's Melech is potentially the Messiah while Richler's Horseman is a kind of golem); and neither author allows a definitive conclusion to the search, so that careful interpretation is required to say exactly what the narrators have found. Family stories about a lost Soviet branch of Richler's mother's family contributed to the invention of the Horseman,[11] but the *structure* of Jake's search makes it clear that Richler had read and learned from *The Second Scroll*. It may even be that Richler had Klein in mind when he came up with the title, *St. Urbain's Horseman*. Within the novel, Richler attributes the title to a line from Isaac Babel's "Sunset," a line that stirred him: "When a Jew gets on a horse, he stops being a Jew."[12] But given Richler's use of Klein, he may also have had in mind *The Second Scroll*, in which Casablanca law, to avoid affront to Arabs, dictates that "no Jew [is] permitted to mount a horse."[13]

The search for the mysterious relative and the philosophical and historical import of that search tie *The Second Scroll* and *St. Urbain's Horseman* to the genre that Patricia Merivale and others have identified as the metaphysical detective story, in which mundane detection figures a broader attempt to uncover a hidden order in the world. In Merivale's formulation, the genre is in evidence whenever the traditional features of the detective story are subverted. I would construe the genre more narrowly, separating metaphysical detective stories – stories in which the detection process seeks a metaphysical object – from *parodies* of the detective story, which may satirize the genre but which don't necessarily lead the reader towards metaphysics. The full flowering of the genre began in the last third of the twentieth century, with such distinguished examples as *The Magus* (1965) and *The Crying of Lot 49* (1966); *The Name of the Rose* (1980) and *The White Hotel* (1981); and, in this decade, Michael Redhill's *Martin Sloane* (2001) and David O. Russell's playful film *I ♥ Huckabees* (2004). It may even be that Klein, along with Borges, is one of the originators of the genre. Other possible progenitors tend to be either high on detection or low on metaphysics (Chesterton's stories and Poe's Dupin stories), or high on metaphysics and low on detection (Poe's *The Narrative of A. Gordon Pym of Nantucket* [1838], Cabell's *The Cream of the Jest* [1917], and Joseph Conrad's *Heart of Darkness* [1902]). Before the middle of the twentieth century, only *Oedipus Rex* and Borges's "Tlön, Uqbar, Orbis Tertius" (1940) seem to combine an emphasis on detection with a distinctly metaphysical goal.

Two broad issues arise out of Richler's structural borrowing from Klein. First, one notices the uses to which Richler put Klein's structure; second, one is confronted with the question of why Richler would rely on a structure seemingly alien to his intentions.

Theodic issues were at the heart of Klein's use of the metaphysical detective structure. These issues were much in Klein's mind, from the time of "Reb Levi Yitschok Talks to God" (written in 1932) through his work on the unfinished novel about Pimontel (ca. 1948),[14] and the final unfinished novel "The Golem" (probably written around the time of Klein's breakdown in the mid-1950s).[15] Leon da Modena of "The Golem" writes a book, *The Perfect Crime*, in which a killer liberally scatters clues about the numberless corpses for which he is responsible, clues that suggest "a vast and inscrutable design." The book the killer writes details his career. It's opening sentence reads: "In the beginning He created the heaven and the earth." The narrator recognizes the scandal inherent in such a line but wants to publish Modena's book in order to rebuke it.[16] With respect to Modena, one could envision Jacques Lacan or Slavoj Žižek weighing in upon the founding act of violence that establishes the symbolic order. Given Klein's biography, it would be all too easy to leap to the conclusion that the narrator is a ruse, that Modena articulates what Klein couldn't say in his proper voice, and that, as Žižek disarmingly puts it, suicide is the only successful act.[17]

In *The Second Scroll* Klein gives us a strictly structured messianic search, working his way allegorically and systematically through several possible approaches – Orthodox Judaism, Bolshevism, Christianity, and social reform – before arriving at the notion that in the miracle of the "Disincarnation" there could be no final sighting of a Messiah. Against the grain of the traditional detective genre, Klein offers us an enigma, or an aporia, since Melech is never located. Yet, the conclusion of Klein's novel is far more concrete than the end of *The Crying of Lot 49* or *The Name of the Rose*. Klein's allegorical approach is governed more by ideas than by representation, and his final reluctance to name God seems to be a religio-philosophical decision. On the level of ideas, the reason that Klein refuses to represent Melech seems straightforward: the Second Commandment prohibits making images of God. The Messiah thus resists representation or, alternatively, in Phyllis Gotlieb's terms, Klein lost his faith and was no longer able to conceive of a literal Messiah. Klein tried to move both forward into modernism and backward into the Jewish past, as Sherry Simon puts it.[18] The novel ends not simply with the burning of Melech, but with muted and sober celebrations, as the beacons announce "new moons, festivals, and set times."[19] The narrator goes forth into order.

The Second Scroll explores theodicy in that Klein finds meaning in history. Either God permits evil in order to bring about a greater good than he could himself, or God is limited by the free behaviour of his creations.[20] In *The Second Scroll* God is not a sufficient explanation for the historical data, and the State of Israel is never interpreted as somehow an adequate recompense for the horrors of Auschwitz. However, theodic arguments have not disappeared; they have simply taken new non-theistic forms. Klein uses a weak form of theodicy in the sense that *The Second Scroll* finds the end of the 1940s and the end of Deuteronomy to be an improvement upon the earlier years of the decade and the century. Klein does not defend history as a rational dialectic per se, yet he seems to find some comfort in the point at which history has arrived in 1949. Klein thus addresses the problem of evil along the lines set down by Jean-Jacques Rousseau and Immanuel Kant. The Messiah is evoked, but supernatural forces are not required to explain the tragedies of Jewish history; instead, we, in our smallness, are responsible for good and evil: "Titus troubled by a gnat ... Titus by the termite tutored."[21] God's responsibility for state and empire devolves to human responsibility for the moral sphere. Yet, as in Kant, in *The Second Scroll* it seems as if a God or some form of transcendence watches over and honours human attempts to take the categorical imperative to heart.[22]

In Richler, we have at once a more direct naysayer to Judaism and Zionism. It is clear that when the Horseman addresses the problem of evil, Richler is repudiating any possibility of theodicy: Why is the Lord God One? the Horseman asks, and receives the answer: "It is because our Lord has such a tapeworm inside him ... that he can chew up six million Jews in one meal.... Two we couldn't afford."[23]

One would expect, then, that Richler would have little use for Klein. His earlier parody of Klein, David Lerner, fit perfectly into *Son of a Smaller Hero* because that novel fits perfectly into the grand narrative of emancipation from tradition and transcendence. Noah frees himself from the strictures of community and faith. In *A Choice of Enemies* and *The Apprenticeship of Duddy Kravitz*, Richler is more sceptical about the Enlightenment narrative, without offering alternatives. What Klein's detective story offered Richler was the idea of a metaphysical quest. Jake's search in *St. Urbain's Horseman* and Moses Berger's search in *Solomon Gursky Was Here* are messianic in tendency, despite the ironies. The Horseman is a curious amalgam of human upstart challenger to God (as Joey Hersh), of golem (as Jake's creation), and of God himself. Unlike Melech, the Horseman does not go through an orderly set of historical stages or philosophically coherent positions, but the detective structure allows Richler to address large questions of being, time, and fate. Kantian notions of moral responsibility also loom large. Evil in *St. Urbain's Horseman* is not ultimately profound and Satanic but, rather, lies within human bounds, whether we are speaking of Jake or the briefly glimpsed Mengele, of Ingrid or Harry Stein. Richler would certainly agree with what Hannah Arendt, following Kantian lines, wished the judges had said of Adolf Eichmann: "We are concerned only with what you did, and not with the possible noncriminal nature of your inner life and of your motives."[24]

At the end of *St. Urbain's Horseman*, Jake makes peace with the here/not-here Horseman. Initially, Richler wanted to avoid a conclusion, but his editor, Tony Godwin, prodded him towards one.[25] Richler's pulling back and forth between an ironic reading of the Horseman and a reading in which he is messianic is seen in Jake's assertion that the Horseman is only "presumed dead."[26] If Jake were to entirely repudiate the Horseman's image, discovering a Horseman too violent (rather than the possessor of an *actor's* gun), or a Horseman too sinister (the full *equivalent* of Harry Stein), it would be possible to argue that Richler intended to finish off transcendence, to let Jake fall completely into the world's appearances.

Although Norman Ravvin argues convincingly that the Holocaust is not *Jake's* trauma and that Jake must ultimately set aside the self-validating fantasy of the Horseman,[27] it is important to remember that Jake does not let go of the Horseman completely, and that Richler gives his blessing to this. Jake was not at Auschwitz, and, all told, he's not such a great opponent of oppression. So Jake is not somehow justified by what happened in the Second World War. Yet, Auschwitz cannot simply be left behind, and without the Horseman there would be no key figure to mediate that particular evil. Klein's suggestion that the photograph of Uncle Melech may be a graven image resonates in *St. Urbain's Horseman* when Jake worries that he has raised the Horseman as a golden calf in contravention of the Second Commandment.[28] By refusing to let the Horseman be overthrown completely, the novel (though perhaps not Richler personally) arrives at a kind of humanist faith.

Richler invested much of himself in the belief that there was no transcendence, yet, on the question of the Holocaust, the brute event could not be sustained by itself. The notation "presumed dead" signals Richler's achievement in *St. Urbain's Horseman*: he could not simply return to the nation (for him Zionism had features of Nazism), and he could not return to God; but he could invent a figure as a place-holder for a seemingly lost transcendence.

If imitation is the sincerest form of flattery, then in *form* Richler flatters Klein. A final piece of evidence for the filial relationship between Klein and Richler can be found in the ending of *Barney's Version*. *Barney's Version* is in many ways a brilliant novel, but I would argue that the weakness of the final denouement, which is meant to prove Barney's innocence, occurred because Richler, wanting to be honest about Alzheimer's, about death, and about his own existential beliefs, tried to ensure that this time his detective story would rely on none of Klein's metaphysical conceits. Richler insists that some greater order *must* exonerate Barney, but he has no faith in such an order. The result is a sinking towards circumstantiality, a bathos that mars a great novel. That, we might say, is Richler without Klein.[29]

Without Klein, Richler might still have become a political gadfly. He might still have written excellent novels in the style of *The Apprenticeship of Duddy Kravitz*, novels that run colloquially through Jewish Montreal. He might still have been an important witness to a particular time and place. Reading Saul Bellow's *Herzog*, he might still have arrived at the autobiographical form that empowered his big novels. But it was Klein who allowed Richler's mature work to expand into a larger philosophical search. Not until he went through Klein did Richler fully become Richler.

LAWRENCE KAPLAN

Uncle Melech and Cousin Joey: The Search for the Absent Hero in A.M. Klein's *The Second Scroll* and Mordecai Richler's *St. Urbain's Horseman*

Despite Mordecai Richler's repeated and vigorous denials that he had in any way been influenced by A.M. Klein, literary scholars and critics now generally agree that Klein's *The Second Scroll*[1] serves as an important literary source of Richler's *St. Urbain's Horseman*.[2] Indeed, the striking resemblances between the two novels fairly leap to view. Nevertheless, until the present chapter, scholars have neglected any single-minded examination of how and to what extent *St. Urbain's Horseman* draws upon *The Second Scroll* and exactly how and to what extent it transforms, and perhaps even critiques, the material upon which it draws. Ira Nadel's discerning, if one-sided, study, "The Absent Prophet in Canadian Jewish Fiction,"[3] discusses these resemblances. Later, passing references to these resemblances are found in Tom Marshall's essay, "Third Solitude: Canadian as Jew,"[4] primarily in an effort to analyze *The Apprenticeship of Duddy Kravitz*, and in Rachel Brenner's monograph, *Assimilation and Assertion: The Response to the Holocaust in Mordecai Richler's Writing.*[5] Most recently, Reinhold Kramer, in his path-breaking critical biography *Mordecai Richler: Leaving St. Urbain*, addresses this subject.[6] Moreover, Nadel, Brenner, and Kramer, in their focus on the structural and thematic similarities between the two novels, tend to downplay (Kramer), if not overlook completely (Nadel and Brenner), the novels' equally important structural and thematic differences.[7] This chapter, then, seeks to chart and map the similarities and differences between the novels more fully and accurately, and in a more balanced fashion, than has been the case until now.

   As has often been noted, *St. Urbain's Horseman* is, to coin a term, an elliptical novel, that is, it, or, perhaps better, the consciousness of its main protagonist, Jake Hersh, revolves around two foci: the Horseman (Jake's cousin, Joey Hersh) and Harry Stein.[8] Both figures serve as alter egos for Jake, as is indicated, among other ways, by the similarity of names. Joey Hersh has the same last name and the same initials as Jake, and this similarity leads to Jake's often being taken for Joey, while Jake addresses Harry Stein by the latter's affectionate Yiddish diminutive, Hershel. Let us regretfully set aside the Harry Stein part of the novel – regretfully, for, as critics generally maintain, the repellent and rancorous, indeed vicious and pathological, but withal not entirely unsympathetic, Harry Stein is one of Richler's most successful literary creations, a judgment with which I thoroughly concur.[9]

Jake Hersh, through whose consciousness most of the novel's narrative is filtered, is a thirty-seven-year-old Jewish film director, born in Montreal in 1930 but living in the novelistic present of 1967 in London with his gentile wife. While Jake is certainly not to be identified with Mordecai Richler, he is, nevertheless, whether in terms of biographical details or cultural and political attitudes, a stand-in for him.[10] Since his childhood, Jake has been obsessed with his somewhat older cousin, Joey Hersh, who takes on heroic, even mythic dimensions in his eyes, despite the fact, or perhaps precisely because, Jake has not seen Joey since Joey was forced to flee Montreal in 1943 when Jake was thirteen. Jake feels that he and his generation have lived on the margins of history, too young to fight in the Spanish Civil War and the Second World War, and too old to be part of the generation and excitement of the 1960s. By contrast, Joey is said to have participated in the great events of his age. He fought on the Ebro in the International Brigade in the Spanish Civil War and rode in the last convoy into Jerusalem in the Israeli War of Independence. In the novelistic present, Joey is in Paraguay where Jake imagines he is hunting down the notorious war criminal Dr Mengele. Jake first becomes Joey's advocate, later his acolyte. He views him as his moral exemplar, as the new, masculine, heroic type of Jew, not afraid to boldly stand up for the underdog, whether the beleaguered Jewish youth of wartime Montreal or the beleaguered Spanish Republic. When Jewish honour is threatened, whether in Montreal or even in Israel, Joey taunts his more passive and timid Jewish compatriots with the challenge: "*What are you going to do about it*" (459). Much of the novel is taken up with Jake's unavailing search for Joey. Reportedly he misses him first in England and later in Israel, with a particularly near miss in Munich. At the novel's end, Joey is reported to have died in a fiery plane crash in Paraguay, his body burned beyond recognition.

Let us now look at *The Second Scroll*. Its main protagonist, this time the anonymous narrator of the work, a Montreal Jewish translator of Hebrew poems, is, whether in terms of biographical details or cultural and political attitudes, a stand-in for the author, A.M. Klein.[11] Like *St. Urbain's Horseman*, *The Second Scroll* is constructed around the obsession and search of its main protagonist, who again appears to be living on the margins of history, for an absent somewhat older relative, his uncle, Melech Davidson, a relative whom, in this case, the narrator has neither seen nor met. Indeed, he has never even seen a photograph of him. Like Joey Hersh in the eyes of Jake, Davidson acquires mythic and symbolic, even redemptive and messianic, significance for the narrator of *The Second Scroll*. For, in his intellectual and spiritual vacillations and peregrinations – from Talmudic prodigy, to victim of a pogrom, to Communist propagandist and dialectician, to Holocaust survivor, to potential convert to Christianity, to author of "dark angelesque meditations" (51) on Michelangelo's paintings on the ceiling of the Sistine Chapel, to demographer and defender of Sephardic Jewry in exile, to Safed sage and mystic – Davidson serves for the narrator, and for the author and readers as well, to encapsulate the tragedies and triumphant events of the Jewish people in the first half of the twentieth century. The novel relates the narrator's near misses of Davidson in Bari, Rome, Casablanca, and finally Israel. At the novel's end, again like in *St. Urbain's Horseman*, Melech Davidson, the absent, long-sought-for-but-never-found heroic mythic relative, dies a fiery death, ambushed by Arabs on a Sabbath eve on the outskirts of Safed. He is shot and gasoline is poured on his dead body in an attempt to burn it. As was the case in the reported end of Joey Hersh, Davidson's body is burned beyond recognition.

Indeed, the similarities between the novels extend beyond the broad contours delineated above to such specifics as names, incidents, and images.

Names

Davidson's name is clearly symbolic, redolent with messianic significance: Melech, King; Davidson, son of David. Of course, as readers may know, the Jewish tradition conceives of the Messiah as being of Davidic descent. Similarly, Joey Hersh takes as a pseudonym the name Jesse Hope. The surname "Hope" speaks for itself. As for Jesse, if "Davidson" in Melech Davidson clearly alludes to the son of David, "Jesse" in Jesse Hope may refer to Jesse, King David's father.

Incidents

Both Melech Davidson and Joey Hersh break with the Jewish establishment's traditional *"Sha shtil,"* non-confrontational policy of quiet diplomacy, negotiation, and accommodation in responding to discrimination and oppression in the exile. Uncle Melech organizes a public but peaceful demonstration by the beggars of the Mellah in Casablanca against the French authorities' mistreatment of Jewish mendicants; Cousin Joey leads the St Urbain Street boys in a street brawl against French-Canadian youth who had previously attacked a Jewish youth. Regarding each of the incidents, the Jewish establishment reacts fearfully and apologetically, and, in its wake, Davidson is forced to leave Casablanca, while Joey Hersh is forced to leave Montreal. At the same time, there are important differences between the incidents, a point to which I shall return.

Images

At the end of the novels both Melech Davidson and Joey Hersh, following their fiery deaths, are referred to as mirrors, though *what* they mirror and *how* they mirror what they mirror differ radically.

This final observation leads me to the differences between the novels. For if the similarities between the novels are striking – and both Nadel and Kramer have pointed out some, though by no means all, of them – the novels' differences, something entirely overlooked by Nadel and not accorded sufficient weight by Kramer, are equally striking. I refer here to the differences between the absent heroes of *The Second Scroll* and *St. Urbain's Horseman* – Melech Davidson and Joey Hersh, respectively – to the differences between the relationships obtaining between the anonymous narrator of *The Second Scroll* and his uncle Melech, and to the differences between Jake Hersh of *St. Urbain's Horseman* and his Cousin Joey.

Nadel describes both Melech Davidson and Joey Hersh as "inherently political individuals."[12] But, while both do at times engage in political activity, in truth, as should be clear from my descriptions of these figures given above, Melech Davidson is primarily a scholar and an intellectual, while Joey Hersh is a fighter. The former is highly cerebral; the latter is intensely physical.

Kramer, as opposed to Nadel, recognizes that "Joey's incarnations – baseball star, gangster, Zionist fighter, country and western singer – run much farther afield than [those of] Klein's Melech ... a teacher of Jewish law, a Bolshevik, a Catholic, an Israeli social reformer."[13] This observation is well taken, but it does not cut deeply enough. It is not just that "Joey's incarnations ... run much farther afield than [those of] Klein's Melech"; rather, the key point, overlooked by Nadel[14] and Brenner[15] and only hinted at by Kramer,[16] is that Joey Hersh is a much more morally ambiguous and problematic figure than Melech Davidson. Thus, to return to the image of Davidson and Joey Hersh as mirrors: Davidson after his martyrdom is eulogized in a public funeral as "a kind of mirror, an *aspaklaria*, of the events of our time" (*Second Scroll* 61), while, after Joey Hersh's purported death, his cousin Jake wonders, "What if the Horseman was a distorting mirror and we each took the self-justifying image we required of him?" (*St. Urbain's Horseman* 460). Or, to take a more prosaic, but nonetheless revealing, image: at one point in *The Second Scroll* Melech Davidson is described as a "philanderer of ideas" (*Second Scroll* 33); Joey Hersh is a philanderer, plain and simple.

To explain and elaborate, Davidson, in all his intellectual vacillations and flirtations, is first and foremost an idealist. When an Italian communist in Rome makes the cynical suggestion that the missing Davidson may be found either in the city's brothels or in its black markets, the narrator scorns to answer: "Uncle Melech in a brothel! Uncle Melech a black-marketeer!" (*Second Scroll* 29). And indeed, in light of everything we know about Uncle Melech, the suggestion is, in truth, both insulting and absurd.

By contrast, one would not be at all surprised to find Joey Hersh in a brothel or black-marketeering. To cite from the description of Joey by his and Jake's rich uncle Abe, who supported Joey, his siblings, and his mother when they lived in Montreal, Joey was a gambler who welshed on his debts, a "gigolo," a "blackmailer" who "squeezed women for money ... a bigamist, and a liar" (*St. Urbain's Horseman* 402, 407). While Abe – never Joey's greatest admirer – may be exaggerating, a close reading of the novel indicates he is not doing so by much. Indeed, it is not really clear why Joey is in Paraguay: to hunt down Dr Mengele? To engage in a lucrative cigarette smuggling operation, or perhaps both? And, by extension, did Joey die in the plane crash hunting down Mengele or smuggling cigarettes? Or perhaps he didn't die in the crash but, rather, as his mother suggests, was in trouble with the police and faked his death in order to evade arrest and so that she might collect on his insurance policy. An even more disturbing question arises: even if Joey had been tracking down Mengele, and even if he might have succeeded in finding him, would he, as Jake liked to think, have first extracted Mengele's gold fillings with pliers and then slit his throat or, rather, would he have, as Uncle Abe liked to claim, blackmailed him?

In light of the above, some critics argue that the heroic Joey is a fantasy, a product of his cousin Jake's imagination and need; that, in truth, Joey is nothing more than a petty thief, a common thug and con man.[17] I think this oversimplifies Richler's portrait. In my view, Cousin Joey is both: a heroic figure and a morally and legally disreputable figure with his eye on the main chance.

And yet, these critics are not entirely wrong. For while Joey is a heroic figure, his heroism itself has an underside. Thus, if Joey rode in the last convoy into Jerusalem in the Israeli War of Independence, he also took part in the "unprovoked" terrorist attack by units of Etzel and the Stern Gang on "the quiescent Arab village of Deir Yassin" (*St. Urbain's Horseman* 256). And here we return to the difference between Melech Davidson's organization of the demonstration by the beggars of the Mellah and Joey's organization of the street brawl by the St Urbain Street boys.

The demonstration organized by Davidson is portrayed as clearly admirable. It was peaceful, injured nobody, and was a justified and measured response to the unjustifiable discrimination against and oppression of the Jews of Casablanca by the French authorities. The criticism levelled against Davidson's demonstration by a representative of the Jewish establishment rings hollow, and it serves only to reveal him and those for whom he speaks as morally craven and complacent. By contrast, the street brawl organized by Joey served to render unconscious an innocent French-Canadian youth who had not been involved in the previous brawl. The dangers Joey's activities posed to the Jewish community in Montreal are portrayed in vivid terms, and Uncle Abe, as a representative of the Jewish establishment, is given a forceful, cogent, and eloquent speech condemning the folly of Joey's use of violence while defending the need of the official community to take a more accommodating stance. Let's call it a draw.

But what is particularly intriguing is that it is not entirely clear why Joey had to flee Montreal. Is it because, as Jake claims, Uncle Abe and the other members of the Montreal Jewish establishment turned Joey in to the authorities? Or is it because, as Uncle Abe claims, Joey had been involved with the wife of an influential Montrealer who set some thugs upon him to teach him a lesson? Again, perhaps there is some truth to both explanations.

In light of the fact that Melech Davidson is so morally admirable while Joey Hersh is so morally ambiguous and problematic, it is not surprising that the admiration on the part of the anonymous narrator of *The Second Scroll* for his Uncle Melech steadily grows and deepens throughout the book, while at the end of *St. Urbain's Horseman,* Jake, while not abandoning either his admiration for or his heroic image of his Cousin Joey, takes a much more chastened view of him. Jake realizes that, by his deliberately having turned a blind eye to Joey's darker and seamier side, he had in effect been making him into a golden calf, had been unduly idolizing him (464).[18]

How are we to account for these differences? In part they stem from generic considerations, that is, from the very different types of novels these two books are. *The Second Scroll* is an unclassifiable novel. As Elizabeth Popham notes, reviewers "described it as a brilliant modernist experiment in form and language, a travelogue with pretensions, and a new Haggadah."[19] Whatever it is, it is not a standard, or for that matter a non-standard, realistic novel. The novel's two main characters, the anonymous narrator and his Uncle Melech, are vague and shadowy figures; we know almost nothing about their personal lives. The ideas they express, the events they mirror, are much more vivid and vital than they. Perhaps we may say that Klein – who was first and foremost a poet and not a novelist, and who lacked the novelist's ability to create living, breathing characters – succeeded in *The Second Scroll* in converting this weakness into a strength.

By contrast, *St. Urbain's Horseman* is a traditional comic, satiric, though realistic, novel, with all the personal and social density, specificity, and sheer messiness generically demanded by such a book. Most of the characters in *St. Urbain's Horseman*, like most of the characters in Richler's novels and in accordance with generic demands, are rounded, three-dimensional figures, ambivalently portrayed, complex and contradictory, ever-shifting blends of light and shadow. The exception here is Richler's portrait of Jake's gentile wife, Nancy, which strikes me, as well as most critics, as being rather idealized and consequently lifeless and unconvincing. Moreover, given Richler's satiric impulse, it would be only natural for him to create a hero with a seamy underside, to construct a heroic image only to deconstruct it, albeit partially. Indeed, we may almost say that Richler constructed the Jake Hersh-Cousin Joey relationship in *St. Urbain's Horseman* by taking the anonymous narrator-Uncle Melech relationship as portrayed in *The Second Scroll* and transposing it into a comic realist key.[20]

But the differences between the two novels stem not only from generic but also from ideological considerations. *The Second Scroll* is clearly a celebratory novel. Its true subject is the history of the Jewish people in the twentieth century; Melech Davidson is described as a "kind of mirror, an *aspaklaria,* of the events of our time" (61). And its true hero, that is to say, Klein's true hero, is not so much the individual Melech Davidson, despite his being a moral exemplar, but the Jewish collectivity. For with Davidson's martyrdom his messianic and redemptive role is taken over by the miraculous reborn and renewed Jewish people in the miraculously newly established State of Israel, where everyday life and language are filled with the marvelous and the miraculous.

By contrast, *St. Urbain's Horseman* is notable for its elliptical qualities. Jake Hersh's identity revolves about, or, perhaps better, is torn between, two foci: (1) Jake's identity as a Jew and his attachment to Jewish history and destiny, as exemplified by his heroic image of his cousin Joey; and (2) his identity as a private individual, an artist, a loving husband married to a gentile wife, who, in the end, realizes that he has made an idol of Joey by deliberately blinding himself to the Horseman's darker and seamier side. And, indeed, with Joey's death or presumed death, *his* place is taken by the decent, albeit clearly unheroic, Jake.

Much of the above, as it relates to Jake, applies to Richler's identity as a person and a writer. Jake's ambivalence regarding his identity reflects a similar ambivalence on the part of Richler. To take just one particularly striking example: Richler ends his very personal, funny, and irreverent essay on Deuteronomy with a description of Ornstein, his friend from cheder days:

> Ornstein, who broke with the Communist Party long ago, is
> still opposed to all kinds of religious mumbo-jumbo, any sort
> of tribalism. A scientist of some renown, he always seems to be
> heading for or just coming back from an important international
> conference in Tokyo, London, or Milan. Last year he was in
> Jerusalem for the first time, and he went to see the Wailing Wall.
> "And you know what?" he said. "I burst into tears. I wept and I
> wept."[21]

The reader might wonder if it is in fact Richler himself being de‑-scribed here.

This ideological difference between the two novels is reflected with particular sharpness in their conclusions. *The Second Scroll* ends with a vision of collective renewal. The anonymous narrator intones "the kaddish ... this wonderful mourner's Magnificat," for his uncle who had no son. And in the novel's last sentence, he turns "for the last time from the city of Safed, holy city on whose hills once were kindled, as now again, the beacons announcing new moons, festivals, and set times" (*Second Scroll* 62).

St. Urbain's Horseman, by contrast, ends on a much more ambiguous note, suspended between public and private, between the Horseman and Jake's gentile wife, Nancy. Jake retrieves the Horseman's journal, finds the page where Jake had written "Died, July 20, 1967, in an air crash," crosses it out, and writes over it "presumed dead." Might this signify that Jake is still attached to his heroic image of the Horseman, albeit a much more sober and chastened image? Or does it suggest that Jake, the private, decent, unheroic individual, is now the true Horseman? I would like to think it signifies both. Then, in the novel's last sentence, Jake "returned to bed, and fell into a deep sleep, holding Nancy to him" (*St. Urbain's Horseman* 462).

In light of the ideological differences between the two novels, I would like to carry my previous argument one step further. I suggested earlier that Richler constructed the Jake Hersh-Cousin Joey relationship in *St. Urbain's Horseman* by taking the anonymous narrator-Uncle Melech relationship as portrayed in *The Second Scroll* and transposing it into a comic realist key. But, given the ideological differences between the novels, I would like to further suggest, if in a more tentative vein, that Richler may have intended the Jake Hersh-Cousin Joey relationship to constitute a tacit and subtle critique of the anonymous narrator-Uncle Melech relationship. That is, Richler may be suggesting that, in real life, if one seeks to move from the margins of Jewish history to its centre by uncritically investing one's absent Jewish relative, who was fortunate or unfortunate enough to participate in the great events of Jewish history, with heroic, mythic, and symbolic significance, it is much more likely that that absent "hero" will end up resembling a Cousin Joey than an Uncle Melech. It is safer and better, Richler appears to be saying, to avoid such misplaced hero worship and to devote oneself to cultivating the more private, decent, if unheroic virtues, as Jake Hersh does at the end of *St. Urbain's Horseman*.

Perhaps Klein would not entirely disagree. For, as we have seen, Melech Davidson, for Klein, is not so much a living, rounded, three-dimensional character as he is a "kind of mirror, an *aspaklaria,* of the events of our time," of the history of the Jewish people in the first half of the twentieth century (*Second Scroll* 61). And, for Klein, as we have also seen, while the life history of any particular Jewish individual may be more or less heroic, the history of the Jewish people as a collectivity, particularly the history of the establishment of the State of Israel, is certainly heroic and, as such, deserves to be celebrated and commemorated. Indeed, it deserves no less than a *Second Scroll*.

At least part of the answer to the question as to whether *The Second Scroll* can speak to us today depends upon whether we are able to see that collective history as heroic. In contrast to my reading, which sees the ending of *The Second Scroll* as affirmative and celebratory, Elizabeth Popham, in her generally informative and insightful introduction to the annotated, critical edition of *The Second Scroll*, sees the novel's ending as chastened and ironic. Part of her reason for doing so may arise from the critical fashion that prefers that the endings of our favourite novels be low-key and ambiguous rather than affirmative and celebratory. But, so I believe, something deeper is at work. In the concluding paragraph of her introduction Popham writes:

> Klein repeatedly argues, as does his narrator, that the establishment of the State of Israel is a "miracle," figuring the redemption of Israel as a people. But, in fiction *and in fact* [emphasis added], as the "dream" of the new state is realized, its symbolic value is undermined by a partial fulfilment ... internal tensions ... external threats ... as well as by political and commercial opportunism. In his acknowledgment of contradictory, unresolved elements ... Klein has given us "a double, a multiple exposure" of jubilation and misgiving right to end of the novel. (Klein, *Second Scroll*, xxiv)

In referring to "internal tensions ... external threats ... commercial and political opportunism ... [and] contradictory, unresolved elements," Popham has in mind certain events in the work and features of the narrative that we need not detail here. In my view these are minor undercurrents that barely disturb the placid, clear-flowing surface of the book's ending – if at all. More significant, I believe, is Popham's throwaway phrase, "and in fact." It appears that Popham is of the view that *in fact* the "symbolic value [of the State of Israel] has [been] undermined by a partial fulfillment ... internal tensions ... external threats ... as well as by commercial and political opportunism." I would suggest, then, that it is precisely Popham's own chastened and ironic, as opposed to an affirmative and celebratory attitude towards the establishment of the State of Israel, and the fact that she, unlike Klein, apparently does not view the establishment of the state as a "miracle," that led her to unjustifiably project a chastened and ironic attitude onto the ending of *The Second Scroll*.[22]

Here my own reading of *The Second Scroll* on purely literary-critical grounds dovetails nicely with my own personal Jewish commitments. That is, precisely because I, as a traditional Jew, share Klein's affirmative and celebratory attitude towards the establishment of the State of Israel, I have no problem in taking the ending of *The Second Scroll* at face value, in reading it as I believe Klein intended it to be read and would have wished it to be read, that is, as unabashedly positive. And in personally resonating to Klein's image of "Safed, holy city on whose hills once were kindled, as now again, the beacons announcing new moons, festivals, and set times," I believe I am responding precisely as Klein intended me and would have wished me and, indeed, all readers to respond (62). Part of Klein's greatness is that he, precisely as a Montreal Jewish writer, has given voice with incomparable poetry and eloquence to what I believe – and what I imagine he believed – to be the miraculous rebirth of the Jewish people in the land of Israel, while avoiding the error of the negation of the Diaspora.

At the same time, I am not immune to Richler's warnings about the dangers of misplaced hero worship and the need to devote oneself to cultivating the more private, decent, if unheroic virtues. Such is Richler's artistry, that although, on a personal level, I can by no means identify with Jake Hersh, I am deeply moved and touched by Jake when he writes "presumed dead" in the Horseman's journal. I am even moved when he "return[s] to bed, and [falls] into a deep sleep, holding Nancy to him" (462).

Both A.M. Klein and Mordecai Richler have given us works that testify to the power of art to illuminate both the human and the Jewish condition, in both the public and private spheres. We should not seek to harmonize, much less homogenize, Klein and Richler – folly even to contemplate this. We need them both.

DAVID LEAHY

A.M. Klein: Mordecai Richler's Versions

A considerable consensus has developed among critics, especially evident since the appearance of Usher Caplan's *Like One That Dreamed: A Portrait of A.M. Klein* (1982), suggesting that much of Klein's life as a writer was tragic, or at least that he agonized about the relative lack of recognition of his oeuvre during his lifetime. This narrative, reproduced in various forms in articles, books, and encyclopaedia entries, goes more or less as follows: after more than two decades of rather prodigious literary and journalistic production, in which Klein established himself as "the first contributor of authentic Jewish poetry to the English language" (Lewisohn, "Appendix," 350),[1] the period in which he also fulfilled significant roles within the Montreal Jewish community as the editor of the *Canadian Jewish Chronicle*, as a candidate for the CCF, and as a speechwriter and public relations adviser to Samuel Bronfman, he slipped into a depression that caused him to withdraw from society and to stop writing. Some observers emphasize a continuous sense of Klein's disappointment at the lack of popular recognition of his literary output – especially of *The Rocking Chair and Other Poems* (1948) and his highly innovative metaphysical detective novel, *The Second Scroll* (1951) – as the primary cause of his emotional crisis. Others characterize Klein's postwar fact-finding trip on behalf of the Canadian Jewish Congress to refugee camps in Europe and North Africa, as well as to Israel, as having motivated his melancholic decline. Whatever the primary origins of Klein's withdrawal from society – and as we know all too well, it could have been the result of, or significantly aggravated by, some kind of bio-chemical or neurological disorder – the aforementioned narrative of Klein's life is reductive and tends to detract from consideration of what was joyous and perhaps even heroic about his life and literary career.

The tragic narrative of Klein's life has been hegemonic, and this chapter addresses how some of the works of another important Montreal Jewish writer, Mordecai Richler, are demonstrative of and have contributed to it. Yet, as Zailig Pollock suggests, even Richler's cruel fictionalizations of Klein mark his continuing centrality to Canadian literature. Furthermore, Richler produced more than one fictionalized version of A.M. Klein, and they are not necessarily consistent across time. In other words, I am suggesting that their significance is not monological.

Reinhold Kramer argues that Richler's fictionalized critical attitudes towards Klein "betray ... a certain ambivalence" regarding Klein's life and art. Kramer's characterization of this tendency is best exemplified by his observation regarding *Solomon Gursky Was Here*:

> By making L.B. Berger/Klein the father of the present-day writer, Moses Berger, Richler was doing two important things. He was acknowledging the crucial role that Klein had played in the genesis of Jewish writing in Montreal and backhandedly confessing how much his own writing owed to Klein. As in *St. Urbain's Horseman*, so in *Solomon Gursky* Richler turned to Klein's brilliant metaphysical detective plot structure in *The Second Scroll* – the search for "I Am That I Am." Secondly, and against that debt, by treating L.B. Berger harshly, Richler was declaring emphatically that he was not Klein, that the elevated spiritual quest in Klein's work must be overcome so that a writer unafraid of human vulgarity could flourish.... Richler's [immediate] literary ancestors ([his mother] Lily, Rabbi Rosenberg, Klein) and non-literary ancestors (his weak father Moe, his hot-tempered grandfather Shmarya) were profoundly unsatisfactory to him. In their place Richler once again invented wished-for ancestors, this time Ephraim and Solomon Gursky: smart and tricky, ruthless, vulgar, humane. (*Mordecai Richler* 312–13)

I am not currently interested in exploring the broad range of Richler's "wished-for [literary] ancestors";[2] rather, I concentrate on Kramer's idea of Richler as a kind of rebellious son of Klein and on two key examples of Richler's shifting attitudes towards Klein as well as towards his own life and art. Moreover, I contend that the cruel portrayal of the cipher for Klein in Richler's story "Mortimer Griffin, Shalinsky, and How They Settled the Jewish Question,"[3] from the late 1950s, may at first glance appear to be synonymous with the cipher for Klein in *Solomon Gursky Was Here*,[4] but this is not ultimately the case.

"That was my time, my place, and I have elected myself to get it right," Richler famously proclaimed in "Why I Write" (19) regarding his narratives' focus upon the Montreal Jewish community in which he came of age, and this is useful for my present purposes. It raises the questions as to whether or not Richler got Klein "right" in *Son of a Smaller Hero* (1955), "Mortimer Griffin," and *Solomon Gursky*, and why he chose to satirize such an obvious target more than once. When Dryden stooped to dismiss contemporaries like Thomas Shadwell and Richard Flecknoe as monarchs of poetic dullness he barely disguised their identities and names; so, too, as shall become apparent, is the case with Richler when satirizing Klein. However, as much as Dryden despised Shadwell and Flecknoe as poets, they were nevertheless his competitors. Klein was never truly a literary competitor of Richler's. Like Kramer, I believe that there is significant evidence that Richler saw Klein as a literary forefather with whom he had to contend. One can perhaps make too much of Richler's early Hemingwayesque disdain for poetry as an effete endeavour of the ineffectual, his concomitant attraction to the idea that *real* writing in the postwar period was synonymous with prose and, hence, that Klein, who saw himself as a kind of poet-prophet, was an obvious if not inevitable target of Richler's disdain. After all, William Weintraub remarks that Richler liked Klein's writing. But it does not necessarily follow that Richler was always able to distinguish between Klein the man and Klein the writer, nor that he ridiculed Klein as often as he did without there being some kind of antagonistic, perhaps even unconscious, motivations that he was trying to work through. Given the several works within which Richler creates pathetic, generally tragic ciphers for Klein – David Lerner in *Son of a Smaller Hero*, I.M. Sinclair in "Mortimer Griffin," and L.B. Berger in *Solomon Gursky* – in opposition to younger, artistically spirited male protagonists who can be interpreted as ciphers for Richler, it would appear that he perceived Klein (likely because of his stature within the Montreal Jewish community and the Canadian literary scene during Richler's formative years) as a passé father-like figure who had to be put to rest. However, during the thirty years that transpired between the writing and the publication of "Mortimer Griffin" and that of *Solomon Gursky*, Richler's semiosis of Klein was not consistent: it evolved and mutated. For as much as these texts' fictionalized versions of Klein can be understood as cruel, *Solomon Gursky* not only evinces a backhanded homage to Klein but also reveals signs of Richler's appreciation of the more tragic *and* heroic aspects of Klein's life. This sympathy may in turn be understood as an acknowledgment, and an imaginative working through, of some of Richler's own anxieties and foibles, such that Moses Berger is not only an inverted, failed version of Richler but also a fictional embodiment of the limitations of the satirist's, or any writer's, ability to get things right.

Kramer suggests that Richler failed to "control the farcical element" in "Mortimer Griffin" (*Mordecai Richler* 139), but this argument holds only if one insists on reading the story as a failed comic realist narrative. It is not just comic but also satiric, and this generic vehicle of much of Richler's prose undermines the possibility of his "get[ting] it right" in any kind of mimetic way, while nevertheless allowing one to identify with Richler's perspectives and values. Among the farcical, rag-tag coterie of characters in "Mortimer Griffin" who irritate and plague the protagonist Griffin until his liberal WASP attitudes and guilt towards Jews are transformed into his accepting himself as a closeted Jew, is the pathetic, modernist poetaster, I.M. Sinclair. The fact that the initials I.M. are homonymous with A.M. are enhanced by the diction and syntax when Sinclair first "confronts" Griffin: "I am I.M. Sinclair." His discourse is that of an arrogant, self-aggrandizing man, who almost sounds like Yahweh – "I am that I am"[5] – but more modestly compares himself to Chekhov and announces: "I'm the only poet in Canada." He then proceeds to recite poetry that the narration suggests he may or may not be "composing on the spot": "I am an old man – an old man in a dry mouth – waiting for rain" (Richler, "Mortimer Griffin," 481). It is unclear whether Sinclair is trying to pass off the botched verse as a paraphrase of the opening verses of Eliot's "Gerontion" (1920) or as his own. He does say "I have turned better lines" (481), but whether he thinks of them as being "better" than his own or Eliot's is unclear. Furthermore, the substitution of "mouth" for "month" is sexually connotative of fellatio and perhaps even impotence (given the "dry[ness]" and the "waiting for rain" motif, which is consistent with how Richler's early fiction often associated poetry and homosexuality with artistic impotence or failure). Furthermore, in the poem by Eliot the first-person "old man" is read to (served) by a boy – an association, I suspect, that Richler expected many readers to make in their semiosis of I.M. Sinclair. In short, one can argue that Richler not only intended I.M. Sinclair to be read as a contemporary, vatic-identified, aging Jewish poet – and who else but Klein would have fit the bill in the contemporary imagination of literary-minded Montrealers and Canadians? – but also as somebody who was unbalanced or disturbed, as Klein was at the time of the story's publication. This psychological association was enhanced by the implicit homophobic charge of Sinclair's enunciation, which drew upon contemporary associations between mental illness and homosexuality.[6]

If my interpretation of the aforecited passage from "Mortimer Griffin" seems to be forcing its point, consider how other critics and readers have faulted Klein for being derivative as a modernist, as in the often cited example "Soirée of Velvel Kleinburger" (1931), which alludes to Eliot's "The Love Song of J. Alfred Prufrock."[7] The figure of I.M. Sinclair embodies a similar penchant with a vengeance when he misappropriates Eliot's "Gerontion." This tendency reappears in Sinclair's direct theft from Auden. Sinclair is said to have "composed a special poem" for Mortimer's Jewish wedding: "*Lay your sleeping head, my love, / human on my faithless arm* ... " (Richler, "Mortimer Griffin," 489). The punning in the adjective "faithless" is ironic given the strangeness of Mortimer's religious conversion. The adjective may be understood not only as an allusion to Griffin's lack of true faith but also to Griffin as a secular goy who has been mistaken for a Jew and cannot be fully trusted. But it may also be interpreted as a satiric comment upon the derivativeness of Klein's modernist-identified, and, at times, devotional verse.

If one is still not convinced of this fictional equation, there is another instance when Griffin and Sinclair first meet in which I.M. Sinclair's poetasting strongly suggests A.M. Klein's poetry. He says: "We have a lot to talk about, Griffin. The moment in the draughty synagogue at smokefall ... " (Richler, "Mortimer Griffin," 481).

This is not an allusion to an actual moment the two characters have shared, since Sinclair and Griffin have just met, though we may infer that Sinclair, like Shalinsky, wants to talk to Mortimer about his supposedly repressed Jewish roots. The anachronistic nature of Sinclair's statement, however, is reminiscent of scenes and the tone in poems by Klein such as "Reb Levi Yitschok Talks to God." Or consider the following verses from "Out of the Pulver and the Polished Lens": "What better than ram's horn blown, / And candles blown out by maledictory breath, / Can bring the wanderer back to his very own, / The infidel back to his faith?"[8]

Consider, beyond the parallels stated so far between A.M. Klein and the fictional character of I.M. Sinclair – the homonymous nature of their initials, their pronounced concern about their reputations, the derivative nature of their modernist poetics, the religiosity of their verses – how the portrayal of I.M. Sinclair in "Mortimer Griffin" is remarkably similar to Richler's portrayal of Klein as L.B. Berger in *Solomon Gursky* some thirty years later. This similarity is highlighted by the devices Richler deploys to satirize I.M. Sinclair in "Mortimer Griffin" and L.B. Berger in *Solomon Gursky*.

As a number of critics recognized when *Solomon Gursky* was published, the Gurskys had "more than a passing resemblance to the Bronfman family" (Prose 7).[9] And most critics were amused rather than disturbed by the ways in which Richler, as he had done in previous narratives, used types like the Gurskys as a means of satirizing vulgar egotism, hypocrisy, a decline in ethical values, and grasping materialism. There has been less unanimity about how to qualify and react to the character of L.B. Berger, who, in his relationship to Samuel Bronfman, is clearly the novel's comic-satiric equivalent of A.M. Klein.[10] In *Maclean's*, Morton Ritts characterizes the figure of L.B. Berger as "a witty caricature" of Klein "in his vanity, erudition, early political beliefs" and in terms of his relationship to the Bronfmans (189). Dennis Duffy asks the muted rhetorical question whether L.B.'s "initials come a little too close for comfort to those of A.M." (190). Russell Brown, in *The Oxford Companion to Canadian Literature,* is more openly disturbed by the figure of L.B. Berger, reading him as "a devastating caricature of A.M. Klein" (1001). In *New York*, as one might expect from an American publication, Rhoda Koenig does not make connections between the Bronfmans and the Gurskys, let alone Klein and

Berger, but she does say that the latter, "the failed poet ... is the most chilling character in the book: Loud and maudlin in his protestations of love for his son, he really wants Moses to fail as well, so he can have more justification for feeling he has been kept down by fools and anti-Semites" (189). And while Montreal's Joel Yanofsky, in a review in *The Village Voice*, shies away from making direct connections between actual people and those of Richler's fiction, he characterizes "L.B., a failed poet turned speechwriter" as being "happily in the pocket of the Gursky family patriarch" (86).

Richler hardly portrays L.B. Berger as being happy about his relationship with the Gurskys, just as in Klein's notebooks and letters we discover his distaste for a number of aspects of his service to Sam Bronfman. Klein anguished about his financial and professional dependency upon him, as in the case of his part-time faculty appointment at McGill, and was repulsed at times by Sam Bronfman's vulgarity and ignorance. Analogously, L.B. Berger frets and is embarrassed by his financial reliance upon Bernard Gursky and the latter's boorishness. More important for my purposes, Klein was haunted by an increasingly profound sense of his not having fulfilled his literary potential, and Berger is portrayed as being so distraught by his failure to achieve a wide literary audience that he malevolently sabotages the *New Yorker*'s acceptance of a story by his son, Moses.

On the other hand, this latter incident is just one of many in which the discrepancies between Klein's life and that of L.B. Berger, like much of the magic-realist, exaggerated portrayal of the Bronfmans as the Gurskys, remind us how much Richler's novel is a work of art that takes poetic liberties and should not be confused with reality. For example, Klein's two sons were never sabotaged by him in attempts at literary careers; rather, they devoted themselves to the law and to architecture, respectively. This said, of all Richler's works of fiction, *Solomon Gursky* features the greatest number of identifiable public figures (however parodic and fictionalized). Moreover, Richler could have easily lampooned the Bronfmans without creating the pathetic figure of L.B. Berger. Doubtlessly, this is one of the reasons Richler shied away from talking about the historical and biographical sources of several of the book's main characters. He presumably wanted the book to be received and enjoyed on the basis of its artistic merits, but he foresaw, on the basis of the previous occasions when people took exception to his books, that *Solomon Gursky* would draw heat without his adding to it. And he must have known that L.B. Berger would be read as a portrait of A.M. Klein, as a cipher that readers might find distasteful and cruel. But Richler might also have contemplated how the "cruelty" of his version of Klein in *Solomon Gursky* was not as dismissive or offensive as it could have been, especially when compared with the absolutely disdainful version of Klein he had created in "Mortimer Griffin."

One of the signatures of Richler's satiric versions of Klein in "Mortimer Griffin" and *Solomon Gursky* involves the way in which he plays with names and initials. I have noted the homonymous nature between the initials for I.M. Sinclair's given names in "Mortimer Griffin" and those of A.M. Klein. It is also worth noting that Berger's name is a slant rhyme for the "burger" of "Kleinburger" in the aforementioned poem by Klein and that, given the self-identificatory coupling of the names "Klein" and "[B]urger" by Klein himself, it is not such a stretch to imagine Richler's uncoupling of them as the literal (and poetic) source of Berger's name. Furthermore, the name of "Moses" (given to L.B. Berger's son) can be related not only to that of Richler's actual father – such that his *real* father becomes a gloss for the intelligent but unsuccessful type that Mordecai Richler could have become – but also to the Book of Exodus and, especially, to Richler's ironic sense of his relationship not only to Klein but also to his Jewish heritage and to contemporary Jewish culture in general. Finally, a far more explicit source of one of the fictional names in *Solomon Gursky* is Klein's wife Bessie, whose name is given to L.B. Berger's wife.

Reinhold Kramer points to the textual evidence that proves that the figure of L.B. in *Solomon Gursky* is based upon Klein. My aim is to examine the generally condemnatory tone of the characterization in order to account for the authorial anger behind it as well as to recognize what distinguishes it from Richler's earlier version of A.M. Klein as I.M. Sinclair.

Consider some analogous aspects of the publishing history of Berger's book of poetry, *The Burning Bush*, and Klein's collection *The Rocking Chair*. We are told that Berger's initially self-published volume eventually gets picked up by Ryerson Press – the press that published *The Rocking Chair* – and the dismissive tone of the narration clearly damns the book's publication as an instance of anti-

Semitic paternalism: "The breakthrough came for L.B. [when] Ryerson Press, in Toronto, brought out their own edition of *The Burning Bush* in their Ethnic Poets of Canada series, with an introduction by Professor Oliver Carson: 'Montreal's Eloquent Israelite'" (*Solomon Gursky* 18). Among the key aesthetic and ideological differences between Klein and Richler is the traditional Jewishness of Klein's humanism and the ways in which this manifested itself in his use of forms, languages, and themes, in contrast with the more pronounced secularism of Richler's humanism and aesthetics. Richler's decision to change the title of *The Rocking Chair*, Klein's most secular and most modernist collection, to *The Burning Bush*, and his decision to dub its author an "Israelite," not only foregrounds Klein's and Richler's philosophical differences but also allows Richler to critique Klein for his traditionalism and his sense of himself as a poet-prophet. This critique, I might add, can be seen to deny what was innovative, modern, and secular about Klein's Governor General's Award-winning book.

Richler's Professor Oliver Carson is clearly meant as a send-up of Lorne Pierce, who, for forty years, was the editor of Toronto's Ryerson Press and who was known for his "liberal" anti-Semitism.[11] The parallel narrative chastises Klein for his willingness to be published by Ryerson Press and, more broadly, for his tendency to place too much faith in the commonality of traditional values as a means of ethnic reconciliation and multicultural peace. Such themes are idealized in poems like "The Rocking Chair" and "Montreal."[12]

Solomon Gursky's fictionalized account of Berger's *Burning Bush* also stands as a comment upon Klein's longing to achieve a wide readership and popularity for his poetry. This is in marked contrast with Richler's preferred role as a satirist and relative pariah who lambasted the major religious and ethno-linguistic communities of his day while nevertheless achieving not only notoriety but also popularity and fame. Richler's fictionalized versions of A.M. Klein and his literary career can be understood as Oedipal in nature: they were attempts on Richler's part to assert and distinguish his literary capital from the likes of Klein, whose more rarefied poetic modernism and devotional verse he considered to be passé (even if he appreciated Klein's talent and significance).

Moses Berger is introduced to the literary life under the aegis of his father. We are told that "when his father mounted the podium" to give a reading "Moses would take up a position ... applauding wildly, torn between rising anger and concern" (*Solomon Gursky* 17–8). Eventually it becomes apparent that there was another piddling audience, and "most nights Moses was lucky to peddle four or five copies of *The Burning Bush*" (18). As Moses grows older and becomes aware of the ways in which L.B. compromises his art for the sake of his family – "Am I not entitled, after all of these years of serving my muse, to put some bread on the table?" (21) – Moses draws the conclusion that his father has become little more than a "lapdog" to Bernard Gursky:

> When L.B.'s poem celebrating Mr. Bernard's twenty-fifth wedding anniversary in 1950 was published in *Jewish Outlook*, it enraged Moses. A committed socialist himself now, he lashed out at his father for having betrayed his old adoring comrades to become an apologist for the Gurskys, one of Mr. Bernard's lapdogs (29).[13]

Moses' disdain deepens once he learns that his father has intercepted and deep-sixed a story by Moses that was accepted by the *New Yorker*. Furthermore, this betrayal confirms Moses in the righteousness of his desire to expose the Gurskys' shady dealings – in part to rub his father's face in it, to make his father pay more than he already has. Yet Moses never succeeds as a writer or as an investigative journalist. In fact, it can be said that he becomes as pathetic in his ignoble quest to revenge himself upon his father as was L.B. in his idealistic hopes for the reception of his poetry and for positive political consequences for Jewry through Bernard Gursky's failed political interventions.[14]

To the extent to which one can read Moses as a cipher for Richler, as an imaginative version of himself as the failed writer he could have become, L.B.'s self-serving, hypocritical lecture to Moses about his son's literary drive to surpass him can be interpreted as yet another fictionalized version of Richler's urge to make light of Klein's more rarefied sense of literature.[15] It acknowledges, too, Richler's recurrent anxieties about striking a balance between literature and the popular:

> Don't you dare look at me like that. I'm your father and it goes without saying that I forgive you this childish business with *The*

New Yorker. It mustn't upset you either because it was only natural. You know your Oedipus and so do I. I never published there – not that I ever wanted to – so you would, administering a slap in the face to old L.B. .... Had they accepted your story you would have gone on to write more formula fiction tailored to their commercial expectations. Moishe, you have escaped a trap. (134)

There are important passages in the novel, in which the righteousness of Moses' Oedipal angst – and by extension Richler's – is challenged. The former Red militant, Gitel Kugelmass, tells Moses he should feel ashamed of his dismissive attitude towards his father: "I never blamed L.B. for writing those speeches for Mr. Bernard. As for the others ... it was envy pure and simple" (73–4). And not long before his literary betrayal by his father, as he peruses L.B.'s *Collected Poems*, Moses contemplates how many

of the poems were clearly vitiated by sentimentality or self-pity. W.B. Yeats he was not. Gerard Manly Hopkins he was not. Yes, but did the poems have any merit? Moses, sliding in sweat ... shirked from deciding, unable to accept such a responsibility. After all, he held a life in his hands. His father's life. All those years of dedication and frustrated ambition. The sacrifices, the humiliations. The neglect. (130)

Tim Callaghan, a former flunky of the Gurskys, assures Moses that his father wasn't "drafted, he volunteered. He didn't have to write those speeches for Mr. Bernard" (162). But we are also told that, as "far as Callaghan was concerned, what redeemed the young Moses, so quick to anger, was that he had not yet grasped that the world was imperfect. He actually expected justice to be done" (163). This discourse is, in turn, echoed by Kaplansky, one of several manifestations of Solomon Gursky, the primary trickster figure of the novel and a kind of surrogate father to Moses: "There is no just kingdom, but only the quest for one, a preoccupation of idiots for the most part, wouldn't you say?" (196).

There is evidence that Moses feels remorseful about his life-long dismissal of his father and that he grudgingly recognizes the heroism of L.B.'s art and life: "Moses glanced at the portrait of L.B., contemplating the cosmos, enduring its weight, and turned away, surprised by tears" (551). In the previous instances of this leitmotif of Moses observing his father's portrait, the tone is suggestive of Moses' judgmental, mocking attitude towards his father. Nor does Richler stoop to put bad and stolen verses into L.B. Berger's mouth, as he does with his fictional version of Klein in "Mortimer Griffin." L.B. Berger dies relatively early in the narrative and is not subjected to fictionalized versions of the increasing isolation, self-doubt, and paranoia that marked the final years of his life.

Just as Moses' investment in his narrow, self-righteous narrative about his father is softened and shaken by the end of the novel, so, too, is Richler's take on Klein. Here we can recognize what is fundamentally different about Richler's "Mortimer Griffin" version of Klein and the one offered in *Solomon Gursky*. In the latter, there is an identification with and sympathy for Klein's humanity as portrayed in the Oedipal dynamic between L.B. and Moses Berger – something that is not present in "Mortimer Griffin."[16]

IAN RAE

Converting Failure in Klein, Cohen, and Michaels

In Montreal there was a tight band of poets. The senior members were Irving Layton and Louis Dudek and other poets – Frank Scott. And they were very, very kind to me. And we would meet regularly in an informal way with drinks, of course, and food and we would read ... each other our poems and then they would be subject to savage, word-by-word criticism. I mean, you couldn't get away with anything. We really wanted to be good writers, good poets, great poets.... We thought we was [sic] the most important thing in the world. We thought every time we met it was a summit conference. You know, we really took seriously – I think it was Shelley who said "poets are the unacknowledged legislators of the world." I mean, an incredibly naïve description of oneself, but we certainly fell for that. We thought it was terribly important, what we were doing. Maybe it was, who knows?

Leonard Cohen, *I'm Your Man*[1]

In a 1964 speech at the Jewish Public Library of Montreal, Leonard Cohen criticized A.M. Klein, a poet he greatly admired, because "Klein chose to be a priest though it was as a prophet that we needed him" (qtd. in Siemerling 147). Convinced that Klein's nervous breakdown in the 1950s was a result of his attempt to reconcile the roles of poet and "theorist of the Jewish party line," Cohen styled his public persona in the 1960s as that of a renegade prophet. However, Cohen's priestly inclinations became pronounced in subsequent years, particularly in *Book of Mercy* (1984). Indeed, Ira Nadel maintains that Cohen "reformulate[s] the voice of the Jewish poet" by "combining Klein's priestly mien with the prophetic energy of Layton" (*Various Positions* 67). Interestingly, however, Cohen insists in his library speech that any attempt to merge the priest and prophet "exhausts itself in failure" (Siemerling, "Leonard Cohen," 150). Nadel is correct in his assessment of Cohen, but the contradiction highlights a central tension in Cohen's writing. Throughout the 1960s, Cohen adopted a series of increasingly radical positions in an attempt to subvert the priestly inclinations that his entire upbringing was designed to foster – as the grandson of a rabbi on his mother's side and of the president of the Shaar Hashomayim congregation on his father's side (Nadel, *Various Positions*, 7–9). In Cohen's works from the mid-1960s onwards, and particularly in his 1966 novel *Beautiful Losers*, failure becomes synonymous with a bold, if necessarily incomplete, challenge to social, institutional, religious, and generic boundaries.

By examining the reception and legacy of A.M. Klein's 1951 novel, *The Second Scroll*, this chapter explores the distinction between the active embrace of failure as a testing of limits and the passive experience of failure as defeat. I argue that we must reconsider the so-called "failure" of Klein's novel in light of the acclaimed poet-novelists who have followed his example, in particular Leonard Cohen and Anne Michaels. Reading *The Second Scroll* as a harbinger of Canadian postmodernism, as well as as a fine example of high modernism, reveals two important continuities in postwar writing that defy the usual division between modern and postmodern. First, experimental "failure" and Canadian nationalism are frequently linked in writing after the Second World War. Second, Klein's poetic prose played a formative role in recuperating the lyric voice for future generations of Canadian authors who wished to respond to the horrors of genocide in the twentieth century despite well known prohibitions against such writing, most notably Theodor Adorno's 1949 assertion that to "write poetry after Auschwitz is barbaric" (34).

Klein's The Second Scroll

The Second Scroll is a quest narrative about a young Canadian journalist's trip to Israel to witness the prophesied restoration of the Jewish homeland and to locate his elusive Uncle Melech. The story derives from journalistic accounts of the emerging Jewish state that Klein published in the *Canadian Jewish Chronicle*, a publication he edited between 1938 and 1955. However, in the novel, Klein combines the documentary narrative with a more symbolic and mystical vision of Judaism derived from kaballistic interpretations of the scriptures (Pollock, *A.M. Klein*, 196–232) and embodied in the character of Melech Davidson, whose name connects him to King David and the Messiah.

Klein clearly set out to write a Joycean masterpiece that would mythologize what he initially perceived as the fulfilment of Jewish prophecy in the State of Israel. To illustrate this ambition, Seymour Mayne cites a letter Klein wrote to A.J.M. Smith in 1951 in which Klein outlines his aims for the novel: "I desired first of all, a record, a conspectus of my pilgrimage to the Holy Land, some heirloom to attest to the fact that I had been of the generation that had seen the Return.... I was struck, furthermore, by the similarity between contemporary Jewish history and my people's ancient saga – I thought I saw in the events of today, in large outline, a recurrence of the events of the Pentateuch" (qtd. in Mayne, "Afterword," 137). The Pentateuch, the five books of the Hebrew Bible, supplies the formal model for Klein's novel. Mayne demonstrates that Klein consciously proceeds from Genesis (a short history of the narrator's youth in Montreal), to Exodus (the trip to Europe), to Leviticus (the priestly book wherein the narrator encounters the Monsignor at the Vatican), to Numbers (a stock-taking of relations between Sephardic Jews and Muslims in Casablanca), and, finally, to Deuteronomy (the Return and Restoration).[2] In proper Talmudic fashion, these chapters are complemented by a scholarly apparatus of glosses that contain Klein's poem "Autobiographical," an elegy for Melech, a lyric essay on the dome of the Sistine Chapel, a verse drama in which an impoverished Jew pleads his case to Muslim authorities in Casablanca, and a selection of prayers.

The two sections of Klein's novel permit very different reading strategies and complicate questions of the novel's genre. Following the cues in the footnotes and reading the book from chapter to gloss, one encounters a novel that exhibits the qualities of an epic quest narrative, including a larger-than-life hero, Melech, who endures exile and a variety of temptations before finding his spiritual home, experiencing the founding of a new state, and inaugurating the victory celebration of a particular ethnic group. On the other hand, Klein's encyclopaedic mix of materials in the glosses is not subsumed into the principal narrative, as is customary for the epic. Indeed, reading the book from cover to cover creates an open-ended effect that counteracts the stasis of "set times" established by Melech's martyrdom and returns the narrative to a state of multiplicity and fragmentation (*Second Scroll* 87). Instead of creating "word by word, phrase by phrase, the total work that when completed would stand as epic revealed!" (78), as Melech's nephew imagines his project in *The Second Scroll*, this reading produces a novel that is elliptical, gestural, and that takes formal cues from some of the poets the narrator meets on his journey, although their poetry does not satisfy the nephew, either. According to the cover-to-cover reading, the imperial genre of epic collapses halfway through the book and fails to impose a lasting order on the diasporic writings the nephew collects.

Klein's "Failure"

The hybrid format of *The Second Scroll* perplexed Klein's early readership. Even Klein's admirers, such as his childhood friend Leon Edel, qualified their enthusiasm for the vibrant language and imagery of *The Second Scroll* by judging it as a "kind of novelistic failure" (Edel 24). Miriam Waddington makes a strong case for the importance of Klein's verse in her 1970 book on the author, but when she turns to his prose her judgment is stark: "I have always admired Klein's poetry," she says, "but I was strongly repelled by the diction of *The Second Scroll*. Although I read it carefully later, I became more and more convinced that the book was a failure" (*A.M. Klein* 116). Waddington finds the novel's diction archaic and "strained," and its characterizations "too sketchy" (118). She recognizes that the two-part structure of the novel is inspired by Talmudic tradition, but she considers the form a "shortcut" that "saves [Klein] the labour of integrating into the text raw material which doesn't quite fit, but is still too good to discard" (ibid.). The theme of exile and return displeases her because it is "narrowly focused on the State of Israel – with all of its Zionist political connotations – as well as on the theological aspects of Judaism in a way which exclude[s] unorthodox believers" (116). Furthermore, according to Waddington, the "line between fiction and autobiography is very wavering" in *The Second Scroll* and presents "serious problems" for the modernist critic (117). On the positive side, Waddington is intrigued by Klein's efforts to combine English and French words with Yiddish idioms and Hebrew syntax (126). Ultimately, however, her only consoling judgment is that the "occasional failure is the price of all experimentation" (130).

Critics further into the postmodern period see the absence of masterful closure in Klein's writing as a positive attribute; his toying with autobiography enhances their theories of plural subjectivity; and his strange diction becomes a pioneering gesture of transculturation. For example, Sherry Simon makes the linguistic prowess of Klein a cornerstone of her excellent book *Translating Montreal*, although she acknowledges that Klein was "a failed translator" if "successful translation is replacing one coherent linguistic system by another.... His strategy was to remain between languages, forcing the limits of English, subjecting it to the strain of alien vocabulary" (63). We need to revisit *The Second Scroll* to apply a similar logic to Klein's narrative method if we are to appreciate the full measure of his brilliance.

Klein was certainly capable of masterful modernist closure, and the conclusion of his poem "Portrait of the Poet as Landscape" demonstrates that he was able to convert the angst of personal defeat into the epiphany of artistic success. However, the magnitude of the tragic subject matter in *The Second Scroll*, wherein Klein set out to celebrate Israel as the "consolation of our people's rescue," as Klein described the Jewish state in a letter to Edel (qtd. in Mayne, "Afterword," 138), perhaps forced him to acknowledge the limits of art and statecraft to redress the horrors of the Holocaust.

Kevin McNeilly offers such an anti-epic reading of Klein in his essay "All Poets Are Not Jews: Transgression and Satire in A. M. Klein." McNeilly is interested in the way that the contortions of the German language in the poetry of Paul Celan force readers to "confront the unspeakable and the untranslatable, and we are led to experience through language the sense of marginality and alienation that Celan as a Holocaust survivor scourged by guilt knows intrinsically as a Jew" (419). McNeilly sees similar contortions and lacunae in Klein's 1944 mock-epic *The Hitleriad*:

No response but satiric grotesquery – its bathos revealing the inadequacy of language to catch the cosmic criminal magnitude of Auschwitz – is possible in such a poem if one accepts anything like Adorno's prohibition on poetry after Auschwitz: to see the human in the engineers of the death camps, to rationalize the unthinkable, to make a poem as anything other than grotesquely bombastic, is to lapse (inadvertently and even understandably, perhaps) into a saccharine humanism that belies the magnitude of the crime itself and that finally makes a mockery – in Adorno's phrase – of the victims' death. Klein has no stylistic choice but poetic failure. Klein's humanism has no alternative but to betray – verbally and poetically – its untenability. (436)

McNeilly's essay draws useful attention to Klein's satirical wit, but the more pressing concern for Klein's legacy remains his use of the lyric voice. McNeilly touches on this issue when he reconstitutes a phrase from Klein's elegy "The Cripples," which draws a comparison between Klein's own early faith and that of the pilgrims at Oratoire St Joseph, and argues that "[Klein's] poetry deliberately and formally acknowledges that it is, as all post-Auschwitz writing must be, *crippled*: 'And I who in my own faith once had faith like this, / but have not now, am crippled more than they'" (McNeilly 436; Klein, *Selected Poems*, 107–8). Following McNeilly's line of argument, one might ask: Did Klein rewrite his journalistic account in the lyric voice in *The Second Scroll* to cripple epic, or perhaps to expose the untenability of epic?

Not quite.

Lyrical Prose

I believe Klein's genius in this novel is to make both epic and lyric readings possible – to place in dialogue two systems and world views across the gap between scrolls. If one reads the novel as Melech's story and moves through it in Talmudic fashion, then it is an epic tale of Zionist unification. However, if one reads the novel in the Western, secular fashion, it becomes the story of a Canadian who outlives his uncle and carries the novel past its midpoint, who resists the pull to move to Israel in favour of the cosmopolitan euphoria and guilt of the Diaspora, who blurs fiction and non-fiction, biography and autobiography, while compiling a multilingual anthology of lyric poetry.

Indeed, if one reads *The Second Scroll* in this fashion, then one has a template for many novels by Canadian poets in subsequent decades. Klein's anthology conceit, which adds a prose framework to the modernist collection of fragments, becomes an organizing principle in Cohen's first novel, *The Favourite Game*, which in its draft version bore the subtitle "*An Anthology*" (Nadel 89). It also helps to make sense of the two-part structure of Anne Michaels' *Fugitive Pieces*, wherein a Canadian scholar collects the fragments of the poet Jakob Beer. Conversely, Michaels' theory of poetry illuminates Klein's elliptical style because Michaels argues that "great poems are steeped in failure. Their measure is the depth of ignorance they reach in us. The mystery contained in the best poems is bottomless" ("Cleopatra's Love" 15). Michaels elevates this failure, which for her represents a confrontation with emotional and cognitive limits, into a stylistic principle to guide her writing: "A real power of words," she says, "is that they make our ignorance more precise. Writing is negative aspiration: to work strenuously towards the moment when failure is confirmed" ("Unseen Formations" 97). This sensibility also affects the manner in which characters comprehend what they have read about the Holocaust in *Fugitive Pieces*: "A camp inmate looked up at the stars and suddenly remembered that they'd once seemed beautiful to him. This memory of beauty was accompanied by a bizarre stab of gratitude. When I first read this I couldn't quite imagine it. But later I felt I understood. Sometimes the body experiences a revelation because it has abandoned every other possibility" (53). Thus, for Michaels, failure is part of the process of developing new forms of empathy and understanding. "Science," as Michaels points out, "is full of stories of discoveries made when one error corrects another" (284). The failure of intention can have productive – if oblique, unforeseen, and limited – outcomes provided that one engage in the search.

Modern Failures

Elizabeth Popham demonstrates that Klein's anthology conceit stems from his 1949 declaration in the *Canadian Jewish Chronicle* that a new Haggadah was waiting to be written in the new state of Israel ("Introduction" vii). The Haggadah is the Jewish book of blessings, anecdotes, parables, and legends connected to the *seder* ritual at Passover. However, Popham also sees modern precedents in Klein's vision of the cultural work performed by anthologists and anthologies. In formulating the character of the nephew, Klein may have had in mind the globe-trotting exploits of his "correspondent and publisher James Laughlin of New Directions Press, compiler of many influential anthologies of modernist writing" (Popham, "Introduction," xiii). Popham also argues that Klein's anthologist is "emulating the nationalist mission of Canadians A.J.M. Smith, Ralph Gustafson, and E.K. Brown, who in the 1940s had attempted to redefine the canon of Canadian literature in their anthologies" (xiii). The nephew tries, but largely fails, to emulate these modernist examples for the Zionist cause. He places the blame for this failure on the inability of modern Jewish poets to articulate Israel's poetic principle, not on his own efforts.

And yet, by the time Klein wrote *The Second Scroll*, many of the major modernist writers in English were already aware of the limits of their totalizing ambitions. Ezra Pound begins his long poem "Hugh Selwyn Mauberley" (1920) by acknowledging the bankruptcy of his early, more traditional compositions:

> For three years, out of key with his time,
> He strove to resuscitate the dead art
> Of poetry; to maintain "the sublime"
> In the old sense. Wrong from the start – (187)

However, the poem immediately deflects blame for this failure onto the poet's audience and age:

> No, hardly, but seeing he had been born
> In a half savage country, out of date;
> Bent resolutely on wringing lilies from the acorn; (187)

The remainder of the poem makes a case for Pound's belief that he gave the world the poetry demanded by the age, a poetry that bears a closer resemblance to "A prose kinema" than to "the 'sculpture' of rhyme" (188). Through the persona of Mauberley, Pound makes claims to literary success and mimesis, even if he despises the age his poetry reflects. Certainly, Mauberley's cinematic vision of poetry as a series of framed images or painterly "medallion[s]" (200) grew in influence over the course of the twentieth century and perhaps goes some way to explaining Klein's reading of the medallions on the ceiling of the Sistine Chapel in *The Second Scroll* and Cohen's fascination with the framed image in *The Favourite Game*.

However, Cohen skewers the hubris of Pound-like artists in his novels. Ultimately, Cohen and Klein address the shortcomings of art from a humble position more akin to that of T.S. Eliot. In *Four Quartets*, a collection of poems rewritten and published in the 1940s, Eliot laments:

So here I am, in the middle way, having had twenty
years –
Twenty years largely wasted, the years of *l'entre deux guerres* –
Trying to learn to use words, and every attempt
Is a wholly new start, and a different kind of failure
Because one has only learnt to get the better of words
For the thing one no longer has to say, or the way in which
One is no longer disposed to say it. And so each venture
Is a new beginning, a raid on the inarticulate
With shabby equipment always deteriorating
In the general mess of imprecision of feeling,
Undisciplined squads of emotion. (Eliot, "Four Quartets,"
182)

Here, Eliot comes dangerously close to the sense of frumpy humiliation that he had earlier mocked in "The Love Song of J. Alfred Prufrock" (1917):

I am no prophet – and here's no great matter;
I have seen the moment of my greatness flicker,
And I have seen the eternal Footman hold my coat, and snicker
(Eliot, "Prufrock," 15)

However, Eliot's "failure" in "Four Quartets" is redeemed by its insistence on bold new ventures, on raiding the inarticulate. Pound may have insisted on a more dominant outcome, but the postmodern position bears a closer resemblance to Eliot's entropic sense of perpetual new beginnings.

Failing in Canada

Michaels' argument against totalizing forms challenges the Zionist reading of *The Second Scroll*, but it doesn't make the novel any less a part of Jewish tradition in Canada. For example, in trying to explain the titular premise of Cohen's *Beautiful Losers* (1966), Patricia Morley observes that there is a strong Jewish-Canadian basis for its attitude towards loss: "Writing of the Jewish community in Canada, Rabbi Stuart Rosenberg notes that the age-old Jewish struggle to draw success out of failure has a general parallel in the shorter Canadian experience. He quotes an unidentified observer to the effect that the Canadian character is marked by the knowledge of failure" (137). Morley supports this argument about national character by demonstrating that the novelist Hugh MacLennan, Cohen's teacher at McGill, wrote an essay entitled "The Canadian Character" in which he makes a similar point. MacLennan's essay reflects his own ethnic bias, but the underlying sentiment resonates with Cohen's work: "The three founding groups of this nation, French, Loyalist and Highland Scots, 'became Canadians because the nations or factions to which they had belonged suffered total defeat in war. It was in their response to the challenge of these three separate defeats, a response which in each case was remarkably similar, that the common denominator in the Canadian character was forged'" (Morley 137–8; MacLennan 10). In *Beautiful Losers*, Cohen adds Jews, Africans, and Aboriginals to this list of what he calls the "pack of failures" (5) who search for a new paradigm of nationhood that will bring about the imagined "Magic Canada" in the conclusion of the novel (172). Cohen thereby links failure to visionary experience such that even falling short of "magic" is preferable to fulfilling more modest ambitions.

Ruth Panofsky's *The Force of Vocation: The Literary Career of Adele Wiseman* suggests one possible explanation for the prevalence of this notion of productive failure in Jewish-Canadian writing. Panofsky demonstrates that, as the child of immigrants from war-torn Russia, Wiseman – who won the Governor General's Award in 1956 for her first novel, *The Sacrifice*, a story about survivors of a pogrom – felt a powerful obligation to use her talents to document the experience of Jews in the postwar period, even if this task necessarily exceeded her abilities:

There was very little of innocence about the world into which I
emerged as a young adult. We were counting our dead.... In the
counting of our dead I had more dead than I could ever count....
I did not feel guilt because I survived; I felt the responsibility,
rather, in some sense to make the dead survive through me. (qtd.
in Panofsky 4–5)

The prosperity and mobility Wiseman experienced as a Canadian
in this period only compounded her sense of duty because she was
empowered to do and say things that were suppressed among her
parents' generation. Like the nephew in *The Second Scroll*, also a
descendent of Ukrainian Jews, Wiseman dedicated her resources to
a literary project of witnessing that was both in demand and impossible: "In my own work, which has for me the force of vocation, to
aim for other than the highest would be not only self-destructive but
worse, boring. To aim for and miss the highest is only failure. Not
to aim for the highest is betrayal" (qtd. in Panofsky 5). Although
the voice Wiseman employs in *The Sacrifice* does not resemble the
priestly or prophetic models developed by Klein and (later) Cohen,
the author's underlying sense of vocation is made clear by Panofsky's
choice of title.

The visionary role of Montrealers in Canadian and Québécois culture and politics, a role Cohen was eager to dramatize in the 1960s,
is placed in a historical context by Peter Van Toorn in his "'Introduction' to *Cross/cut: Contemporary English Quebec Poetry*." Van
Toorn argues that, in both English and French, poets who assume
this visionary role have to confront a foundational sense of loss and
reinvent their respective cultures with this loss in full view:

What such an indigenous Québécois poetry (as distinct from a
colonial or derivative poetry) does seem to bear out is a commitment to becoming adjusted to origins. This commitment to locat-
ing a source, an original starting point, a free slate, redeemed
from history, is a commitment to a particular experience, one of
defeat, resignation, containment, endurance, ascesis, and faith
rooted in social vision. This attention to origins, to an authentic
point of arrival, is also an attention to final things, to a radiant
point of departure. Such an apocalyptic attention must arrange
itself in metaphors of becoming to match the unconscious

ambivalence of the Canadian imagination to history itself. (Van Toorn 54)

The apocalyptic conclusions of *The Second Scroll* and *Beautiful Losers* animate this process of becoming by trying to convert an experience of loss into one of growth through the creation of a sacred space from which a new social order emanates.

However, whereas English-Canadian authors and politicians in the nineteenth century could at least dream of a dominant anglophone culture from sea to sea, francophones have been much more acutely aware of their precarious condition, as well as the crucial role of Quebec in sustaining the French language in North America. Émile Martel succinctly described this condition at the 2008 conference entitled Are We American? Canadian Culture in North America. The poet, translator, and diplomat argued that the strength of Québécois culture derives from a creative tension produced by the confrontation of francophones with the demographic mass that surrounds them in North America. Out of this tension emerges a creativity and an *américanité* that distinguishes the Québécois from their counterparts in France: "Notre force est grande parce que nos racines historiques sont profondes, mais aussi parce que nous sommes en état de résistance face à tous qui nous entourent. Et cette résistance exclue la victoire. C'est la tension maintenue entre notre groupe minoritaire et la majorité qui nous entoure qui nous nourris, nous explique, et nous légitime" (Martel).[3] Klein saw commonalities between the minority experience of French Catholics and Jews in North America, and he admired the Québécois for the resilient ways in which they combine language, faith, and a strong sense of place (Popham, "Introduction," xi). When Klein turns his attention to Israel in *The Second Scroll*, he sees a small Jewish population confronting a large Muslim population in Palestine, and he makes allusions to Jonah's emerging from the belly of a whale – allusions that would not have been out of place in a Catholic sermon in Quebec in the 1950s. A decade later, in the secularizing era of the Quiet Revolution, Cohen embraced the cultural politics of Québécois artists who were aggressively confronting the anglophone majority in Canada. In 1968, Cohen turned down the Governor General's Award for poetry out of sympathy for the process of decolonization Quebec was undergoing – although his support stopped short of advocating for the outright separation of Quebec as an independent state. When one looks for precedents for Cohen's openness to Québécois culture, one does not look to Irving Layton and Mordecai Richler, the Montreal authors to whom Cohen is most frequently compared, but to Klein.

Reappraising the Montreal Moderns

And yet, by stressing these overlooked connections to Klein, I do not want to dismiss the influence of Layton. A recent example of how Cohen converts the passive sense of failure as defeat into an active embrace of failure as a medium for producing difference can be found in "Layton's Question," a short poem in *Book of Longing* (2006) that was perhaps inspired by Cohen's visits to his ailing mentor:

Always after I tell him
what I intend to do next,
Layton solemnly inquires:
Leonard, are you sure
you're doing the wrong thing?
(87)

Cohen also affirms his debt to Layton, Klein, and the Montreal moderns on his 2004 album *Dear Heather*. The album begins with a cover of "Go No More A-Roving" that is dedicated to Layton and features a Cohen drawing of Layton in the liner notes (1). Six songs later, Cohen adapts to music F.R. Scott's "Villanelle for Our Time" and includes a drawing of Scott by his wife Marian Scott (8), a leading member of the Beaver Hall group of painters who pioneered an urban vision of modern painting in Canada. Four songs later, Cohen adapts to music his early poem "To a Teacher," which is dedicated to A.M. Klein. The album's liner notes include a Cohen drawing of Klein with his mind wreathed in holy fire (12). The Klein tribute is followed by a song called "The Faith," which is "based on a Québec folk song" (13), and follows a pattern of French-English translation that is fundamental to Cohen's merging of American folk music and *les chansons québécoises et françaises*. Confronted with the passing of the moderns as a generation and the decline of cultural productions (such as the *chanson*) and value systems (such as the faith-based communities of Jewish and Catholic Montreal) that shaped Cohen's youth, the artist seems determined to position his legacy in relation to them. The album is therefore dedicated to the "memory of / Jack McClelland / 1922–2004," Cohen's long-time publisher at McClelland and Stewart and a driving force behind literary nationalism in Canada in the 1960s and 1970s (15). This dedication page also features a photograph of Cohen in formal attire with his head bowed near a painted portrait of his father (a clothing manufacturer) and beside a replica of a tall ship with a cross-shaped mast, which evokes the Catholic mariner's church in Montreal's Old Port that Cohen made famous in his song "Suzanne."

Zailig Pollock's thesis in *A.M. Klein: The Story of the Poet* (1994) helps to make sense of Klein's position in relation to postmodern authors such as Cohen and modern authors such as Scott. Pollock argues that Klein's career as a writer revolves around "retellings [of] the story of the poet" as a unifying figure in a chaotic world, "drawing on the same basic set of characters, images, and gestures, and unfolding the same central vision, a vision of the One in the Many" (3). The key image in this story is the artist's "unfolding" of truth from the divine scroll. However, Pollock cautions that "any adequate account of Klein's achievement must go beyond the metaphor of unfolding and its claim to mastery, to acknowledge the impotence in the heart of Klein's struggle with his subject – and Klein's growing awareness of this impotence" (7), which reaches a state of crisis when Klein tries to make sense of the Holocaust in *The Second Scroll*. Pollock argues that the heroic conclusion of Melech's narrative is strained and unconvincing because it depends on the Christian notion of the Messiah as martyr; and this martyr is celebrated as a national hero even though, in his short time in Israel, Melech had "remained in relative obscurity, known only to a small circle of kabbalists in Safed" (250). Likewise, Pollock argues that the nephew's quest "to find the great Israeli poet, the new Bialik, has been a failure. His attempt to find a substitute for this poet in the inventions of copywriters, who exploit the language of the Bible to advertise insurance, dry-cleaning, or ice cream, is paradoxical to say the least. Elsewhere, Klein expresses contempt for the debasement of language by commerce, and for the connivance of poets in the process" (248–9). Given Klein's inability to find symbolic or poetic redress for the horrors of the Holocaust, Pollock endorses

Edward Alexander's assertion that writing on the Holocaust and its aftermath is "one of those problematic human enterprises in which some degree of failure or inadequacy is almost a precondition of success, in which we can expect no more than a shattered majesty and a noble imperfection" (251). On the other hand, Pollock maintains that the novelist's failure to encompass the historical event is not a defeat of the novelist on the level of craft because Klein makes the reader aware of his artifice. There is an element of self-reflexivity in the short novel that calls attention to the impossibly huge task the author has set himself. The glosses seem specifically designed to accentuate the author's fallibility as well as the limitations of language and logic. For example, the nephew's elegy for Melech in Gloss Beth was composed prior to Melech's death and then recast as a "premonition" of the uncle's demise after Melech briefly re-entered the nephew's life (23, 92–6).[4]

To understand the element of fallibility in Klein's novel, it would be useful to reprise an argument Elizabeth Popham has made that the self-as-centrepoint of time and space guided Klein's writing practice until the 1950s, when that unifying point was somehow decentred. I would argue that *The Second Scroll* marks this splitting point because the Zionism it dramatizes also forced Klein to choose between two great loves: Israel and Montreal. Klein was, on the one hand, a Zionist enthralled by the mythic force of reunification and, on the other hand, "a man who felt profoundly at home in the public spaces as well as in his own personal place in Montreal," as D.M.R. Bentley demonstrates through a reading of Klein's architectural metaphors (22). Mayne notes how this split marks the principal characters in the novel: "Both nephew and uncle find immediate source and relation in Klein himself, the writer who put poems and prose passages first published under his own name into the mouths, so to speak, of his two key characters. That these voices echo each other suggests how much Klein invested of himself into this work, perhaps more so than in any other of his writings except for a few signature poems" ("Afterword" 141). The Melech-oriented reading favours the choice of Israel and situates Melech at the "centre of a whirlwind" of Jewish reunification (*Second Scroll* 86); however, the translator-oriented reading anticipates the recursive and fragmented narratives that subsequent poet-novelists would employ to pair questions of formal and social innovation in milieux where cultural unity is an impossibility. The two main characters also represent different kinds of subject formation. Whereas Klein connects Melech to the synthetic, modernist ideal of "efflorescent impersonality" (79), which is everywhere felt but nowhere incarnate, the translator on his journey through Montreal, Rome, Casablanca, and Jerusalem explores the various positions of "I" – a distinction Cohen noted was crucial to his own appreciation of Klein's more vulnerable and incarnate moments (Siemerling, "Leonard Cohen," 147).

Although Cohen and Waddington criticized Klein for conforming to an ideological "line," it is worth noting that Klein led the move from Yiddish to English in Montreal and sought alternatives to strictly Jewish modes of expression and conduct. Naïm Kattan reports that Klein was haunted by accusations of hypocrisy because he did not support his praise of Israel by actually moving there (*A.M. Klein* 80), and Rachel Feldhay Brenner points to one of Klein's final publications, "In Praise of the Diaspora" (1953), as evidence that he too sought alternatives to the Zionism that unsettled Waddington (*A.M. Klein* ii). I would therefore point to a need for critics to pay closer attention to the unorthodox translator who refuses to abandon Canada and enjoys concocting fantasies about his uncle as a Communist leader or a Jewish Pope that are, by his own admission, "perverse" (Klein, *Second Scroll*, 38) – but perverse in a fashion that foreshadows the cross-cultural journeys of the protagonists in novels by Cohen and Michaels.

Conclusion

Klein pushed the modernist impulse as far as any Canadian writer, and he crashed headlong into the problems of indeterminacy and the failure of grand narratives that become the central preoccupations of postmodernism. For Klein this collision was tragic, as Pollock demonstrates. The legacy of a writer is not determined principally by how well he lives up to his youthful dreams and adult ambitions but, rather, by how readers and writers of subsequent generations respond to his work.

Following Klein there is an abundance of Canadian writers who emphasize the failures of Canada to fit the standard templates of nationhood in order to highlight the innovative potential of Canadian writing. For example, in "For Play and Entrance: The Contemporary Canadian Long Poem," Robert Kroetsch argues that the "long poem, by its very length, allows the exploration of the failure of system and grid. The poem of that failure is a long poem" ("Play and Entrance" 118). Arguing that the grand gestures of epic have been rendered undesirable by the cataclysmic events of the twentieth century, Kroetsch states in *Completed Field Notes* that "the eloquence of failure may be the only eloquence remaining in our time" ("Author" 269). These quotations are worth keeping in mind when one considers that George Bowering adds *The Second Scroll* to his list of great twentieth-century long poems in *The New Long Poem Anthology* (351). However, Kroetsch adapts his theories of the long poem to a more general statement about writing in Canada in *The Impossible Sum of Our Traditions: Reflections on Canadian Culture*. There, Kroetsch argues that "Canada is as timeless as winter, a nightmarish dream of what might and cannot be .... The Canadian writer must uninvent the word. He must destroy the homonymous English and American languages that keep him from hearing his own tongue. But to uninvent the word, he knows, is to uninvent the world. He writes ... knowing that ... to succeed is to fail" (23). If, according to this logic, Klein destroyed the homonymous English and American languages that kept him from hearing his own tongue and drew instead on his vast knowledge of Jewish and Latin cultures, then his writing might be considered a postmodern success. For instance, Klein undoes centuries of Christian theology and art history through an "audacious act of creative misreading" of the panels of the Sistine Chapel in the lyrical essay that Pollock considers a key to understanding the processes of dismemberment and "re-membering" in Klein's oeuvre (*A.M. Klein* 220–30). The self-consciously errant nature of this reading, as Pollock observes, becomes a standard trick of postmodern writing.

To conclude, I would argue that the genre of the novel did not defeat Klein; rather, he reinvented it for subsequent poets, such as Cohen, Michaels, Kroetsch, Michael Ondaatje, Joy Kogawa and George Elliott Clarke, all of whom make use of the hybrid form to address the devastation and fragmentation of their respective cultures as well as their reinvention in Canada. As Tom Marshall argues, "Klein has bequeathed to his successors the task of creating their country" (*A.M. Klein* xxv) so that questions of Canadian cosmopolitanism rise directly out of Jewish ones, yet without positioning religion as the absolute basis of group identity.

Notes

1 This comparison was suggested to me by Richler's biographer, Charles Foran, in conversation.

ELIZABETH POPHAM

1 Klein shared his anxieties on the issue with Kennedy and solicited his assistance placing reviews in mainstream publications. Typical of their exchanges is Kennedy's letter of 6 May 1940 (Klein Fonds, LAC, ms 83), in which he writes that he has sent notice of the publication of *Hath Not a Jew* ... to a number of potential reviews but advises Klein to publish a volume of "non-sectarian stuff" as soon as possible. On 12 November (Klein Fonds, LAC, 110–12), he cautions: "You say that you are interested in being reviewed in other journals than the Anglo-Jewish group ... but if you're not publishing other than the Menorah and Jewish opinion type of thing, the answer is that you won't get reviewed outside the Anglo-Jewish field, unless they're written by pals like myself."

2 For Richler, the most damning evidence of Klein's role as Bronfman's "indentured poet" was that "degrading himself and his sullen craft, Klein obliged with more than one hosanna in verse" (*Saturday Night*, July/August 1992, 15).

3 As Caplan admits in the preface to *Like One That Dreamed*, his modus operandi is not conventionally academic. As the archivist who, in 1973, organized the Klein Papers and prepared the finding guide for the National Archives of Canada, Caplan had extraordinary access to Klein's unpublished writing. The "montage" he assembled from images,

interviews, and fragments from Klein's published and unpublished writing creates a powerful portrait of the writer and his milieu, which has subsequently been elaborated, but not superseded, in such studies as Zailig Pollock's literary biography *A.M. Klein: The Story of the Poet.*

4 For a transcription of the full application, see Heft, "Lost A.M. Klein."

5 Like Usher Caplan in *Like One That* Dreamed (218), I feel that the absence of draft material in the Klein Papers points to Klein's destruction of the Joyce commentary sometime after 15 October 1952 when he wrote to Leon Edel that he was "putting my Joyce work aside" (Edel Papers, McGill). Harold Heft, in "Some Apocalyptic Discoveries: A History of A.M. Klein's Troubled Involvement in James Joyce Studies," is more cynical: "there is no proof that Klein at any time in his life, was in the habit of destroying his work, regardless of his or the public's attitude toward it. Surely he would never have destroyed anything that he was as proud of as his Joyce scholarship?" (216). Heft's position is that Klein had completed very little in the way of commentary prior to the commencement of his correspondence with Mason, that he "borrowed" the ideas for his three published articles on Joyce from Mason, and that his progress on the Joyce commentary effectively ceased in 1949 with the end of their exchange of letters (219–27). An equally plausible conclusion is that the line-by-line commentary had been initially set aside in favour of the more discursive commentary attempted in Klein's articles – a venue in which Klein was able to preempt Mason's objections to his piecemeal annotations. There is no doubt that Klein's best critical work was written in real or imagined debate, and that his correspondence with Ellsworth Mason provided a catalyst for his published articles, particularly in the case of their shared interest in Vico. Subsequent exchanges with Leon Edel and Joyce critic John J. Slocum show Klein intermittently returning to his project between 1949 and 1952, though with less intensity than evidenced in the Mason letters.

6 Many letters include secretarial notations (e.g., "AMK/FP"). In his letter to A.J.M. Smith dated 5 November 1943, Klein's second postscript reads: "Pardon the rudeness of a dictated letter. I began by writing it by hand, but found I could not reread it."

7 Sandor Klein, himself a lawyer, describes Klein's legal style as distinctly impersonal.

8 The book is literally a work of art, with – as we are informed on pages devoted to "The Artists" and "The Printer" – thirty-one "specially commissioned" illustrations (ten in full colour) and nine maps by prominent

Canadian artists, including W.J. Phillips and F.H. Varley, printed on "a cream finish Paragon Book paper of Canadian manufacture which was made especially for the book."

9 The difficulties were apparently insurmountable, and the French edition was not published.

10 Caplan notes that this dedication was "found among Klein's hand-written drafts for the personal inscriptions that Sam Bronfman was to write in his gift copies of Stephen Leacock's history of Canada" (*Like One That Dreamed* 86). These provide fodder for Mordecai Richler's denigration of Klein as Bronfman's "indentured poet" in "Speak Easy of Sam Bronfman": "Complimentary copies were sent to George VI Rex Imperator, Haile Selasse, Jack Benny, and Marshall Joseph Stalin, each with a handwritten dedication composed by A.M. Klein and signed by Sam" (*Saturday Night*, July/August 1992, 15).

11 In *Solomon Gursky Was Here*, "L.B. would stand at the back of the hall listening to Mr. Bernard, watching him rake in acclaim for a poet's unacknowledged eloquence. Edgar Bergen and Charlie McCarthy, that's us, L.B. thought. It stung. But there were compensations" (18). In "Speak Easy of Sam Bronfman," Richler dismisses Bronfman's biographer, Michael R. Marrus, as a "house-broken academic" and a "fool": "Mind you, many years earlier, a better writer, A.M. Klein, was hired to fill the humiliating office of Sam's poet laureate" (*Saturday Night*, July/August 1992, 15).

12 A number of speakers at the Concordia conference, The Poet as Landscape: A Portrait of A.M. Klein Today (18–20 October 2007), speculated on the nature of Klein's relationship with Samuel Bronfman, viewing it through the lens of Richler's portrayal in *Solomon Gursky Was Here*. The issue was addressed most directly by David Leahy, in his "A.M. Klein: Mordecai Richler's Version," on 20 October.

13 Letter to Shonie Levi, Education Director for National Hadassah, 22 January 1948 (Shonie Levi, private collection).

14 In "Those Who Should Have Been Ours," Klein particularly "mourns" Shapiro's "denial" of his heritage because "[a] voice such as his had not been heard in American poetry – a perfect, an impeccable recreation in words of the very sound and texture of the American scene" (*Canadian Jewish Chronicle* [16 November 1945]; *Literary Essays and Reviews* 250, 248). In "Annotation on Shapiro's *Essay on Rime*," Klein had commented on Shapiro's "uncertainty about his position as a Jew in American letters ..., this feeling of alien-ness [that] disturbs Shapiro, disturbs him so much

that it takes on a pathogenic form" (*Canadian Jewish Chronicle* [22–29 March 1946]; *Literary Essays and Reviews* 175–6). By 1948, however, Shapiro had begun work on a series of autobiographical poems addressing his Jewish identity, later published as *Poems of a Jew* (New York: Random House, 1958). In addition, as one of the fellows in American Literature of the Library of Congress, he had voted against the controversial decision in 1948 to award the Bolligen Prize to Ezra Pound, and he had done so on the grounds of Pound's overt anti-Semitism.

15 On 25 June 1943, Louis E. Levinthall of the Jewish Publication Society had written to accept the collection, but negotiations continued throughout the fall as the press was demanding revisions to poems that members of the board found objectionable or "obscure," and Klein responded with detailed explanations of his poems (Jewish Publication Society Papers, box 24, Philadelphia Jewish Archives Center).

16 Letters to James Laughlin, New Directions Press, 12 January 1944 and 10 September 1943, respectively (New Directions).

17 Charney's letter of 16 January 1941 is in Yiddish. I am grateful to Mildred Gutkin for this translation.

18 Reviewer and anthologist, Clifton Fadiman hosted a radio program called *Information, Please*. Louis Untermeyer was a prominent poet, translator, and anthologist, who would be featured in the 1950s on the television show *What's My Line?* Bennett Cerf, publisher of Random House Books and the Modern Library series, also held forth on a popular radio show called *Books Are Bullets* in which he presented books that "conformed to the accepted interpretation of the war" (Farrell *Fate of Writing*). Keimberg (referred to in Klein's letters to Laughlin as "Kip") may be a misspelling of the surname of poet and anthologist Alfred Kreymborg, whose name seems to have been added to the list primarily because the letter "K" filled out Klein's acronym.

19 Ironically, Klein's public relations campaign for *The Hitleriad* was modelled point-by-point, right down to seeking the approval of Roosevelt, on Clifton Fadiman's guide to making a "best seller" found in the informal prologue to the anthology *Readings I've Liked* (1941).

20 Evidence that Laughlin shared Klein's opinions is provided in his correspondence with another of his authors, Delmore Schwartz. Writing to ask for a "blurb" from Schwartz for his *The World Is a Wedding* (1948), Laughlin alludes to his difficulties with Klein's *The Hitleriad*:

> You must write the blurb for the book yourself. I cannot handle the Jewish question. If I write that you describe the lives and thoughts of

the Jews more lovingly and more observingly than I have ever read before, then there will be people who will resent the fact that I single out Jews as being Jews and not just people. It is all too complex for me. In the case of Klein, I pointed out that he was a Jew and so offended all the crossed-over Jews like Untermeyer, Fadiman, Cerf etc., who like to see Jews succeed in the world but do not like to have them labelled as such. There is certainly no solution to the problem except that every-one should marry a Jew at one time and obliterate the tribe. Is that not right? (31 January 1948, qtd. in Phillips, *Delmore Schwartz*, 247–8)

21 Letter to Father Stanley Murphy, 28 June 1956 (Klein Fonds, LAC, MS 841). Klein did speak on Hopkins in Assumption College's Christian Culture series in October 1956. It was his last public lecture.

ROBERT MELANÇON

1 Klein, *Complete Poems*, 2:689, lines 1–6.
2 Klein, *Beyond Sambation*, 318.
3 Klein, *Complete Poems*, 2:678, line 1.
4 Ibid., 1:183, line 5.
5 Ibid., 2:634, line 1.
6 Ibid., 2:634. line 4.
7 Klein, *Beyond Sambation*, 340–1.
8 Klein, *Complete Poems*, 2:678, lines 1–4.
9 Ibid., 2:679, line 18.
10 Ibid., 2:651 lines 1–4.
11 Klein, *Second Scroll*, 23–5.
12 Klein, *Complete Poems*, 1:176.
13 Klein, *Second Scroll*, 32–3.
14 Klein, *Complete Poems*, 2:622, lines 25–32.
15 Klein, *Second Scroll*, 63.
16 Klein, *Comple.e Poems*, 2:622, line 33.
17 Ibid., 2:624, lines 1–8.
18 John Donne, *Devotions Upon Emergent Occasions and Death's Duel, Meditation xvii. Nunc Lento Sonitu dicunt, morieris*, 2. Available at www.anglicanlibrary.org/donne/devotions/devotions17.htm (viewed 27 September 2010).
19 Klein, *Complete Poems*, 1:168–9.
20 Klein, *Beyond Sambation*, 230–1.
21 Ibid., "Little Red Riding Houde," 46–7.

22 Klein, *Second Scroll*, 52.
23 Ibid.
24 Klein, *Beyond Sambation*, 463–77.
25 Ibid., 468–9.

REBECCA MARGOLIS

1 Brown, *Jew or Juif*, 159, asserts that this norm characterized the history of early Jewish immigration to Canada.
2 See Harshav, *Meaning of Yiddish*.
3 Letter to Shmuel Niger, cited in Caplan, *Like One That Dreamed*, 87. The letter is discussed more fully later in this study.
4 Waddington, *A.M. Klein*, 97, 133n5.
5 Fuerstenberg, "From Yiddish," 79, 70.
6 Pollock, *A.M. Klein*, 27–8.
7 Simon, "A.M. Klein as Pimontel," 65.
8 Fuerstenberg, "From Yiddish," 67.
9 Klein, *Collected Poems*, 271.
10 It was not until after the death of his mother in 1946 that Klein moved away from Yiddish as a living, spoken language. Comment by Sandor Klein following my lecture, *"Ken men tantsn af tsvey khasenes?"*
11 In 1931, only 3 percent of Jews declared themselves unable to speak English. By 1951, the Yiddish Mother Tongue statistic had fallen to less than half. See Rosenberg, *Canada's Jews*, 257, 255.
12 It was through this club that, in 1924, he met David Lewis, a recent immigrant from Poland. Klein taught Lewis English and engaged in lively discussions about Jewish politics in Yiddish with him and his father in their home. See Caplan, *Like One That Dreamed*, 35.
13 Fuerstenberg, "From Yiddish," 66–9; Kattan, *A.M. Klein*, 30–1.
14 Caiserman, *Yidishe dikhter in kanade*, 167.
15 See Roskies, "Yiddish in Montreal."
16 Klein, *Beyond Sambation*, 3.
17 Ibid., 8.
18 Klein, *Literary Essays and Reviews*, 4.
19 Menkis points to articles by David Lewis that promote the simultaneous existence of two literatures – Yiddish and Hebrew – in the *Judaean*. Menkis, "A.M. Klein and Jewish Youth Cultures."
20 Pollock "To Be Talked About."
21 Waddington, *A.M. Klein*, 61–2.

22 *Judaean* 5.2 (June 1932): 2, 5, 6; *Canadian Jewish Chronicle* (hereafer CJC), 23 September 1932, 5, 16; CJC, 7 April 1944, 9–10; CJC, 30 August 1946, 6.

23 CJC, 28 November 1952, 5, 12, 19; CJC, 26 December 1952; CJC, 2 January 1953, 4.

24 Klein, *Literary Essays and Reviews*, 109, 113.

25 For example, *Der Keneder Adler* (hereafter KA), 10 May 1939, 6; and CJC, 12 May 1939, 4.

26 For example, CJC, 14 June 1940, 3; and CJC, 12 September 1952, 3.

27 For example, CJC, 28 April 1939, 4.

28 CJC, 19 May 1939, 3; CJC, 31 March 1944, 4.

29 CJC, 8 December 1939, 3; CJC, 14 May 1943, 3; CJC, 2 December 1949, 3, 15; CJC, 12 March 1954, 3, 6.

30 KA, 2 January 1941, 6; and CJC, 3 January 1941, 4, 16; CJC, 4 February 1944, 4, 15; CJC, 16 November 1945, 14; CJC, 5 October 1945, 8.

31 11 September 1942, reproduced in Klein, *Beyond Sambation*, 166.

32 27 April 1945, reproduced in Klein, *Beyond Sambation*, 233.

33 Waddington, *A.M. Klein*, 7.

34 Ibid., 98.

35 Cited in Caplan, *Like One That Dreamed*, 87.

36 Ibid.

37 Ibid.

38 Ibid.

39 Ibid., 140.

40 Cited in Klein, *Collected Poems*, appendix, 350.

41 Caplan, *Like One That Dreamed*, 141.

42 Cited in Caplan, *Like One That Dreamed*, 164.

43 Pollock, *A.M. Klein*, 19.

44 Fuerstenberg, "Yiddish Influences," 75.

45 Caplan, *Like One That Dreamed*, 65.

46 Waddington, *A.M. Klein*, 6–29, 88–9, 126–30.

47 Waddington, *Folklore in the Poetry of A.M. Klein*.

48 Gotlieb, "Hassidic Influences," 47–64.

49 CJC, 19–27 March, 19–26 September, 1939.

50 The *purimshpil* is a tradition of public performances for the Jewish holiday of Purim that arose in the Middle Ages. See Sandrow, *Vagabond Stars*, 1–20.

51 Fischer, "A.M. Klein's Forgotten Play," 42.

52 Fuerstenberg, "Yiddish Influences," 75–7, 84.

53 Caplan, *Like One That Dreamed*, 188.

54 *CJC*, 25 July 1941, 3; *CJC*, 26 September 1952, 4.

55 These translations appeared between 1944 and 1947. See Pollock et al., *A.M. Klein*, 31–4, for a complete listing.

56 Pollock, *A.M. Klein*, 30.

57 *CJC*, 9 September 1932, 5.

58 Rozmovits, "Klein's Translations."

59 Ibid., 3.

60 Ibid., 7.

61 Cited in Rozmovits, "Klein's Translations," 5.

62 Rozmovits, "Klein's Translations," 7.

63 Rozmovits, "Klein's Translations."

64 Esther Frank, personal interview, 2007.

65 Kaplan, "A More Contemporary Voice," 132.

66 Rozmovits, "Klein's Translations," 7; Pollock, *A.M. Klein*, 30.

67 A handful of translations appeared between 1931 and Segal's death. See Pollock et al., *A.M. Klein*, 30–3, for a complete listing.

68 *CJC*, 14 November 1930, 14–8; *CJC*, 2 November 1945, 8, 16; *CJC*, 9 June 1950, 5.

69 Fuerstenberg, "From Yiddish," 67.

70 Klein, *Literary Essays and Reviews*, 10.

71 *CJC*, 1 November 1945, cited in Klein, *Literary Essays and Reviews*, 49.

72 Klein, *Literary Essays and Reviews*, 50.

73 Ibid., 87.

74 This is the title of Klein's review of Segal's *Sefer yidish* [The Books of Yiddish] 1950.

75 Fuerstenberg, "From Yiddish," 70.

76 Waddington, *A.M. Klein*, 82–8.

77 Caplan, *Like One That Dreamed*, 112.

78 Greenstein, *Third Solitudes*, 35.

79 Waddington, *A.M. Klein*, 98–9.

80 "Literarishe velt" [Literary World], *KA*, 8 September 1944, 7.

81 Klein, *Collected Poems of A.M. Klein*, 206.

82 "Literarishe velt" [Literary World], *KA*, 15 September 1944, 7.

83 Caplan, *Like One That Dreamed*, 114.

84 Ibid.

85 Wolofsky, *Journey of My Life*.

86 Anctil, "Wolofsky *ibergesetst*."

87 CJC, 11 October 1940. Cited in Klein, *Literary Essays and Reviews*, 22.
88 Reider, "Modern Renaissance of Jewish Music," 64; Werner, "Of Jewish Music," 277.
89 Norich, *Discovering Exile*.
90 Klein, *Beyond Sambation*, 477.
91 *A.M. Klein: Portrait of a Poet as Landscape*. VHS. Directed by David Kaufman.
92 Ibid.
93 Caplan, *Like One That Dreamed*, 213.

IRA ROBINSON

1 Caplan, "Introduction," in *A.M. Klein*, xiii.
2 On A.M. Klein, see Pollock, *A.M. Klein*; Marshall, *A.M. Klein*; Caplan, *Like One That Dreamed*; Waddington, *A.M. Klein*; Fischer, *In Search of Jerusalem*; Lester, "Of Kith and Kin." Cf. Pollock, Caplan, and Rozmovits, *A.M. Klein*.
3 Cited in Caplan, *Like One That Dreamed*, 8, 71.
4 Pollock, *A.M. Klein*, 33, cf. 40.
5 Spiro, *Tapestry for Designs*. Solomon B. Isaac (1040–1105), known to Jews by the acronym "Rashi," wrote the most definitive medieval Jewish commentaries on the Hebrew Bible and Babylonian Talmud. For nearly a millennium, Jews have looked to him as the commentator "par excellence".
6 Bulkeley, "Hypertext Bible Commentary."
7 Pollock, *A.M. Klein*, 27.
8 Caplan, "Introduction," in *A.M. Klein*, xiii.
9 Jacobson, *Modern Midrash*, 45–62; On Klein's translations of Bialik, see Kaplan, "A More Contemporary Voice."
10 Wolofsky, *Journey of My Life*.
11 It was published in 1930 under the title *Oyf Eybiken Kvall: Gedanken un batrachtungen fun dem hayntigen idishen leben un shtreben, in likht fun unzer alter un eybig-nayer tora, eingeteylt loyt di parshiyos fun der vokh* [From the Eternal Source: Thoughts and Observations from Contemporary Jewish Life and Aspirations in the Light of Our Old and Eternally New Torah, Organized According to the Weekly (Torah) Portions]. On this work, see Robinson, *Rabbis and Their Community*, 119–26. An English translation of this work was completed by Moishe Dolman and Ira Robinson.

12 Wolofsky, *Oyf Eybiken Kvall*, 7. Wolofsky was, in this attitude, similar to many immigrant Orthodox rabbis of his generation. Cf. Caplan, *Orthodoxy in the New World*.

13 It seems necessary to me that both Hebrew and Yiddish be used in this project because some of the poems speak to me in Hebrew, while others speak to me in Yiddish.

14 Cited in Caplan, *Like One That Dreamed*, 87.

15 Cf. Pollock, *A.M. Klein*, 71.

16 "To the Jewish Poet," 12. All citations of Klein's poetry come from Klein, *Collected Poems*, edited by Miriam Waddington.

17 Isaiah 6:10.

18 Klein, *Collected Poems*, 78–9.

19 Ibid., 144–5.

20 Klein, *Selected Poems*, 158.

21 Klein, *Collected Poems*, 128.

22 Ibid., 158.

23 Ibid., 181.

24 Ibid., 221.

25 Cf. Leviticus 14:5, 50; Numbers 19:17; Zachariah 14:8.

26 Klein, *Collected Poems*, 224.

27 Ibid., 225.

28 Rabbi Solomon ben Isaac (Rashi), commentary on Genesis 2:11.

29 Klein, *Collected Poems*, 283.

30 Ibid., 343.

31 Ibid., 345.

PIERRE ANCTIL

1 Klein, *Second Scroll*, 6.

2 Klein, *Complete Poems*, 1:298, lines 1–8.

3 Caiserman can be translated as follows: "His first poem appeared in *Menorah Journal* in 1927. The author then published in various Canadian and American literary journals. He was ready to go to press with a large book of poetry." *Yidishe dikhter in Kanade*, 219.

4 On Klein and proverbs see A.M. Klein Fonds, Library and Archives Canada, R3590. See also Peretz, *Selected Stories*, 96–102.

5 Caplan, *Like One That Dreamed*, 81.

6 Wolofsky, *Mayn lebns rayze*, 35.

7 My translation. Klein decided not to translate this passage into English.

8 Wolofsky, *Mayn lebns rayze*, 41.

9 My translation. Klein decided not to translate this passage into English.
10 Wolofsky, *Mayn lebns rayze*, 70.
11 My translation.
12 Wolofsky, *Journey of My Life*, 52.
13 Ibid., *Mayn lebns rayze*, 72.
14 My translation.
15 Wolofsky, *Journey of My Life*, 53.
16 Ibid., *Mayn lebns rayze*, 117–18.
17 My translation.
18 Wolofsky, *Mayn lebns rayze*, 219.
19 My translation.
20 Wolofsky, *Journey of My Life*, 154.
21 Ibid., 152.
22 Ibid., *Mayn lebns rayze*, 215.
23 My translation.
24 Wolofsky, *Journey of My Life*, 152.
25 Ibid., *Mayn lebns rayze*, 205.
26 My translation.
27 Wolofsky, *Journey of My Life*, 143.
28 Peretz, *Selected Stories*, 95.

LIANNE MOYES

1 I would like to thank Sherry Simon and Norman Ravvin for the impetus
   to work on Klein; Pierre Anctil and Rivka Augenfeld for suggesting I
   read Klein in the context of Yiddish-language poets; Shannon Hodge
   and Eiran Harris at the Montreal Jewish Public Library for their assistance in the Segal Archive; and Jozef Kwaterko and Robert Majzels for
   their critical dialogue. I am also grateful to Richard Cassidy for his
   library work in the early stages of the project. This chapter is excerpted
   from a longer discussion of Klein and Segal that will appear in my
   forthcoming book. Translations from French are mine unless otherwise
   specified.
2 Shtern arrived in Montreal in 1927.
3 Simon comments helpfully on the significance of Anctil's "translational
   act" (112).
4 Maze arrived in Montreal in 1908 and was, throughout the 1920s and
   1930s, a mentor for many writers.
5 Gotlib arrived in Montreal in 1930. His poetry collection *Montreal* was
   published posthumously in 1968.

6 Halpern arrived in New York in 1908. He lived in Montreal from April to October 1912. See Anctil's note (Shtern 338n100). See also the photograph of Halpern dated 1912, taken on l'Île Sainte-Hélène (Shtern 95).

7 Segal arrived in Montreal in 1911.

8 See Fuerstenberg, "From Yiddish," for a detailed discussion of various traces of Klein's relationship with Segal. Segal, it is worth noting, was editor at *Der Keneder Adler* from 1938 to 1945, roughly the same period that Klein was co-editor at the *Canadian Jewish Chronicle*. These two publications shared offices and printing facilities on St-Laurent (Fuerstenberg, "From Yiddish," 68–71).

9 Date of original publication, not of composition.

10 I have not been able to determine the year "Late Summer in Montreal" was written or, specifically, whether it predates or postdates Klein's "The Mountain," composed in 1947. The Segal Archive at the Montreal Jewish Public Library (in Yiddish) is indexed. Under the category "Poetry Manuscripts" (J.Y. Segal Microfilm S–1 through S–10) there are numerous boxes of manuscripts in no particular order. Segal did not date or consistently title his manuscripts. There are several boxes of clippings under the listing "Published Poems" (J.Y. Segal Microfilm S–14 and S–15), but "Late Summer in Montreal" is not among them. Given that Segal published a book in 1944 (*Lider un loybn*), I am assuming that "Late Summer in Montreal" was written between 1944 and 1950. More research is needed to determine if Segal, who was a prolific writer, collected his poems in approximately the order in which he wrote them. (The poem in question is printed on page 461 of *Seyfer Yidish*, a collection of 584 pages.)

11 Throughout the chapter, in parenthetical references to poems in Yiddish, I cite the translation I am using followed by the Yiddish-language original. For the purposes of continuity, I give preference to English-language translations where they exist.

12 "resplendent in the harsh light of the snow."

13 "All night the cross shines / who knows, for eternity?"

14 "Over great distances, it sends out its light / however pallid and wan."

15 Given that Halpern died in 1932, his visit to Shtern in Montreal must have taken place in the early 1930s. Shtern arrived in Montreal in 1927 but was at the Mont-Sinai sanatorium in Sainte-Agathe from 1928 to 1930.

16 See, for example, the poem "Strange" ["Fremd"] (qtd. in Friedman 23; Segal, *Lyric*, 267) as well as Segal's 1933 prose passage: "Here I run

around in the city already for two decades and still feel as strange as if I had just stepped off the boat" (qtd. in Fuerstenberg, "Transplanting Roots," 66).

17 Rue de la Gauchetière, site of present-day Chinatown, still bears traces of the old downtown Jewish district (Baker 45; Anctil, *Tur Malka*, 67).

18 "like a flight of savage birds / in a grey sky."

19 In this context, Pollock makes reference to Linda Luft Ferguson's argument that Klein all but ignored the "connotations assigned to Mount Royal in the literature and lives of the Québécois" (Ferguson 63). Ferguson refers here to Gabrielle Roy's *Bonheur d'occasion*, in which, in her words, "the mountain looms over the Québécois in working-class Montreal as a symbol of English wealth and power" (63). What Ferguson forgets, however, is that the mountain has more than one peak: the "mountain" of Roy's novel is the residential neighbourhood of Westmount; the "mountain" of Klein's poems is the public park designed by Frederick Law Olmsted in 1877. It would be unlikely for Klein's speaker, resident of the immigrant district to the east of Mount Royal, to have the same relation to Mount Royal Park that the residents of St. Henri had to Westmount.

20 This was not the first time Klein gave a mountain human qualities. A note in his "Raw Material" file from around 1943 (*Notebooks*) is far more explicit: "Mountains get lonely. Have only each to each to speak to. Get tired, look about for others. Sometimes will speak even to hills. After all a hill is a mountain lying down" (Klein, "Raw Material," 20).

21 Eliyah-Chaim Sheps ("E. Almi") suggests that the narrow streets of the Plateau Mont-Royal with "Shabbat candles lit in the window" allowed Segal to dream he was still in Korets; but they also meant that he went on longing for Korets rather than becoming acclimatized to Montreal (qtd. in Friedman 26).

22 Simon makes a related argument about Olmsted's park, which, she suggests, "has survived as a militantly non-denominational space devoted to a poetics of reverie" (*Translating Montreal* 195).

SHERRY SIMON

1 Klein, *Complete Poems,* 1:191, line 50; 1.198, line 16; 1:142, line 25.

2 However, more than Dublin, it is Joyce's Trieste that can be seen as a parallel to Klein's Montreal as a multilingual crucible of literary modernity.

Trieste was the Austrian city in which Joyce spent some of the most creative years of his life, from 1905 to 1915. Like Montreal, Trieste was a city of many languages – at the margins of Europe and at the crossroads of Germanic, Italian, and Slavic culture. The "Tergestis Exul" was a crucial period of Joyce's life (McCourt 252) and, of all the different kinds of education Joyce received there – including his introduction to Jewish culture (219) – his "linguistic" education would be most intimately linked to this city. It was the local dialect, Triestino, that became the base language of *Finnegans Wake*, the *Wake* itself being constructed upon an exaggerated, exploded Triestino.

3 It is true, as has been emphasized by Brian Trehearne, that neither Jewish languages nor Jewish experience is a part of the mix in "Montreal". But as Trehearne points out, "there are countering forces at work ... which serve to reinstate the centrality of Jewish culture in the city by figuring the poem's speaker as its metaphoric body" (Trehearne 162–3). The poet is the "chiefest I" and the supreme "eye" of the poem. The bardic impersonal nature of the poem does not preclude an intense subjectivity, and therefore the real felt presence of the Jewish poet.

4 Another example by Jolas:

> La grande migration is not yet over in our time
> Here in the milltown crucible je regarde les étrangers
> Die dunklen stunden der einsamkeit kommen zurueck
> And I remember a blizzard wept itself to death
> On the roof of the typewriter-clattering city-room
> C'était il y a si longtemps I was still an immigrant
> lad
> Ero americano and all my friends were aliens
> Dont les yeux regardaient tristement les usines
> fumantes
> Dans les aubes sales de las horas electro-mécanicas
> Tutto il mundo de la macinas era disgraziato
> Metallic parrots chattered odes to a dark age
> Travailing stickfuls danced on the city editor's
> desk..
> The languages floated together into a sad chant
> We are always amerigrating on a long journey ...
> (Perloff n.p.)

ROBERT SCHWARTZWALD

1 On the major tour he began in September 1949, following his return from Israel, Europe, and North Africa, and on another in 1951, he specifically addresses the situation of Iraqi Jews. The *Jewish Post* reports how, in his United Jewish Appeal dinner speech in Winnipeg, "for a vivid image, the poet went to the works of Edgar Allan Poe" to evoke how Jews were caught between the pit and the pendulum. He calls upon the contemporary Jewish generation in the west, "the happiest and wealthiest in Jewish history," to help resettle them. "Jews Caught Between the Pit and the Pendulum," *Jewish Post* (hereafter *JP*), 3 May 1951, 1.

2 "Klein Launches Tour of West Points for CJC." *JP*, 30 September 1949, 5.

3 When I complained about this treatment, my father understood my feelings as, years before, he had studied under the same choirmaster.

4 My grandparents sent their sons to Talmud Torah and, pointedly, *not* to the Bundist and Yiddishist I.L. Peretz School; however, at least they heard, and sometimes spoke, Yiddish at home. What I have retained from my half-hearted instruction is the ability to read the alphabet and to recognize some vocabulary and grammatical elements thanks to my academic studies in Hebrew and German. Thus, I am able to navigate headlines and advertisements, aided by transliterations of English and Hebrew.

5 My account of the history of the Jewish press in Winnipeg is based primarily on Levendel's *Century of the Canadian Jewish Press*, esp. 175–208.

6 Levendel, *Century of the Canadian Jewish Press*, 175.

7 Ibid., 175–6.

8 Ibid., 160.

9 "A.M. Klein, poet-laureate of Canadian Jewry, will speak in Winnipeg on Tuesday, May 1 ... as part of the month-long Festival of Jewish Culture"; "Big Names at Culture Festival," *JP*, 29 March 1951: 3. My knowledge of Yiddish is sufficient to allow me to scan the Yiddish press for evidence of such appearances.

10 *JP*, 14 January 1937, 8.

11 Ibid., 7 January 1937, 3.

12 Ibid., 6 September 1951, 2.

13 Srebrnik, "Birobidzhan on the Prairies," 174. My discussion of Birobidjan is drawn largely from Srebrnik's essay.

14 Ibid., 176.

15 Ibid., 182.

16 Ibid., 183. In an article from 1940 originally published in the *Canadian Jewish Chronicle* and reprinted in the *Jewish Post*, Klein takes Zhitlovsky to task for urging Jews to be patient with, and "tolerant" of, Hitler. Zhitlovsky was not alone: these were the years of the Stalin-Hitler pact, when Communist parties and fellow travellers capitulated to the Comintern line and muted their attacks on the Nazi regime. See "Shadow and Substance," *JP*, 29 August 1940, 8.

17 Ibid., 187.

18 Ibid., 189.

19 Waxman, *History of Jewish Literature*, 1:228.

20 Levendel, *Century of the Canadian Jewish Press*, 202.

21 Waddington, "Outsider: Growing Up in Canada," in Waddington, *Apartment Seven*, 38.

22 Waddington, "The Cloudless Day: Klein's Radical Poems," in Waddington, *Apartment Seven*, 120–38.

23 See, for example, Mann's "I Accuse the Hitler Regime," *JP*, 18 March 1937.

24 *JP*, 7 January 1937, 1.

25 Ibid.

26 Trachtenberg, "Jews and Left Wing Politics," 139.

27 Wiseman, "Jewish Politics," 160.

28 Ibid., 161.

29 *JP*, 10 August 1944, 8.

30 Ibid.

31 Ibid.

32 *JP*, 13 October 1949, 3.

33 Ibid. These themes receive more profound and sustained treatment in Klein's "In Praise of the Diaspora," in *Beyond Sambation*, 463–78.

34 Ibid.

35 Ibid.

36 Ibid.

37 *JP*, 1 September 1949, 1.

38 William Eggleston, "The Causerie," *Winnipeg Free Press*, 27 August 1949, 19.

39 The *JP* reported on this in "Klein First Jew to Win Poetry Award," in its High Holidays supplement, 22 September 1949, 106.

40 Ibid.

41 Ibid.

42 Ibid.

43 To be fair, a brief article, "High Point in Literary Year," accompanied by a photo, did appear in the *JP* on 15 November 1951, 10, on the occasion of Klein's presenting a copy of *The Second Scroll* to the library of the Canadian Jewish Congress in Montreal: "The novel has been widely acclaimed as one of the finest expressions of modern Jewish idealism in the English language [and] one of the finest sections of the book deals with the Jewish society of Montreal early in the century."

44 *JP*, 21 September 1972, 6.

45 *Yiddish Press*, 1 September 1972, 7.

46 Ibid.

47 Levendel, *Century of the Canadian Jewish Press*, 27.

48 *Canadian Jewish Chronicle*, 13 June 1942, 4.

REINHOLD KRAMER

1 See Hyman, 33 and 36.

2 Klein, *Notebooks*, 129.

3 Draft of *Barney's Version*, 336; Richler Fonds, acc. no. 680/21.4.

4 Richler, *Solomon Gursky*, 22.

5 Richler, *Son of a Smaller Hero*, 143.

6 Klein, *Complete Poems*, 2:640, lines 1–4, 10.

7 It's not clear when the lampoon of L.B.Berger was written, and only a careful study of the *Solomon Gursky* manuscripts will provide an answer. Richler initially began work on the novel in the early 1970s.

8 Richler makes much of Klein's inscription to Stalin, his birthday odes to Sam Bronfman, and his willingness, as late as 1957, when his advanced mental illness had caused him to set aside almost all other labours, to work on a coat of arms for Bronfman. Richler, *Belling the Cat*, 26-7, 36–7.

9 Weintraub interview.

10 Brenner, *Assimilation and Assertion*, n.p.

11 See Kramer, *Mordecai Richler*.

12 Richler, *St. Urbain's Horseman* (Toronto: McClelland and Stewart, 1991), 34.

13 Klein, *Second Scroll*, 42.

14 Pimontel wants to be a rabbi, but loses his faith, decides to become a writer, then a translator, then a police detective (Klein, *Notebooks*, 129–36). The last leap seems counterintuitive to Sherry Simon ("A.M.

Klein as Pimontel" 71), but it fits with *The Second Scroll* (as Simon points out), where the Klein-like narrator moves away from his father's faith. He does not move counter to his father into Marxism or Christianity; instead, he tries to discover the sources of his father's faith, going over the same territory but with a wider education, looking, often in vain, for the spoor of God. He is a metaphysical detective who has lost the old faith but is not ready to set it aside. Possibly deluding himself, Pimontel believes that the detection of crime is "a priestly office involving the daily asseveration of right order and the administrative implementation of the will of God" (Klein, *Notebooks*, 136). Such a formulation implies theodicy. Klein introduces the problem of evil when, in postwar Purim celebrations, a Jew wonders: "insofar as [the six million] are concerned, who won, Mordecai or Haman?.... I come because there's nowhere else to go.... But don't tell me, while a great emptiness yawns in our midst, of miracles and salvations" (Klein, *Notebooks*, 139).

15 Pollock, "Introduction," Klein, *Notebooks*, xvi.

16 Klein, *Notebooks*, 157–60.

17 See Žižek, *Enjoy Your Symptom*, chap. 2.

18 Simon, *Translating Montreal*, 63.

19 Klein, *Second Scroll*, 62.

20 See, for example, Wainwright, 75–96.

21 Klein, *Second Scroll*, 57.

22 See Neiman, *Evil in Modern Thought*, 81.

23 Richler, *St. Urbain's Horseman*, 265.

24 Arendt, 278.

25 Notes on *St. Urbain's Horseman* by an unidentified editor (internal evidence suggests Tony Godwin), Richler Papers, msc 36.30.1, p. 3. Godwin also asked that the Horseman denouement and the trial outcome be brought together.

26 Richler, *St. Urbain's Horseman*, 462. The question of Richler's irony raises the possibility that the Horseman is a fetishistic psychological device, such as Freud delineated in *The Future of an Illusion*. For Freud, the heavenly father (and, by implication, theodicy) is a reaction-formation, a fantasy via which we flee from the real. If Jake has made real gains in maturity by the end of the novel, from a psychoanalytic perspective he ought not to let his idols keep breathing. That Richler has him write "presumed dead" suggests that the novel doesn't dismiss the metaphysical aspect of Jake's quest as simply a holdover from childhood.

27 Ravvin, 37, 43, 45.

28 Richler, *St. Urbain's Horseman*, 464.

29 *Joshua Then and Now* presents a challenge to my claim about the import-
    ance of the metaphysical detective story to Richler's mature work. The
    detection involved in *Joshua Then and Now* (the search for a reason why
    Joshua was wearing women's panties) is almost entirely tongue-in-cheek,
    yet the novel is an artistic success and doesn't sink towards bathos. A
    preliminary response might be to point towards Reuben's ambiguous
    function: he is a way of keeping Judaism and transcendence around. He
    is often treated satirically, to be sure, but he generally appears as a philo-
    sophical naïf who doesn't fully see the ironies in his stance rather than as a
    cynic who undermines Judaism.

LAWRENCE KAPLAN

1 Klein, *The Second Scroll*. Toronto: University of Toronto Press, 2000.

2 Richler, *St. Urbain's Horseman*. Toronto: McClelland and Stewart,
   1991.

3 Nadel, "Absent Prophet," 86.

4 Marshall, "Third Solitude," 154.

5 Brenner, *Assimilation and Assertion*, 113.

6 Kramer, *Mordecai Richler*, 227–8.

7 See notes 14–16, 18, and 20.

8 See, for example, Waugh, "St. Urbain's Horseman."

9 See Cameron, "Aren't We All Made of Flesh."

10 See Cranford, *Fiction and Fact*, 84–5: "Of the many merits in [*St. Urbain's
    Horseman*], critics have pointed to the extraordinary amount of autobio-
    graphical material suffusing the obviously sensational, fictional plot....
    And truly it is sometimes hard to tell where Jake Hersh begins and Richler
    leaves off."

11 See, for example, Popham, "Introduction," Klein, *Second Scroll*, xii–xiii.
    Popham, in speaking of "the extent to which Klein's novel is rooted
    in autobiography," points to the "numerous detailed correspondences
    between the unnamed narrator's life experiences and Klein's own." After
    spelling out those "detailed correspondences," she notes: "In a more gen-
    eral sense, the literary concerns and aspirations of the author and his circle
    are also reflected in the characterization of the narrator," a point upon
    which she expands considerably.

12 Nadel, "Absent Prophet," 86.

13 Kramer, *Mordecai Richler*, 228.

14 Thus Nadel, in his essay, does not address the morally questionable nature
   of Joey's organization of the street brawl by the St Urbain Street boys,
   the real motivation for his leaving Montreal, the dubious circumstances
   surrounding his visit to Paraguay, his participation in the "unprovoked"
   terrorist attack by units of Etzel and the Stern gang "on the quiescent
   Arab village of Deir Yassin" (*St. Urbain's Horseman* 256), or, finally, Jake's
   growing ambivalence towards him. And Nadel's suggestion ("Absent
   Prophet" 83) that Joey performs "the task of the genuine prophet," as
   described in Martin Buber's classic essay, "Prophecy, Apocalyptic, and the
   Historical Hour," is exaggerated. If anything, Joey turns out to be more of
   a false prophet than a true one.

15 Thus, Brenner, in *Assimilation and Assertion*, writes: "Joey found Israel
   as complacent and indifferent about the Holocaust as the rest of the
   world. He left Israel contemptuous for and disgusted with its betrayal of
   the dead. Evidently Richler doesn't see Israel as a satisfying answer to the
   Jewish need for just retribution. Nor does he consider the Israeli as a role
   model for the Diaspora Jews" (13). But, in light of Joey's, to say the least,
   morally dubious and often self-justifying and self-rationalizing character,
   it is impossible to assume that he can be viewed here as a spokesman for
   Richler himself.

16 Kramer, in *Mordecai Richler*, writes: "More canny than Klein, Richler
   knew that a Messiah who could pass for Bugsy Siegel would make a big-
   ger dent on the literary market than one who sounded like Gershom Scholem" (228). While there may be some truth to this, the idea that Richler
   endowed Joey with Bugsy Siegel-like characteristics primarily "to make
   a ... dent on the literary market" ultimately trivializes Richler's moral
   critique.

17 See Marshall, "Third Solitude," where he describes Joey as "a common
   thug" (154).

18 Kramer, in *Mordecai Richler*, claims that "Klein's suggestion ... that
   the photograph of Uncle Melech may be a graven image, influenced *St.*
   Urbain's Horseman, where Jake senses that he has raised the Horseman
   as a golden calf, in contravention of the Second Commandment" (228).
   This seems a stretch. First, it is not the novel's anonymous narrator who
   suggests "that the photograph of Uncle Melech may be a graven image";
   rather, at the very beginning of *The Second Scroll* (6–7) the narrator
   relates that, as a young boy, curious as to what Uncle Melech, at the time
   a brilliant and strictly Orthodox Talmudic scholar "looked like, I asked
   my mother one day whether she had a photograph of [him] ... My mother

was shocked. 'Don't you know that Jews don't ... permit themselves to be made into images? That's the second commandment. Uncle Melech wouldn't think of going to a photographer!'" And if one chooses to read any larger symbolic significance into this charming anecdote, it is that one cannot and should not try to reduce Uncle Melech to a single image for, as we have seen, it is precisely the sweep of his intellectual and spiritual vacillations and peregrinations that enable him to encapsulate the great events in the history of the Jewish people in the first half of the twentieth century. Thus, even if one chooses to link the "graven image" motif of *The Second Scroll* with the "golden calf" motif of *St. Urbain's Horseman*, the former serves as moral praise, the latter as moral critique.

In this connection, one may ask how it is that critics generally as astute as Nadel, Brenner, and Kramer have overlooked or downplayed the morally problematic and seamy side of Joey's character. I would suggest that we have here an example of the "halo effect." That is, precisely because these critics have properly taken note of the similarities between the functions that the absent heroes of *The Second Scroll* and *St. Urbain's Horseman*, Uncle Melech and Cousin Joey, respectively, play in the two novels, they – particularly Nadel – have tended to transfer some of the morally admirable features of Uncle Melech to Cousin Joey, despite the fact that the latter does not merit them. On the other hand, those critics who have focused solely on *St. Urbain's Horseman*, and who have not been, as it were, distracted by the comparison with *The Second Scroll*, have been better able to perceive the less admirable, darker, even seamy and thuggish features of Joey's character.

19 Popham, "Introduction," Klein, *Second Scroll*, vii.
20 Kramer, in *Mordecai Richler*, correctly notes that "Richler owed nothing stylistically [to Klein]. Where Klein was Joycean and formal – sometimes overformal and pompous – Richler was colloquial and direct" (228). He goes on, however, to say: "But structurally he owed a great deal" (228). This is certainly the case. We may say that perhaps Kramer does not sufficiently appreciate how, despite the novels' important and significant structural and thematic similarities, their stylistic and generic differences give rise to equally important and significant structural and thematic differences.
21 Richler, "Deuteronomy," 17.
22 Popham, "Introduction," *Second Scroll*, xxiii–xxiv. Popham, in order to see the novel's ending as more chastened and ironic, drives a rather dubious wedge between *The Second Scroll*'s anonymous narrator and its implied

author. That Klein intended the ending of *The Second Scroll* to be affirmative and celebratory is, however, substantiated by the fact that many of the narrator's affirmative and celebratory statements are taken directly, almost verbatim, from Klein's own "Notebook of a Journey," which served as important raw material for the novel (see Appendix A: Selections from "Notebook of a Journey," Klein, *Second Scroll*, 181–203). Popham, of course, is aware of this. How does she respond? Let us look again at the concluding paragraph of her introduction: "Klein repeatedly argues, as does his narrator, that the establishment of the State of Israel is a 'miracle,' figuring the redemption of Israel as a people ... In his acknowledgment of contradictory, unresolved elements ... Klein has given us 'a double, a multiple exposure' of jubilation and misgiving right to end of the novel" (xxiv). Who is the first "Klein" of this conclusion, and who is the second? Popham would appear to be suggesting that we should not only differentiate between the novel's anonymous narrator and "A.M. Klein," its implied author, but also between the rather blatantly ideological real-life A.M. Klein, the author of the unambiguously affirmative "Notebook of a Journey," and the more subtle, artistic, and nuanced A.M. Klein, the implied author of *The Second Scroll*, with its supposed "acknowledgment of contradictory, unresolved elements." I must say that such a suggestion, assuming I have understood Popham properly, strikes me as a counsel of desperation.

One minor ambiguous note in the novel's end may be pointed out. The last sentence of *The Second Scroll* does not read "I turned for the last time *to* the city of Safed, holy city" but "I turned for the last time *from* the city of Safed, holy city" (emphasis added). That is, the narrator, despite his celebration of the miraculous rebirth of the Jewish people in the State of Israel, chooses not to be part of that rebirth. He turns from the holy city of Safed and returns home to the Diaspora (as did Klein himself after his visit to Israel, which served as the inspiration for and basis of the novel) to resume his somewhat marginal position as a Montreal Jewish poet, editor, lawyer, and translator of Hebrew poems. Still, this cannot change the fact that the novel closes with the image of "the city of Safed, holy city on whose hills once were kindled, as now again, the beacons announcing new moons, festivals, and set times" (62).

DAVID LEAHY

1 Lewisohn, "Foreword" (reprinted as Lewisohn, "Appendix").

2 See Kramer, *Mordecai Richler*, for an impressive account of Richler's auto-
    biographical sources of fictional characters and their names.

3 Originally published as "Mortimer Griffin, Shalinsky, and How They
    Solved the Jewish Problem," *Tamarack Review* 7 (Spring 1958): 477–89.
    I cite from Smith, *Canadian Century*. Hereafter the story is referred to as
    "Mortimer Griffin."

4 Hereafter referred to as *Solomon Gursky*.

5 The phrase is pronounced by God to Moses (Exodus 3:14). It is also a
    turn of phrase that Solomon Gursky uses when testifying in court and cor-
    responding with Moses Berger.

6 I pursue how Richler's fiction evinces homophobia, homosexual panic,
    and male anxieties about sexual potency and gender roles as well as
    critiques of traditional male-dominant culture in my unpublished paper
    "Homosexual Panic in Mordecai Richler's Early Novels."

7 I would also suggest that critics have not appreciated the parodic nature
    of Klein's poem, "Soirée of Velvel Kleinburger"; his "low" appropria-
    tion of Eliot's famous "high modernist" poem can be understood as a
    form of homage and perhaps even as an ironic commentary on Eliot's
    anti-Semitism.

8 Both of these poems were published by Klein in *Hath Not a Jew* ... (1940),
    whose title ends in ellipsis, as does Sinclair's truncated allusion to "the
    draughty synagogue at smokefall..."

9 See also Bell, "Canada Wry"; Leonard, "Sermon on the Mountie"; Clute,
    "Tricksters from the Heart of the North."

10 This was almost never remarked on by American or British reviewers.
    See Prose, "Hopping Mad"; Bell, "Canada Wry"; and Koenig, "Canadian
    Club."

11 Lorne Pierce's *A Canadian People* (1945) seems at first glance to offer an
    anti-racialist, or what some might now call a transnationalist, vision of
    immigrants as citizens-in-waiting rather than as threats to the established
    ethno-linguistic franchises. But his views are more troubling: "If Canada
    must accommodate itself to a noisy and intransigent minority, then can
    not the Jew bide his time and demand by the force of numbers, economic
    power, control of newspapers, radio, motion pictures, drugs or tailoring, a
    place in the sun? .... A people is either one or it is two; and if it is two then
    it is on its ways to join the dodo" (79). That the threatening, diminutive
    signs of the "noisy and intransigent minority" are synecdochically associ-
    ated with "the Jew" is not only consistent with the common perception of
    the day of Jewish immigration as problematic and odious but also with

the book's overall presumption that the only culture worth preserving is English-Canadian.

12 Other passing references to L.B. Berger's being published in *Poetry* (Chicago), the *Canadian Forum* and the *Northern Review* (19), and to his "poems, stories, and fiery editorials for the *Canadian Jewish Herald* on the plight of the Jews in Europe" (Richler, *Solomon Gursky*, 17), are true enough to the publishing venues for Klein's poetry, and close enough to his variegated contributions to the *Canadian Jewish Chronicle*, to make the biographical link obvious. Likewise, see the reference to L.B. Berger's being "a proficient punster" (19).

13 This chronology is consistent with the period of the 1940s and early 1950s in which Richler came of age in the St Urbain community and subscribed to socialism, alongside the late period of Klein's importance as a poet, speaker, and public figure.

14 For parallels to Sam Bronfman, see Abella and Troper, *None Is Too Many*; and Newman, *Bronfman Dynasty*.

15 See Kramer, *Mordecai Richler*, for several examples of Richler's mother as a failed writer and his attempts to distance himself from her, often by identifying more strongly with his far less "literary" father.

16 I would like to thank my colleague at Concordia University, Peter Webb, and also acknowledge Gerald Lynch in influencing this chapter.

IAN RAE

1 This is my transcription of the interview of Cohen conducted by Lian Lunson, the director of the film.

2 See Klein's letter to A.J.M. Smith, cited by Mayne in his afterword to *The Second Scroll*, 140.

3 This is my transcription of the Martel speech.

4 In the McClelland and Stewart edition (1994), the footnote's instruction "See Gloss Beth, page 98" directs readers to Gloss Gimel. The correct page number is given in the University of Toronto edition (2000).

Bibliography

Archives

Abraham Moses Klein Fonds, Library and Archives Canada (LAC), Ottawa, Ontario.

A.J.M. Smith Papers, Thomas Fisher Rare Book Library (FRBL),University of Toronto, Toronto, Ontario.

Canadian Jewish Congress Papers, Canadian Jewish Congress Archives. Montreal, Quebec.

David Lewis Fonds, Library and Archives Canada (LAC), Ottawa, Ontario.

Ellsworth Goodwin Mason Fonds, Library and Archives Canada (LAC), Ottawa, Ontario.

James Joyce Collection, Beinecke Rare Book and Manuscript Library, Yale University. New Haven, Connecticut.

James Laughlin Papers, New Directions Publishing Corporation. New York, New York.

Jewish Publication Society (JPS). Philadelphia Jewish Archives Centre (PJAC). Philadelphia, Pennsylvania.

John Simon Guggenheim Memorial Foundation Archives. New York, New York.

Lavy Becker Fonds, Library and Archives Canada (LAC), Ottawa, Ontario.

Mordecai Richler Papers, Special Collections, University of Calgary Library.

Leon Edel Papers, McClennan Library, McGill University, Montreal, Quebec.

Shonie Levi Papers. Privately owned.

Usher Caplan Fonds, National Library of Canada (LAC), Ottawa, Ontario.

YIVO Institute for Jewish Research. New York, New York.

Other Works

Abella, Irving, and Harold Troper. *None Is Too Many: Canada and the Jews of Europe, 1933–1948*. Toronto: Lester and Orpen Dennys, 1982.

Adorno, Theodor. "Cultural Criticism and Society." In *Prisms*, 17–34. Trans. Samuel and Sherry Weber. Cambridge: MIT,1981.

A.M. Klein: The Poet as Landscape. VHS. Dir. David Kaufman. 1980.

Anctil, Pierre. "À la découverte de la littérature yiddish montréalaise." In *New Readings of Yiddish Montreal*, ed. Pierre Anctil, Norman Ravvin, and Sherry Simon, 19–30. Ottawa: University of Ottawa Press, 2007.

– "A.M. Klein: The Poet and His Relations with French Quebec." In *The Canadian Jewish Studies Reader*, ed. Richard Menkis and Norman Ravvin, 350–72. Calgary: Red Deer Press, 2004.

– "Les communautés juives de Montréal." In *Le patrimoine des minorités religieuses du Québec, richesse et vulnérabilité. Patrimoine en mouvement*, ed. Marie-Claude Rocher and Marc Pelchat, 37–60. Montreal: Presses de l'Université Laval, 2006.

– Introduction to *Poèmes Yiddish* by Jacob Isaac Segal, 7–21. Montreal: Noroît, 1992.

– *Le rendez-vous manqué: Les Juifs de Montréal face au Québec de l'entre-deux-guerres*. Montréal: Institut québécois de recherche sur la culture, 1988.

– *Saint-Laurent, la Main de Montréal*. Sillery: Éditions du Septentrion et Musée Pointe-à-Callière, 2002.

– "Sholem Shtern, écrivain Montréalais." In *Nostalgie et tristesse: Mémoires littéraires du Montréal Yiddish*, by Sholem Stern, 295–324. Montreal: Noroît, 2006.

– *Tur Malka: Flâneries sur les cimes de l'histoire juive montréalaise*. Sillery: Éditions du Septentrion, 1997.

– "Wolofsky *ibergesetst* ou pourquoi Klein traduit?" Paper delivered at The Poet as Landscape: A Portrait of A.M. Klein Today, conference held at Concordia University, Montreal, QC, 20 October 2007.

– "Writing as Immigrants: Yiddish Belles-letters in Canada." In *What Is Your Place? Indigeneity and Immigration in Canada*, ed. Hartmut Lutz, 118–42. Augsburg, Deutschland: Wisner-Verlag, Beiträge zur Kanadistik 14, 2007.

Apter, Emily S. *The Translation Zone: A New Comparative Literature*. Princeton: Princeton University Press, 2006.

Arendt, Hannah. *Eichmann in Jerusalem: A Report on the Banality of Evil*. New York: Viking, 1963.

Arnold, Janice. "A.M. Klein Letters Reveal Obsession with Being Recognized." *Canadian Jewish News*, 1 November 2007. Available at www.cjnews.com (viewed 24 September 2010).

Baker, Zachary M. "Montreal of Yesterday: A Snapshot of Jewish Life in Montreal during the Era of mass Immigration." In *An Everyday Miracle: Yiddish Culture in Montreal*, ed. Ira Robinson, Pierre Anctil, and Mervin Butovsky, 39–52. Montreal: Véhicule, 1990.

Begley, Louis. *The Tremendous World I Have Inside My Head: Franz Kafka – A Biographical Essay*. New York: Atlas, 2008.

Bell, Pearl. K. "Canada Wry." *New Republic*, 7 May 1990, 42–4.

Bentley, D.M.R. "Klein, Montreal, and Mankind." *Journal of Canadian Studies* 19, 2 (1984): 34–57.

– "'New Styles of Architecture, a Change of Heart'? The Architexts of A.M. Klein and F.R. Scott." In *The Canadian Modernists Meet*, ed. Dean Irvine, 17–58. Ottawa: University of Ottawa Press, 2005.

Borges, Jorge Luis. "The Approach to al-Mu'tasim." In *The Aleph and Other Stories, 1933–1969*, ed. and trans. Norman Thomas di Giovanni, 45–51. New York : E.P. Dutton, 1970.

Bowering, George. "Author's Statement." *The New Long Poem Anthology*, ed. Sharon Thesen, 351–2. Toronto: Coach House Press, 1991.

Brenner, Rachel Feldhay. *A.M. Klein: The Father of Canadian Jewish Literature*. Lewiston: Edwin Mellen Press, 1990.

– "A.M. Klein's The Rocking Chair: Toward the Redefinition of the Poet's Function." *Studies in Canadian Literature* 15, 1 (1990): 94–116.

– *Assimilation and Assertion: The Response to the Holocaust in Mordecai Richler's Writing*. New York: Peter Lang, 1989.

Brown, Michael. *Jew or Juif: Jews, French Canadians, and Anglo-Canadians, 1759–1914*. Philadelphia: The Jewish Publication Society, 1987.

Brown, Russell. "Mordecai Richler." In *The Oxford Companion to Canadian Literature*, ed. E. Benson and W. Toye, 999–1002. Toronto: Oxford University Press, 1983.

Bulkeley, Tim. "Hypertext Bible Commentary – Amos." 1996–2005. Available at www.bible.gen.nz (viewed 4 October 2010).

Cameron, Donald. "Aren't We All Made of Flesh." Review of Mordecai Richler's *St. Urbain's Horseman. The Nation*, 14 June 1971.

Caplan, Kimmy. *Orthodoxy in the New World: Immigrant Rabbis and Preaching in America, 1881–1924*. Jerusalem: Zalman Shazar Center for Jewish History, 2002.

Caplan, Usher. *Like One That Dreamed: A Portrait of A.M. Klein.* Toronto: McGraw-Hill Ryerson, 1982.

– "The A.M. Klein Papers." In *The A.M. Klein Symposium,* ed. S. Mayne, 31–6. Ottawa: University of Ottawa Press, 1975.

– "Introduction." In *A.M. Klein: Literary Essays and Reviews,* ed. Usher Caplan and M.W. Steinberg, xi-xxiii. Toronto: University of Toronto Press, 1987.

– "The Making of the Second Scroll." *Canadian Jewish Quarterly: Viewpoints* 2, 4 (1981): 38–45.

Caiserman, H.M. *Yidishe dikhter in Kanade* [Jewish poets in Canada]. Montreal: Farlag "Nyuansn," 1934.

Charters, Ann, ed. *Jack Kerouac: Selected Letters, 1940–1956.* New York: Viking, 1995.

Chisvin, Sharon. "Interview with Abe Arnold" (11 June 1996). Recorded interview in the collection of the Jewish Heritage Society of Western Canada, Winnipeg.

Cliche, Anne Élaine. *Poétiques du Messie: L'origine juive en souffrance.* Montréal: xyz éditeur, 2007.

Clute, John. "Tricksters from the Heart of the North." *Times Literary Supplement,* 15–21 June 1990, 653.

Coetzee, J.M. "What Is a Classic?" *Stranger Shores.* London, UK: Secker and Warburg, 2001.

Cohen, Leonard. *Beautiful Losers.* 1966. Toronto: McClelland and Stewart, 1991.

– *Book of Mercy.* Toronto: McClelland and Stewart, 1984.

– *Dear Heather.* Columbia Records, 2004.

– *The Favourite Game.* 1963. Toronto: McClelland and Stewart, 2008.

– "Layton's Question." *Book of Longing.* Toronto: McClelland and Stewart, 2006.

– "Suzanne." *Songs of Leonard Cohen.* Columbia Records, 1967.

Cohen, Nathan. "The Jews of Independent Poland: Linguistic and Cultural Changes." In *Starting the Twenty-First Century: Sociological Reflections and Challenges,* ed. Ernest Krausz and Gitta Tulea. 161–75. New Brunswick: Transaction Publishers, 2002.

Compagnie des tramways de Montréal. *Route Map of Bus and Tramways in Montreal.* Montreal: Montreal Tramways Co., 1944.

Cranford, Ada. *Fiction and Fact in Mordecai Richler's Novels.* Lewiston: Edwin Mellen, 1992.

Croteau, Jean-Philippe. "Le financement des écoles publiques à Montréal entre 1869 et 1973: Deux poids, deux mesures." PhD diss., Université du Québec à Montréal, 2006.

Cunnell, Howard. "Fast This Time: Jack Kerouac and the Writing of *On the Road.*" In *On The Road: The Original Scroll*, ed. H. Cunnell. 1–52. New York: Viking: 2007.

Dickstein, Moishe. *From Palestine to Israel*. Montreal: Eagle Publishing, 1951.

Donne, John, *Devotions Upon Emergent Occasions and Death's Duel, Meditation xvii*. Available at www.anglicanlibrary.org/donne/devotions/devotions17.htm.

Dudek, Louis, and Irving Layton. *Canadian Poems, 1850–1952*. Toronto: Contact Press, 1952.

Dudek, Louis, and Irving Layton. "Introductory Note." In *Canadian Poems, 1850–1952*, 13–17. Toronto: Contact Press, 1952.

Duffy, Dennis. "Review of *Solomon Gursky Was Here.*" *Queen's Quarterly* 97, 2 (1990): 325–7.

Edel, Leon. "Marginal *Keri* and Textual *Chetiv*: The Mystic Novel of A. M. Klein." In *The A.M. Klein Symposium*, ed. Seymour Mayne, 15–29. Ottawa: University of Ottawa Press, 1975.

Eliot, T.S. "Four Quartets." In *The Complete Poems and Plays of T.S. Eliot* [1969], 171–98. London: Faber and Faber, 2004.

– "The Love Song of J. Alfred Prufrock." In *The Complete Poems and Plays of T.S. Eliot* [1969], 13–17. London: Faber and Faber, 2004.

Fadiman, Clifton. *Readings I've Liked: A Personal Selection Drawn from Two Decades of Reading and Reviewing*. New York: Simon and Shuster, 1941.

Farrell, James T. *The Fate of Writing in America*. New York: New Directions, 1946.

Ferguson, Linda Luft. "*The Rocking Chair*: Portrait of the Poet as Province." *Journal of Canadian Studies* 19, 2 (1984): 58–65.

Finkel, Alvin. "The Decline of Jewish Radicalism after 1945." In *Jewish Radicalism in Winnipeg, 1905–1960*, ed. Daniel Stone, 192–203. Winnipeg: Jewish Heritage Centre of Western Canada, 2003.

Fischer, Gretl K. *In Search of Jerusalem: Religion and Ethics in the Writings of A.M. Klein*. Montreal: McGill-Queen's University Press, 1975.

– "A.M. Klein's Forgotten Play." *Canadian Literature* 43 (1970): 42–53.

Friedman, Shari Cooper. "J.I. Segal: Between Two Worlds." MA thesis, McGill University, 1988.

Fuerstenberg, Adam. "Yiddish Influence in the Work of A.M. Klein: Folk Character in *Hershel of Ostropol.*" *Yiddish* 4 (1982): 74–85.

– "From Yiddish to 'Yiddishkeit': A.M. Klein, J.I. Segal and Montreal's Yiddish Culture." *Journal of Canadian Studies* 19, 2 (1984): 66–81.

– "Transplanting Roots: J.I. Segal's Canadian Perspective" *Yiddish* 4, 3 (1981): 63–76.

Fuks, Haim-Leib. *Hundert yor Yidishe oun Hebreyshe Literature in Kanade: Cent ans de literature yiddish et hébraïque au Canada* Montréal. 1980. Trans. Pierre Anctil. Sillery: Éditions du Septentrion, 2005.

Garfinkle, Ode, and Mervin Butovsky. "The Journal of Yaacov Zipper, 1925–1926." In *An Everyday Miracle: Yiddish Culture in Montreal*, ed. Ira Robinson, Pierre Anctil, and Mervin Butovsky. 53–68. Montreal: Véhicule, 1990.

Ginsberg, Allen. *Howl and Other Poems* [1956]. San Francisco: City Lights, 1993.

Golfman, Noreen, "Semantics and Semitics: The Early Poetry of A.M. Klein." *University of Toronto Quarterly*, 51 (Winter 1981–82): 175–91.

Gonick, Cy. *A Very Red Life: The Story of Bill Walsh.* St John: Canadian Committee on Labour History, 2001.

Gotlib, Noah-Isaac. *Montreal.* Montreal: Eagle Publishing, 1968.

Gotlieb, Phyllis. "Hassidic Influences in the Work of A.M. Klein." In *The A.M. Klein Symposium*, ed. Seymour Mayne, 47–64. Ottawa: University of Ottawa Press, 1975.

Greenstein, Michael. *Third Solitudes: Tradition and Discontinuity in Jewish-Canadian Literature.* Montreal: McGill-Queen's University Press, 1989.

Harshav, Benjamin. *The Meaning of Yiddish.* Stanford: Stanford University Press, 1990.

Heft, Harold. "The Lost A.M. Klein Guggenheim Application." *Canadian Poetry* 32 (Spring-Summer 1993): 73–81.

– "Some Apocalyptic Discoveries: A History of A.M. Klein's Troubled Involvement in James Joyce Studies." *Essays on Canadian Writing* 61 (Spring 1997): 215–31.

Hyman, Roger. *Aught from Naught: A.M. Klein's The Second Scroll.* No. 81 Monograph Series. English Literary Studies, University of Victoria, 1999.

Jacobson, David C. *Modern Midrash: The Retelling of Traditional Jewish Narratives by Twentieth-Century Hebrew Writers*. New York: State University of New York Press, 1987.

Jolas, Eugene. *Man from Babel*. Ed. Andreas Kramer and Rainer Rumold. New Haven: Yale University Press, 1998.

Kaplan, Lawrence. "A More Contemporary Voice: A.M. Klein's Original and Revised Translations of the Hebrew Poems of Hayyim Nahman Bialik." *Prooftexts* 25, 1/2 (2005): 128–52.

Kattan, Naïm. *A.M. Klein: Poet and Prophet*. Trans. Edward Baxter. Montreal: XYZ Publishing, 2001.

– *Les villes de naissance*. Montréal: Leméac, 2000.

Kelly, Darlene. "A.M. Klein and the 'Fibbiest Fabricator of Them All.'" *Canadian Poetry: Studies, Documents, Reviews* 43 (Fall-Winter 1998): 70–102.

Kerouac, Jack. "About the Beat Generation." In *Portable Jack Kerouac*, ed. Ann Charters, 559–61. New York: Viking, 1995.

– "Beatific: The Origins of the Beat Generation." *Portable Jack Kerouac*, ed. Ann Charters, 565–73. New York: Viking, 1995.

– *On the Road*. New York: Viking, 1957.

Kertzer, J.M. "Personality and Authority: A.M. Klein's Self-Portrait." *Canadian Poetry: Studies, Documents, Reviews* 15 (Fall-Winter 1984): 31–47.

Klein, A.M. *Literary Essays and Reviews*. Ed. Usher Caplan and M.W. Steinberg. Toronto: University of Toronto Press, 1987.

– *Beyond Sambation: Selected Essays and Editorials, 1928–1955*. Ed. M.W. Steinberg and Usher Caplan. Toronto: University of Toronto Press, 1982.

– *The Collected Poems of A.M. Klein*. Ed. Miriam Waddington. Toronto: McGraw-Hill Ryerson, 1974.

– *Complete Poems*. 2 vols. Ed. Zailig Pollock. Toronto: University of Toronto Press, 1990.

– *Hath Not a Jew …*. New York: Behrman's Jewish Book House, 1940.

– *The Hitleriad*. New York: New Directions, 1944.

– *Notebooks: Selections from the A.M. Klein Papers*. Ed. Zailig Pollock and Usher Caplan. Toronto: University of Toronto Press, 1994.

– "From the 'Raw Material' File." In *Notebooks: Selections from the A.M. Klein Papers*, 3–50.

– "Untitled Manuscript" (Pimontel). In *Notebooks: Selections from the A.M. Klein Papers*, 129–41.

- "Poet of a World Passed by." *Canadian Jewish Chronicle*, 9 June 1950, 5.
- "Portrait of the Poet as a Nobody." *First Statement* 31 (June/July 1945): 3–8.
- *The Rocking Chair and Other Poems* [1948]. Toronto: Ryerson, 1951.
- *The Second Scroll*. New York: Knopf, 1951.
- *The Second Scroll*. Ed. Elizabeth Popham and Zailig Pollock. Toronto: University of Toronto Press, 2000.
- *The Second Scroll*. Toronto: McClelland and Stewart, 1994.
- *Selected Poems*. Ed. Zailig Pollock, Seymour Mayne, and Usher Caplan. Toronto: University of Toronto Press, 1997.
- *Short Stories*. Ed. M.W. Steinberg. Toronto: University of Toronto Press, 1983.
- "Words in Their Season: Mr. Samuel Bronfman's Congress Address." *Canadian Jewish Chronicle*, 11 August 1939, 3.
Koenig, Rhoda. "Canadian Club." *New York*, 16 April 1990, 95–6.
Kramer, Reinhold. *Mordecai Richler: Leaving St. Urbain*. Montreal: McGill-Queens University Press, 2008.
- "Richler, Son of Klein" (abstract). Paper delivered at conference entitled "The Poet as Landscape: A Portrait of A.M. Klein Today," Concordia University, Montreal, 20 October 2007.
Kroetsch, Robert. "Author's Note." In *Completed Field Notes: The Long Poems of Robert Kroetsch*. Toronto: McClelland and Stewart, 1989, 269.
- "For Play and Entrance: The Contemporary Canadian Long Poem." In *The Lovely Treachery of Words*, 117–34. Toronto: Oxford University Press, 1989.
- *The Impossible Sum of Our Traditions: Reflections on Canadian Literature*. Toronto: McClelland and Stewart, 1986.
Layton, Irving. "Requiem for A.M. Klein." In *The Pole-Vaulter*, 28–9. Toronto: McClelland and Stewart, 1974.
Leahy, David. "Classic Realist Ethnic, Gender and Class Fictions in Quebec, 1939–1945." PhD diss., Concordia University, 1995.
Leonard, John. "Sermon on the Mountie." *The Nation*, 4 June 1990, 785–6, 788–91.
Lester, Roslyn. "'Of Kith and Kin': A Biographical and Critical Study of Cultural Influences on the Prose of A.M. Klein." MA thesis, Concordia University, 1984.

Levendel, Lewis. *A Century of the Canadian Jewish Press, 1880s–1980s*. Ottawa: Borealis Press, 1989.

Levine, Elimelekh. *Kinder ertsyung ba Yidn, a historishe nakhforshung*. Montreal: sine nominee (s.n.), 1910.

Lewisohn, Ludwig. "Appendix." In *The Collected Poems of A.M. Klein*, ed. Miriam Waddington. Toronto: McGraw-Hill Ryerson, 1974.

– "Concerning a Jewish Poet." *Jewish Standard* 7, 9 (1936): 8, 39.

– "Foreword." In A.M. Klein, *Hath Not a Jew* ... . New York: Behrman's, 1940.

Lunan, Gordon. *The Making of a Spy*. Montreal: R. Davies, 1995.

– *Redhanded: Inside the Spy Ring That Changed the World*. Maxville: Optimum Publications International, 2005.

Lunson, Lian, dir. *Leonard Cohen: I'm Your Man*. Christal Films and Lionsgate Films. 2005.

MacLennan, Hugh. "The Canadian Character." In *Cross-Country*, 3–20. Toronto: Collins, 1949.

Malcolm, Janet. *The Silent Woman: Sylvia Plath and Ted Hughes*. New York: Knopf, 1994.

Marrus, Michael. *Mr. Sam: The Life and Times of Samuel Bronfman*. Toronto: Viking, 1991 (Toronto: Penguin, 1992).

Marshall, Tom. *A.M. Klein*. Toronto: Ryerson Press, 1970.

– "Third Solitude: Canadian as Jew." In *The Canadian Novel: A Critical Anthology*. Vol. 1: *Here and Now*, ed. John Moss, 147–55. Toronto: NC Press, 1978.

Martel, Émile. "Sommes-nous américain?" Paper delivered at conference entitled Are We American? Canadian Culture in North America, McGill University, Montreal, 13–15 February, 2008.

Mayne, Seymour. "Afterword." In A.M. Klein, *The Second Scroll*. Toronto: McClelland and Stewart, 1994.

– *A Rich Garland: Poems for A.M. Klein*. Montreal: Véhicule Press, 1999.

Mayne, Seymour, and B. Glen Rotchin, eds. *A.M. Klein Symposium*. Ottawa: University of Ottawa Press, 1975.

McNeilly, Kevin. "All Poets Are Not Jews: Transgression and Satire in A.M. Klein." *English Studies in Canada* 28, 3 (2002): 413–45.

McCourt, John. *The Years of Bloom: Joyce in Trieste, 1904–1920*. Dublin: Lilliput Press, 2000.

Melançon, Robert. "Réédifier Jérusalem." In *Montréal: L'invention juive*, 25–49. Montreal: Département d'études françaises, Université de Montréal, 1991.

Menkis, Richard. "A.M. Klein and Jewish Youth Cultures in Interwar Canada." Paper delivered at The Poet as Landscape: A Portrait of A.M. Klein Today, conference held at Concordia University, Montreal, 19 October 2007.

Merivale, Patricia, and Susan Elizabeth Sweeney, eds. *Detecting Texts: The Metaphysical Detective Story from Poe to Postmodernism.* Philadelphia: University of Pennsylvania Press, 1999.

Michaels, Anne. "Cleopatra's Love." *Poetry Canada* 14, 2 (1994): 14–15.

– *Fugitive Pieces.* Toronto: McClelland and Stewart, 1996.

– "Unseen Formations." *Open Letter* 8, 4 (1992): 96–9.

McNeilly, Kevin. "All Poets Are Not Jews: Transgression and Satire in A.M. Klein." *English Studies in Canada* 28, 3 (2002): 413–45.

Morley, Patricia. *The Immoral Moralists: Hugh MacLennan and Leonard Cohen.* Toronto: Clarke, Irwin, 1972.

Nadel, Ira. *Various Positions: A Life of Leonard Cohen.* Toronto: Random House Canada, 1996.

– "The Absent Prophet in Canadian in Jewish Fiction." *English Quarterly* 5 (Spring 1972): 83–92.

Neiman, Susan. *Evil in Modern Thought: An Alternative History of Philosophy.* Princeton: Princeton University Press, 2002.

Nepveu, Pierre. *Intérieurs du Nouveau Monde: Essais sur les littératures du Québec et des Amériques.* Montréal: Boréal, 1998.

Newman, Peter C. *Bronfman Dynasty: The Rothschilds of the New World.* Toronto: McClelland and Stewart, 1978.

Norich, Anita. *Discovering Exile: Yiddish and Jewish American Culture during the Holocaust.* Stanford: Stanford University Press, 2007.

Panofsky, Ruth. *The Force of Vocation: The Literary Career of Adele Wiseman.* Winnipeg: University of Manitoba Press, 2006.

Peretz, I.L. *Selected Stories.* Ed. Irving Howe and Eliezer Greenberg. New York: Schocken Books, 1974.

Perloff, Marjorie. "'Logocinéma of the Frontiersman': Eugene Jolas's Multilingual Poetics and Its Legacies." *Kunapipi.* 20, 3 (1999): 145–63. Available at http://wings.buffalo.edu/epc/authors/perloff/jolas.html (viewed 15 October 2010).

Phillips, Robert, ed. *Delmore Schwartz and James Laughlin: Selected Letters.* New York: W.W. Norton, 1993.

Pierce, Lorne. *A Canadian People.* Toronto: Ryerson Press, 1945.

Pollock, Zailig. *A.M. Klein: The Story of the Poet.* Toronto: University of Toronto Press, 1994.

- "'To Be Talked About': A.M. Klein's Reputation." Keynote address at The Poet as Landscape: A Portrait of A.M. Klein Today, conference held at Concordia University, Montreal, QC, 18 October 2007.

Pollock, Zailig, Usher Caplan, and Linda Rozmovits, eds. *A.M. Klein: An Annotated Bibliography*. Toronto: ECW Press, 1993.

Popham, Elizabeth. "Apologia pro vita sua: The Letters of A.M. Klein." Paper delivered at The Poet as Landscape: A Portrait of A.M. Klein Today, conference held at Concordia University, Montreal, QC, 18 October 2007.

- "Introduction." In *The Second Scroll*, ed. Elizabeth Popham and Zailig Pollock, vii–xxvi. Toronto: University of Toronto Press, 2000.

Pound, Ezra. "Hugh Selwyn Mauberley." In *Personae: The Collected Poems of Ezra Pound*, 185–204. New York: Boni and Liveright, 1926.

Prose, Francine. "Hopping Mad in Montreal." *New York Times Book Review*, 8 April 1990, 7.

Rabinovitch, Israel. *Jewish Music Ancient and Modern*. Montreal: Book Centre, 1952.

- *Muzik ba Yid oun andere esayn oyf muzikalishe temes*. Montreal: Eagle Publishing, 1940.

Ravvin, Norman. *A House of Words: Jewish Writing, Identity, and Memory*. Montreal: McGill-Queen's University Press, 1997.

Reider, J. "The Modern Renaissance of Jewish Music by Albert Weisser." *Jewish Quarterly Review* 45, 1 (1954): 62–4.

Reitblat, Abram I. "The 'Novel of Literary Failure.'" *Russian Studies in Literature* 40, 1 (2003). 11–25.

Richler, Mordecai. *Belling the Cat*. Toronto: Knopf, 1998.

- "Deuteronomy." In *Broadsides: Reviews and Opinions*. Markham: Viking, 1990.

- "Mortimer Griffin, Shalinsky, and How They Solved the Jewish Question." In *The Canadian Century: English-Canadian Writing since Confederation*. Vol. 2: *The Book of Canadian Prose*, ed. A.J.M. Smith, 477–89. Toronto: W.J. Gage, 1973.

- "Mr. Sam." In *Belling the Cat*, 21–40. Originally published as "Speakeasy of Sam Bronfman," *Saturday Night*, July/August 1992.

- *Solomon Gursky Was Here*. Markham: Penguin, 1989.

- *Son of a Smaller Hero* [1955]. Toronto: McClelland and Stewart, 1982.

- "Speak Easy of Sam Bronfman." *Saturday Night*, July/August 1992, 13–16, 61–9.

- *St. Urbain's Horseman* [1971]. Toronto: McClelland and Stewart, 1991.

– "Why I Write." In *Shovelling Trouble*. Toronto: McClelland and Stewart, 1972.

Ritts, Morton. "Witness to His Time: Mordecai Richler Creates a Virtuoso Novel." *Maclean's Magazine*, 13 November 1989, 64–7.

Robinson, Ira. *Rabbis and Their Community: Studies in the Immigrant Rabbinate of Montreal, 1896–1930*. Calgary: University of Calgary Press, 2007.

Rome, David. *On the Jewish School Question in Montreal, 1903–1931*. Montreal: Montreal, National Archives, Canadian Jewish Congress, 1975.

– *The First Jewish Literary School*. Montreal: Canadian Jewish Congress Archives, 1988.

Rome, David, and Pierre Anctil. *Through the Eyes of the Eagle: the Early Montreal Yiddish Press (1907–1916)*. Montreal, Véhicule Press, 2001.

Rosenberg, Louis. *Canada's Jews: A Social and Economic Study of the Jews in Canada in the 1930s*. Montreal: Bureau of Social and Economic Research, Canadian Jewish Congress, 1939 (Ed. Morton Weinfeld. Montreal: McGill-Queen's University Press, 1993).

Roskies, David. "Yiddish in Montreal: The Utopian Experiment." In *An Everyday Miracle: Yiddish Culture in Montreal*, ed. Ira Robinson, Pierre Anctil, and Mervin Butovsky, 22–38. Montreal: Véhicule Press, 1990.

Rozmovits, Linda. "Klein's Translations of Moyshe Leib Halpern: A Problem of Jewish Modernism." *Canadian Poetry: Studies, Documents, Reviews* 22 (Spring/Summer 1988): 1–9.

Sandrow, Nahman. *Vagabond Stars: A World History of Yiddish Theater*. Syracuse: Syracuse University Press, 1996.

Segal, Jacob Isaac. *Di drite sude*. Montreal: N.p., 1937.

– *Foun mayn velt*. Montreal: sine nominee (s.n.), 1918.

– "Late Summer in Montreal." Trans. Miriam Waddington. *Viewpoints: Canadian Jewish Quarterly* 2, 3 (1967): 56.

– *Letste lider*. Montreal: J.I. Segal Committee and Canadian Jewish Congress, 1955.

– *Lider un loybn*. Montreal: Y.Y. Sigal Komitet, 1944.

– *Lyric*. Montreal: N.p., 1930.

– *Mayn nigun*. Montreal: N.p., 1934.

– *Poèmes Yiddish*. Trans. Pierre Anctil. Montreal: Noroît, 1992.

– *Seyfer yidish*. Montreal: J.I. Segal Committee and Canadian Jewish Congress, 1950.

Shtern, Sholem. *Nostalgie et tristesse: Mémoires littéraires du Montréal Yiddish*. Trans. Pierre Anctil [1982]. Montreal: Noroît, 2006.

Siemerling, Winfried. "Leonard Cohen – 'Loneliness and History: A Speech Before the Jewish Public Library.'" In *Take This Waltz: A Celebration of Leonard Cohen*, ed. Michael Fournier and Ken Norris, 143–53. Ste Anne de Bellevue: The Muses' Company, 1994.

– "A Political Constituency That Really Exists in the World: An Interview with Leonard Cohen." In *Take This Waltz*, ed. Michael Fournier and Ken Norris, 154–69. Ste Anne de Bellevue: The Muses' Company, 1994.

Simon, Sherry. *Translating Montreal: Episodes in the Life of a Divided City*. Montreal: McGill-Queen's University Press, 2006.

– "A.M. Klein as Pimontel: the Risks of Diasporic Translation." In *New Readings of Yiddish Montreal: Traduire Le Montréal Yiddish*, ed. Pierre Anctil, Norman Ravvin, and Sherry Simon, 65–71. Ottawa: University of Ottawa Press, 2007.

– "A.M. Klein: Pimontel et les Ratés de la traduction." *Voix et Images: Littérature Québécoise* 30 (Spring 2005): 31–42.

Smith, A.J.M. *The Canadian Century: English-Canadian Writing since Confederation*. Vol. 2: *The Book of Canadian Prose*. Toronto: W.J. Gage, 1973.

The Soncino Chumash: The Five Books of Moses with Haphtaroth. Ed. Rev. Dr A. Cohen. London: Soncino Press, 1971.

Spandoni, Carl. "Leacock's *Canada*: The Book That Booze Bought." *Papers of the Bibliographical Society of Canada* 26 (1987): 88–105. Spenser, Edmund. *The Faerie Queene*. Ed. A.C. Hamilton, Hiroshi Yamashita, and Toshiyuki Suzuki. Toronto: Pearson Longman, 2007.

Spiro, Solomon Joseph. *Tapestry for Designs: Judaic Allusions in The Second Scroll and The Collected Poems of A.M. Klein*. Vancouver: UBC Press, 1984.

Srebrnik, Henry. "Birobidzhan on the Prairies: Two Decades of Pro-Soviet Jewish Movements in Winnipeg." In *Jewish Radicalism in Winnipeg, 1905–1960*, ed. Daniel Stone, 172–91. Winnipeg: Jewish Heritage Centre of Western Canada, 2003.

Stone, Daniel, ed. *Jewish Radicalism in Winnipeg, 1905–1960*. Proceedings of a conference organized by the Jewish Heritage Centre of Western Canada, 8–10 September 2001. Winnipeg: Jewish Heritage Centre of Western Canada, 2003.

Tamony, Peter. "Western Words – Beat Generation: Beat: Beatniks." *Western Folklore* 28, 4 (1969): 274-7.

Trachtenberg, Henry. "Jews and Left Wing Politics in Winnipeg's North End, 1919-40." In *Jewish Radicalism in Winnipeg, 1905-1960*, ed. Daniel Stone, 132-55. Winnipeg: Jewish Heritage Centre of Western Canada, 2003.

Trehearne, Brian. *The Montreal Forties: Modernist Poetry in Transition.* Toronto: University of Toronto Press, 1999.

Tulchinsky, Gerald. *Branching Out: The Transformation of the Canadian Jewish Community.* Toronto: Stoddard, 1998.

– *Taking Root: the Origins of the Canadian Jewish Community.* Toronto: Lester, 1992.

Van Toorn, Peter. "'Introduction' to *Cross/cut: Contemporary English Quebec Poetry* (1982)." In *Language Acts: Anglo-Québec Poetry, 1976 to the 21st Century*, ed. Jason Camlot and Todd Swift, 46-65. Montreal: Véhicule, 2007.

Waddington, Miriam. *A.M. Klein.* Toronto: Copp Clark, 1970.

– *Apartment Seven: Essays Selected Old and New.* Toronto: Oxford University Press, 1989.

– *Folklore in the Poetry of A.M. Klein.* The Pratt Lecture. St John's: Memorial University, 1974.

Wainwright, William J. *Philosophy of Religion.* Belmont: Wadsworth, 1999.

Waugh, Auberon. "St. Urbain's Horseman." *London Spectator*, 11 September 1971, 377-8

Waxman, Meyer. *A History of Jewish Literature.* Vol. 4, pt. 1 [1941]. New York: Thomas Yoseloff, 1960.

Weintraub, William. *City Unique: Montreal Days and Nights in the 1940s and '50s.* Toronto: McClelland and Stewart, 1996.

Weisbord, Merrily. *The Strangest Dream: Canadian Communists, the Spy Trials, and the Cold War.* Toronto: Lester and Orpen Dennys, 1993.

Werner, Eric. "Of Jewish Music, Ancient and Modern by Israel Rabinovitch, A.M. Klein." *Notes* 10, 2 (1953): 275-7.

Wiseman, Adele. *The Sacrifice.* 1956. Toronto: McClelland and Stewart, 2001.

Wiseman, Nelson. "Jewish Politics and the Jewish Vote in Comparative Perspective." In *Jewish Radicalism in Winnipeg, 1905-1960*, ed. Daniel Stone, 156-71. Winnipeg: Jewish Heritage Centre of Western Canada, 2003.

Wisse, Ruth. *The Modern Jewish Canon: A Journey through Language and Culture.* New York: Free Press, 2000.

Wolofsky, Hirsch. *Journey of My Life: A Book of Memories.* Trans. A.M. Klein. Montreal: Eagle Publishing, 1945.

– *Mayn lebns rayze, un demi-siècle de vie yiddish à Montréal* [1946]. French translation by Pierre Anctil. Sillery: Éditions du Septentrion, 2000.

– *Mayn lebns rayze, zikhroynes foun iber a halb yorhundert Yidish lebn in der alter oun nayer velt.* Montreal: Keneder Adler, 1946.

– *Oyf Eybiken Kvall: Gedanken un batrachtungen fun dem hayntigen idishen leben un shtreben, in likht fun unzer alter un eybig-nayer tora, eingeteylt loyt di parshiyos fun der vokh.* Montreal: Eagle Publishing, 1930.

Yanofsky, Joel. "Funny, You Don't Look Canadian." *Village Voice*, 1 May 1990, 86.

Žižek, Slavoj. *Enjoy Your Symptom! Jacques Lacan in Hollywood and Out.* 2nd ed. New York: Routledge, 2001.

Contributors

PIERRE ANCTIL has a PhD in social anthropology. He has written several monographs on the history of the Jewish community of Montreal and on ethnic pluralism in the city, among which are translations from Yiddish to French of the memoirs of Jewish immigrants in the first half of the twentieth century. Professor of history at the University of Ottawa, in 2008 he was awarded a Killam fellowship for a project entitled "Parcours migrant, parcours littéraire canadien, le poète yiddish Jacob-Isaac Segal."

LAWRENCE KAPLAN, professor of rabbinics and Jewish philosophy in the Department of Jewish Studies at McGill University, specializes in both medieval and modern Jewish thought. Among his recent articles are "Joseph Soloveitchik: Halakhic Man," in *The Cambridge Companion to Modern Jewish Philosophy*, and "A More Contemporary Voice: A.M. Klein's Original and Revised Translations of the Hebrew Poems of Hayyim Nahman Bialik," in *Prooftexts: A Journal of Jewish Literary History*.

REINHOLD KRAMER has published *Scatology and Civility in the English-Canadian Novel*, the award-winning *Walk Towards the Gallows: The Tragedy of Hilda Blake, Hanged 1899* (with co-author Tom Mitchell) and, most recently, *Mordecai Richler: Leaving St. Urbain*. Kramer is professor of Canadian literature at Brandon University.

DAVID LEAHY is currently a sessional head of the MA and PhD programs in comparative Canadian literature at the Université de Sherbrooke. His research interests and publications focus upon sex-gender, class, and political issues from cultural studies, new historicist, and postcolonial perspectives. His current research project is "'Embourgeoisement' and the Cultural

Fatigue of Québec." He is also a collaborator with Roxanne Rimstead (Université de Sherbrooke) on her "Culture-from-Below" research project.

REBECCA MARGOLIS is assistant professor in the Vered Jewish Canadian Studies Program at the University of Ottawa, where her courses include Yiddish language and culture. Her articles on Canadian Yiddish culture have appeared in *The Canadian Jewish Studies Reader*, *Traduire le Montréal Yiddish*, and *Juifs et Canadiens français dans la société québécoise* as well as in scholarly journals.

ROBERT MELANÇON is professor emeritus of the Université de Montréal, where he taught French literature from 1972 to 2007. With Charlotte Melançon he translated A.M. Klein's *The Second Scroll*, winning the Governor General's Award for translation in 1992. He has published four books of poetry.

LIANNE MOYES, associate professor of English at Université de Montréal, specializes in Canadian and Quebec literature. She is editor of *Gail Scott: Essays on Her Works*, and co-editor of *Adjacencies: Minority Writing in Canada*. Her recent work on Anglo-Montreal writing has appeared in *Québec Studies*; *Études canadiennes*; *Voix et images*; *Canadian Literature*; and in the collections *Language Acts: Anglo-Québec Poetry, 1976 to the 21st Century*; *Trans.Can.Lit: Resituating Canadian Literature*; and *Wider Boundaries of Daring: The Modernist Impulse in Canadian Women's Poetry*.

ZAILIG POLLOCK has taught at Trent University since 1976. He is chair of the A.M. Klein Research and Publication Committee, which has overseen the publication of *The Complete Works of A.M. Klein* (University of Toronto Press), and he has been directly involved in editing Klein's poetry and notebooks as well as his novel *The Second Scroll*. He has also published a study of Klein's work entitled *A.M. Klein: The Story of the Poet*. He is a general editor of the *Collected Works* of both E.J. Pratt and P.K. Page. He edited *The Filled Pen: Selected Prose of P.K. Page* (University of Toronto Press) and is currently at work on an edition of Page's *Complete Poems*.

ELIZABETH POPHAM is associate professor and chair of the Department of English Literature at Trent University. She is a member of the Editorial Committee of the A.M. Klein Research and Publication Committee, co-editor with Zailig Pollock of A.M. Klein's novel *The Second Scroll* (University of Toronto Press, 2000), and editor of the *Letters of A.M. Klein* (University of Toronto Press). She is currently editing the *Letters of E.J. Pratt* for print and hypertext publication.

IAN RAE is an assistant professor in the Department of Modern Languages at King's University College at the University of Western Ontario. He is a specialist in Canadian literature and is presently writing a monograph on Anne Carson as well as papers on Al Purdy, Alice Munro, and the creative economy in Canada. He published *From Cohen to Carson: The Poet's Novel in Canada* in 2008 with McGill-Queen's University Press.

NORMAN RAVVIN, currently the chair of the Concordia University Institute for Canadian Jewish Studies, is a critic, writer, and teacher. His books include *A House of Words: Jewish Writing, Identity and Memory*; *Hidden Canada: An Intimate Travelogue*; the novel *Lola by Night*; and the story collection *Sex, Skyscrapers and Standard Yiddish*. His novel *The Joyful Child* appeared in 2011.

IRA ROBINSON is professor of Judaic studies in the Department of Religion, Concordia University. His 2007 book, *Rabbis and Their Community: Studies in the Eastern European Orthodox Rabbinate in Montreal, 1896–1930*, won the 2008 J.I. Segal Prize in Canadian Jewish Studies. His latest book is *Translating a Tradition: Studies in American Jewish History*. He is president of the Canadian Society for Jewish Studies.

ROBERT SCHWARTZWALD has been professor and chair of the Département d'études anglaises at the Université de Montréal since 2005. Many of his publications explore relationships between notions of literary and national modernities in the 1930s and 1940s, especially in Quebec and France. In 2008, he was the recipient of the Governor General's International Award for Canadian Studies.

SHERRY SIMON is the author, most recently, of the award-winning *Translating Montreal: Episodes in the Life of a Divided City* (2006), which appeared in French translation in 2008 (Fidès), and co-editor of *New Readings of Yiddish Montreal* (2007, with Pierre Anctil and Norman Ravvin). She is a professor in the French department at Concordia University and is a fellow of the Royal Society of Canada.

Index